WAIMARINO COUNTY

WAIMARINO COUNTY
& other excursions

MARTIN EDMOND

AUCKLAND UNIVERSITY PRESS

First published 2007

Auckland University Press
University of Auckland
Private Bag 92019
Auckland
New Zealand
www.auckland.ac.nz/aup

© Martin Edmond, 2007

ISBN 978 1 86940 391 1

Publication is kindly assisted by ꝫcreative
nz
ARTS COUNCIL OF NEW ZEALAND *Toi Aotearoa*

National Library of New Zealand Cataloguing-in-Publication Data
Edmond, Martin.
Waimarino County : & other excursions / by Martin Edmond.
ISBN 978-1-86940-391-1
I. Title.
NZ824.2—dc 22

Cover photograph: View of Mt Ruapehu taken from Ohakune, 1938.
1/4-038726-F, Alexander Turnbull Library, Wellington, New Zealand.
Cover design: Sarah Maxey

Printed by Printlink Ltd, Wellington

A l'adolescent que je fus.

— RIMBAUD

Contents

3 ILLUSIONS

4 VOICES

1
AUTOBIOGRAPHIES

Waimarino County

I

A wagon load of shattered glass on a siding beneath a sky bright with rain. A two-stroke motor, whining like a mason bee in the cells of my prodigal mind. A cross-eyed railway clerk and an enormous Maori in a swanndri. Two kids ride by on bicycles, weaving between the steel girders holding up the corrugated iron roof of the station veranda. In a forgotten nook between the station proper and the toilet block, a sullen girl in a checked shirt and jeans is whipper-snippering the waist-high grass. Soaking wet stems churn in the teeth of the blade, showing piddle yellow as the seed heads go down.

The rain falls from a white sky. Wisps of cloud catch in the greeny-black trees across the tracks, where three identical railway houses stand unnaturally far apart from each other, their back doors to the hidden mountain. The girl sighs and gives up her mowing. The cross-eyed clerk puts on a peaked cap and climbs down on to the rails. The Maori strides into a big red shed from which, impressively, he emerges at the controls of a diesel engine. This he hitches, with the help of the clerk, to the front of a long line of trucks. The goods train passes slowly through the station. The rolling stock is the property of the TransAmerica Corporation; some trucks are labelled *Warning: Poison*.

The two-stroke starts up again. The kids ride round and round, round and round. I walk up to the end of Thames Street and then I walk back down again. I buy two oranges at the general store and eat them under the leery eyes of the clerk. I read the *Wanganui Chronicle* from cover to cover. The front-page story tells how sixteen police outfitted in full riot control gear dealt with the drunken antics of a bottle-smashing, rock-throwing crowd outside a party on Saturday night in the River City. The rain gets heavier. I can hear it now on the tin roof of the veranda, the single event inside an immensity of time on a small town railway platform in the back country on a wet Monday afternoon. What am I doing here.

II

It was just before Christmas, 1980. I had ridden the daylight train down from Auckland, planning to meet a friend from Wellington at Ohakune Junction. He was driving up, with camera. I had this idea of using a series of photographs of the district to illustrate a piece of writing. Whether the writing would be about the photographs or the photographs about the writing, I didn't know. But I knew what I wanted photographed: empty, derelict houses. This is twenty-five years ago now and it's hard to recall exactly why I wanted these particular images. Perhaps I thought they could be an objective correlative to my rather studied melancholy. Maybe I thought they would say something about time and change. Or it might have been that I hoped to find in them traces of something lost.

When Barry arrived we drove into town and then out the other side again. We were going down to see the place in Moore Street where his grandmother once lived. It was a rundown 1950s weatherboard house inside a picket fence. The tops of the pickets were carved into reclining crescent moons with five-pointed stars in their cusps. Hearts, diamonds, spades, clubs from the

3

playing card pack crowned other pickets outside other houses. You could see they had been painted blue and white and red and purple and gold. They were insignia of the Ratana Movement, which once had many adherents in this part of the country.

Our old family home in nearby Burns Street was a dilapidated wooden villa standing naked among the tough grass where somebody's sheep were grazing. It was for sale. I remembered the honeysuckle hedge, the snowball and the lilac, the beech tree and the palm tree. Round the back there was a walnut, an almond, a greengage, a nectarine, a quince. There were pungas, a row of outhouse sheds, a vegetable garden, the chook run, the back fence beyond which the river ran. It was all gone now, as were most of the other places where our neighbours with their hieratic names lived: Mrs Clancy, the Magees, the Rochforts, the Reynolds, the Williams, the Jenkins, the Chamberlains, Miss Seth-Smith, Charlie Herkt, the Aubreys, the Jamiesons, the Morrises, the Prams . . . the houses that were still standing had shrunk with the years. Over the road, where my sisters kept their horses, where in the manuka the girl next door once pulled down her pants to show me her fanny, were a couple of brand new Neill Homes.

Barry knew the address of a boarding house. The Lodge was the property of the Teachers' Training College Mountain Club in Palmerston North, run by a bloke called Gil. He was about sixty, lean, tall, sandy, balding, wearing thick glasses before swimming eyes. Genuinely affable, especially when we handed over the money. We went inside to meet the wife. They had a black poodle called Smoky. The TV blared. A smell of dog and cigarette smoke mingled with stale cooking fat. A closed interior in a cold climate. You stay there long enough, you don't notice any more.

Out the back where the rooms for hire were, you could look away over emerald green grass to the shrouded mountain. In the still falling rain, the rotting wood of gone dwellings leached back into the soil it was milled from only fifty years before. I remembered something curious about this town: in his MA thesis my father mentions that the houses here were too few and built too far apart from each other to make rating economic. A disproportionate distance had to be covered if the Council was to provide essential services like water and sewage to each domicile. It seemed an apt index of the desolation all around.

III

We went down Dreadnought Road to see the Ruapehu Hotel. It was still there then. You could make out the letters of its name fading along the weatherboards of the right-hand gable. In the overgrown garden, red-hot pokers raised their vivid cones in the air. The veranda sagged. One of the dormer windows, broken, was stuffed with boards and straw. The front door opened and a woman came out.

She was big-boned and barefoot and did not look her sixty-five years. She said she'd raised seventeen children and six grandchildren in that house. No regrets, except perhaps the lack of royalties from the many who came to photograph her gothic mansion. Mr Smiles, selling pictures of it in his shop on Cuba Street. Someone else had made place mats. There were tea trays too. There ought to be a law. What else? You have to be patient. You have to wait out the silences, staring into the white distance between one remark and the next. The slight rain drifted down Dreadnought Road towards us.

It rains more since they milled the bush, she offered.

She remembered when there were thirty sawmills within an eight-mile radius of the town. Then the bad years after the boom was over, the Depression, the War, the long slow post-war decline, which the opening of the ski fields reversed. A fifty-year slump between the bush and the mountain. She didn't ask us in, but through the half-open door I caught a glimpse of wonders . . . a glass-doored tallboy full of bric-à-brac . . . a painted plaster parrot won at the Taihape Show . . . little ornamental dolls a sailor son brought back from Japan . . . pieces of kauri gum . . . postcards from Spain . . . a cuckoo clock. In a falling-down garage round the side of the house was a 1955 FJ Holden Special, pristine, before a lawn edged with white-painted car tyres upon which stood a single cabbage tree.

IV

The day wore on. The sky, without clearing, became more brilliant, turning a transparent yellow. Below, in the mortal world, that heavenly light illuminated less and less. The electric grass, the macrocarpa hedges, the wet grey fence battens covered with pale green beards of lichen, reserved their contours to themselves, without insistence, without shadow, until they faded to mere presences in the gloom.

Driving out along the Rangataua Road, we came across an abandoned four-room cottage whose twin windows and gaping door resembled the face of some gaunt survivor of the deluge. We climbed the fence, walked through the dripping grass to the house and went inside. It was full of ghosts. Cold fingers on shivering flesh, tears starting in my eyes. That their lives had come to this.

Through a broken window, dark green foliage of the macrocarpa looked like hectic paint strokes. On a wall next to the fireplace, someone had scratched the word HELP in high quavery letters. And again by the doorway leading into the hall. Across the floor, a scatter of barbed wire, broken glass, rotted wood. In the tiny kitchen, as if built for dwarfs, the red rust and debris of the shattered coal range. And on the bedroom wall, torn from newspapers and pasted up, image after image of brides and grooms on their wedding days, the men's dark suits greying, the brides' white dresses gone brown with the years.

V

Further on is Karioi, where the first sheep stations were, the site of race meetings, feasts and hui a hundred years ago. Further on again, is the railway bridge at Tangiwai, replacing the one a lahar out of the crater lake on Ruapehu tumbled into the turbid waters of the Whangaehu on Christmas Eve, 1953, taking with it the northbound *Limited Express*. One hundred and fifty-three people died that night. The engine and some of the carriages remained in the river bed for years, for years you could find debris from the wreck down there; the concrete piles of the old bridge still lie out in the water.

A quarter of a century later, the only signs we found were a rusty bolt in the sand and a cross nearby made of two bits of wood nailed together. It was painted white and on it was written in black the time and the date of the accident, the name of the place, the number of the dead and the words: *In Memory Of Those Who Died Here*. Beyond, the sinister, yellow-grey waters of the Whangaehu swirled. We used to come out here sometimes to get sand for the sandpit. As kids we believed if you went too close to the river you'd be sucked under and drowned, mouth and nose and eyes and ears clogged with fine sulphuric silt, the voice of the volcano grumbling in your skull as the water closed over.

There was also an effluent pipe discharging into the river just down from the new railway bridge. The colour of the discharge was the same as that of the river, but it had a distinct, pungent, chemical smell, making the brimstone waters seem wholesome in comparison. This pipe ran from the Winstone Pulp plant up the way, where pine trees from the 17,000-acre Karioi State Forest were being mashed. This was perhaps the final destination of whatever poison was in those railway trucks belonging to the TransAmerica Corporation. They chased us out of there with a jeep.

VI

Next morning we went up the mountain. To get there you have to pass the elephant's grave. The ghost of Rajah stands gate-keeper at that entrance to the Tongariro National Park. He came with Wirth's Bros Circus back in the 1950s, and remains because he ate tutu berries in autumn when they are poisonous to animals. For the burial, they bulldozed a hole in the ground just across the railway tracks, winched the elephant in then bulldozed the earth back over him. I remember as a child going to look at the mound of dirt; perched on top was a tiny bouquet of flowers, bittersweet, so funny, so sad.

We entered a forest of huge trees, tawai, rimu and matai. As we climbed the trees shrank, thinned out, changed, until the bush was mostly just mountain beech and mingi mingi. The sealed road gave way to a dirt track that got rockier and rougher the higher we went. Errant watercourses cut across it, scarring the bare earth. The wind was moaning across the razorbacks, skidding great rent sheets of cloud down the valleys. A cold, wet rain fell in violent showers. In between, the blazing white sky cleared so we could see red rock stretching for miles in the intermittent light; the foaming, bubbling waters running off the mountain made it look like a huge ice-cream cone, melting.

We had Talking Heads' *Remain in Light* playing on the tape deck, the song was 'Once in a Lifetime':

> *Letting the days go by*
> *Let the water hold me down*
> *Letting the days go by*
> *Water flowing underground*
> *Into the blue again*
> *In the silent water*
> *Under the rocks and stone*
> *There is water underground . . .*

We stopped once on the way down. I walked out on to a bluff overlooking the beginnings of the river that would become the Mangawhero, the one in which, further down, lazy mountain trout swam in golden pools, the one that ran behind our old house in Burns Street. The waterfall was a vivid slash of white across the red rocks and brown volcanic earth. The air was very cold. The tall columns of the rain strode from ridge to ridge behind me. I remember thinking if I was going to make bones, this would be a good place to leave them. It would be like ending where I had begun. I was very melodramatic in those days.

VII

On a high green hill just outside Raetihi stands a Ratana church with twin domed towers upon which *Arepa* and *Omeka*, Alpha and Omega, are traditionally written. We stopped the car by a clay bank on one side of a cutting through the hill, stepped through the fence and climbed up a steep slope luxuriant with gone-to-seed grass towards the church.

Flags were flying on the marae next to the church – the Ratana flag, the Union Jack, the New Zealand flag, the Rising Sun. A light rain was falling as we walked over to where a young girl sat on the steps of the whare kai. She got up and went into the building. Peering after her into the gloom, I could see the long trestle tables covered with newsprint, the orange and yellow and green and red of the bottles of soft drink, the big plates of sliced buttered bread. A man with red-rimmed eyes and a distracted air came out. He looked doubtful.

The church? he said. *It might be a bit difficult, you know, because we're having a tangi here today.*

He stood on the porch looking out at the falling rain.

I don't know about the church, he said at last. *I'm not a Ratana, see. There's a fella in there who's a Ratana. He might be able to help you more than I can.*

9

He turned and, stooping slightly, went back into that dark interior. He came out again with a younger man, short, stocky, well built. This man radiated that inner certainty and strength called mana. The deep, regular lines round his eyes were like the ravines we had seen up on the mountain.

Well, it's a bit difficult really, the Ratana began. *It's not us younger ones you see, it's the old people . . . maybe not if it was any old time, but today, with this tangi on for one of our elders . . .*

Both men lit cigarettes, Rothmans, using a Bic suspended in a leather pouch on a thong round the Ratana's neck. A scatter of kids drifted nearer.

How many go to the church? Barry asked.

About two, said the Ratana. *No, I mean it. Two or three.*

The church is down there now, said Redeye, gesturing with his thumb towards the town.

Down the pub, said the Ratana.

A thin woman came up, trailing a couple more kids. She lifted a smoke from Redeye.

I'm going home now, she said. *There's no place for kids here.*

She rubbed her thumb and forefinger together. Redeye reached into his pocket and pulled out some crumpled notes. He offered her a two, but her bony fingers extracted a five instead. While this was going on, another character appeared out of the darkness of the building. He was very black. The whites of his eyes glittered strangely in the gloom of the afternoon. He looked like a Dravidian.

Hey, why don't you get Him to turn the tap off up there? he said to the Ratana, jerking one hand towards the sky.

It would just come down again somewhere else, was the equable reply.

The Dravidian's eyes gleamed. He went off down the side of the building muttering to himself. There was a pause.

You can go in, but you can't take photographs. You can photograph the outside and you can have a look inside.

Inside was a little piece of heaven. The same segmented five-pointed star inside the cusp of the crescent moon was carved into the pew ends. Each segment of the star has its own colour: blue for the Father, white for the Son, red for the Holy Ghost; purple for the Angels and gold for the Mangai, T. W. Ratana. Everything in the church was painted, even the altar, which was strewn with flowers. On the wall behind it were murals, copies of the originals at the temple at Ratana.

They had been painted by a youth who was held to be a reincarnation of the prophet's son, Arepa; like Arepa, like Ratana's son Omeka, this boy died when his work was done. The murals tell the story of the movement, especially during the 1920s, when a crusade went out into the world: to the USA, to the League of Nations, to England to see the king. At Geneva the New Zealand representative to the League made sure the delegation was not received. In London, George V, King-Emperor, refused Ratana an audience.

In Japan, however, he was greeted with great ceremony by Bishop Juji Nakada of the Methodist Episcopal Church. Gifts were exchanged, marriages made. Ratana taught that both Maori and Japanese were among the lost tribes of Israel. The idea grew that Ratana had married the Maori race to the Japanese race, had enlisted their support for Maori grievances and prophesied the coming of a world war between the non-white and white races: this is why the Rising Sun still flew over Te Puke marae next to the Haahi Ratana at Raetihi.

VIII

About ten miles north of the church is the largest graveyard of cars in the country. Here you can find parts for any old vehicle you care to mention. If the make got to New Zealand, parts got to Horopito. Especially pre-war American models. Even in the 1950s, there were still quite a few Model T Fords driving around the district, kept going by frequent visits to Horopito.

We used to go there for blackberries. The bushes were huge, yards across, so you could pick only at the edges. They grew the biggest, sweetest berries. I remember the tearing sensation of spines on my skin as I reached too far for a specially luscious one. The red of blood mingled with the purple stains of the fruit on my sun-browned arms. My mother would make blackberry jam. She'd bottle the surplus with peeled and cut-up Granny Smiths and in winter we'd have blackberry and apple pie.

This day, glazed with rain breaking like long stems of glass on the hulks of cars rusting in the distance, green with the luxuriant growth of grasses through falling-down sheds and houses, white with the distance of the unseen mountain, Horopito was just a place to stop and listen to the eternity of the weather.

Down a back road nearby, we found a house behind a plain picket fence with a green corrugated iron roof and white weatherboard walls; a bay window on one side at the front and a veranda on the other; a corrugated iron water tank on the tank stand outside the kitchen; a straggly plum tree leaning over the roof, a row of hydrangea bushes and a macrocarpa tree. There was a thick plume of wood smoke rising from the chimney, for inside, perhaps, they were burning black matai or maire logs from the felled forest, so durable one might last a whole evening in the grate.

I couldn't help feeling a stab of nostalgic pain. It looked like our house in Burns Street had when it was the family home. Even though this house stood all alone without neighbours down an empty road. In the fields of knee-high grass round about, the bright cones of the lupins rose up like signal fires: blue, white, red, purple, yellow, in the falling rain.

IX

Out on the main road we stopped to take some pictures of an old barn. I went inside and peered through a window for Barry to photograph me. I was trying to appear like a spirit. I wanted to inhabit the barn, I wanted to inhabit all these falling-down old places. I wanted a living presence to replace the absence so powerfully articulated in these abandoned buildings. I wanted the sadness of dereliction to yield to my hot irrefutable heart and longing soul.

Near the barn we found a house with a cut-out, corrugated iron, turreted castle topped by a weather vane on the roof. In fact the entire structure was decorated with these curious cut-outs, so that it resembled an angular, wavy gingerbread house. Every door and every window was ornamented, each one in a different pattern; and on the letter box there was a piece of tin inscribed with the words: *Bleak House*.

It was empty. The camera had run out of film. We were looking through a window round the back when there was a shower of metal on the road out front. Up pulled a Valiant Charger with a trailer attached. Three huge men got out, one about fifty, one maybe thirty, the last a mere youth: a man and his two sons. A gigantic plumber's wrench in the back pocket of the youngest showed they meant business. The trailer had jack-knifed as they braked; the elder son picked it up and lifted it into line behind the car again. The older man came over to us.

We just come to get the tank off the back there, he said. *Our one's holed, but this one's still good. What? Yeah, amazing old place really. Plumber lived here 'til last year. Nah, dunno who did all that. Musta been years ago now. Waste of bloody time if you ask me . . .*

X

At the turn-off to the Chateau we sat in the car while I rolled a joint. There was a cop parked nearby but he took no notice of us. We smoked it then headed for Tokaanu and the hot springs. You go past Rotoaira on that road, the dark secret lake set among raupo swamps, overlooked by the sombre mountain. From here, the land slopes away in all directions to the coasts where most of the people live.

Suddenly everything fell into place. I could see the forests of rimu and matai and maire and rata and tawai that grew here in the heart of the land. I could see the shining lakes and hear the endless unscored symphony of bird song filling the forests. I even glimpsed, fleetingly, among the fern fronds and the purple and white sails of the toi toi, the shapes of women and men like trees walking.

The Hallelujah Chorus

I

My father's arrival at Huntly College was greeted with shouts of joy. By the end of the first day of school, the tangata whenua knew their new principal was not going to practise his golf swing on the backs of their pants, as had his predecessor, and were celebrating. I was happy to bask in his reflected glory. Four stressed years of upright Anglicanism in Greytown had taught me only that prayer was of no use when the big Maori boys were determined to extract from you a confession of your impotence. Here they jerked their chins, flicked their eyebrows and smiled: *E hoa!*

Three years later, what remained of my family had gone back down south to Upper Hutt and I was in my dead grandmother's upstairs room in our otherwise empty house on Dudley Avenue with Jean Paki. I lost my virginity with a nurse from Hamilton on a camp stretcher at Jake McManus's place, but I learned more about love from Jean Paki, Maisie Pohutuhutu, Bernice Heta, Hine Wawati.

My official girlfriends were all Pakeha. Julie Till. Judith Carter. Judy Singer. Julie was beautiful and sweet and became a secretary later on, but my love for her was of the despairing kind that knows it will never be answered. Judith was Catholic and not disposed to sin with me or anyone else. Judy became a good friend. Her brother gave me my dog, Mungo, a Labrador cross. She married Riki Muru, a nephew of the queen, Te Ata i Rangi Kaahu, who lived just across the river at Waahi, where later the power station would be built. They've always been big on the generation of power in the Waikato, but hardly anyone in Huntly knew the queen lived there. All the boys played rugby for the school on Saturdays and league on Sunday for Taniwharau. Some of them were geniuses with the ball. The hundred taniwha of the river: Riki Muru, Charlie Tohe, Peter Toka, Dolly Toka, Niki Tipene, Bruce Berryman, Alan de Thierry. Royalty.

That summer, of '67 and '68, I threw a party for my friends in the empty house after the family left and then went haymaking with Graeme Eyre and Trevor McLeish. We lived in the shearers' quarters on the Eyres' farm. This seems to call for some explanation but I can no longer give it. All I remember is a cluster of images around a central drama, the Pentecostal meeting at the Embassy Theatre in Hamilton.

Listening to Cream doing 'White Room' on the radio on a sunny day off with all the curtains in the long bare room pulled, for instance, I learned about LSD before I'd ever taken any. When one of the blokes we worked with was asked what he got for Christmas, he said *Three fucks and a bottle of wine*, silencing us for the rest of the afternoon. Beer tastes better from a cold bottle when your mouth is full of the daylong dust. Inexplicably, on New Year's Eve, we got drunk on apple cider and threw potatoes at the black telephone on the wall where our work was phoned through to us.

One day we rambled over the hills with Graeme's .22. A hawk landed in the bush across the gully. *Give me the rifle*, I said. *And I will shoot it.* The sights were crooked and I had never fired a gun before, but the bird fell dead to the ground. We found a possum up a tree and shot bullet after bullet into it before beating its brains out against the trunk. I felt sicker than I did when I killed the hawk, but I didn't say anything.

This was in Naike out the back of Rotowaro, Pukemiro, Glen Afton, coal mining towns that don't exist any more. Trevor McLeish was from Glen Afton. He lived with his family in a cottage clinging to a steep hillside near the mine. When I first met Trevor, three things impressed me: the hairiness of his legs, his attitude and his technique of smoking at lunchtime. He and Billy Dunlop used to walk slowly away down the grounds towards the bridge, inhaling the smoke and blowing it out down the fronts of their jerseys. You'd see these hairy legs and this cloud of smoke, retreating. They stank all afternoon, but none of the teachers ever had them on about it. Later Trevor learned that, although I was the headmaster's son, I liked to smoke as well, and we became friends.

Graeme Eyre was different. He was lanky and tall and loose-limbed, with distant eyes, and he never said much. For some reason this garnered him a lot of respect. He was a lock forward, good in the lineout. It was his idea that Trevor and I spend the summer haymaking and living on his farm. Graeme moved out of the house and into the shearers' quarters with us, behind the briar rose and the thistles and the long grass.

On the days we worked, which could be any day it wasn't raining, the phone would ring in the morning and we'd be told where to go and what time to be there. We'd pile into Graeme's khaki Simca, drive out to a paddock somewhere and pick up the bales of hay until they were all in. The baler went around the paddock and the truck followed with a ramp bolted to its side. So long as the bales were in a line, they ran smoothly up the ramp to be stacked on the tray.

Lining up the bales was a job. Sometimes you had to pull them out of gullies where they'd rolled. Taking the bales off at the top of the ramp was another. Someone to stack. Someone to drive the truck. When the tray was full you went and put the bales in the barn. We worked until midnight or later, the truck bumping through the gloom, its headlights catching weirdly in the stubble. Then drove miles home through the dark backward

of the Lower Waikato with something like Glen Campbell
singing 'Wichita Lineman' on the car radio.

II

I don't remember anything about Mr and Mrs Eyre. I don't think
I ever went up the house. What happened was, Graeme said one
day we were going into Hamilton to a meeting, and we went.
Trevor said no, so we dropped him off at Glen Afton and then
it was just Graeme and me in the Simca. His parents took their
own car and we met up outside the theatre and went in together.
The Embassy was a picture theatre at the south end of Victoria
Street, backing on to the river.

The place was packed. It was chocker. They all looked like
farming folk. Laconic, rangy men with faraway eyes. Plump
women who never quite look you in the eye. Gaggles of kids
round knees. Crowding into this place with a buzz of anticipation
which hushed when the Preacher began. I don't remember him
that well either. An impression of a well-filled green shirt, maybe
seersucker, and a white suit. He was from Lower Hutt.

He had a voice and he had it easy. These people were primed.
Hours alone tractoring over the stolen land worrying about the
mortgage perhaps, hours watching out the kitchen window for
the shape of the hills to change, left them ready for anything.
The Preacher spoke about the power of Jesus Christ to redeem
their sinful lives. There was a murmuring. He cited examples
to show the ordinary nature of their shameful doings. There
was a restlessness in the auditorium. He told them they did
not need to feel the way they felt all the time. A roar began to
build.

The place was simmering when the testimonies began.
A gasp went through the room when an ash blonde with an
hourglass figure stepped to the microphone and said she had
broken the Ten Commandments – all of them. She said she had

been possessed by demons who made her commit the evils they brought to her mind. She fought, to no avail. Her husband left her. Her children became alienated. At last she was dragged into the presence of the Preacher, who bent her over his kitchen table and began to exorcise her.

The struggle was long and dreadful as they wrestled among the utensils. Her body bucked and twisted as the demons tried to elude the Preacher's righteous hands. At the moment of truth they threw her from the table on to the floor, where her foot gashed open on a piece of glass from a shattered milk bottle and her blood flowed across the linoleum. It was through the wound so made that the demons fled her body.

It was impossible not be impressed by this alarming tale as told by a simple woman in a grey tailored suit; so when the Preacher joined her on stage and began to exhort the faithful to show their appreciation, people began to *Glory* and *Hallelujah*. He took her hand and they stood forth in pillars of light like angels calling us to *Rise Up* and *Praise the Lord*.

The Eyres shot upright in the instant. I stayed where I was, unwilling to miss the show but equally uncertain of my allegiances. Then Graeme gave me a look so I did get up. And it was as if at that moment the whole cinema full of people rose to its feet and began ardently to *Hallelujah*.

What fixed and fanatic eyes they had! In the hot summer night, how the sweat stood out on their throbbing temples and rolled down their faces and under their shirts and blouses! The way their fists were punched towards the ceiling! The bellowing that bent the perfervid air!

Now the Preacher was calling for the sick in body, the sick at heart, the soul sick, to come forward and give themselves to Jesus. In the cacophony of the theatre, people were going down the carpeted aisles towards the stage. Some were halt and some were lame and some were in wheelchairs, but all received alike the laying on of the Preacher's hands, or of the Blonde's, or of one of those others who had also testified before. (There was paperwork to complete as well, but that was done backstage afterwards.)

And as these sinners declared themselves, the chanting in the theatre rose in pitch and fervour and intensity until there came above the thunderous chorus a weird, high ululation from the stalls on the front left-hand side. I had never heard people speaking in tongues before. Glossolalia sounds like someone yodelling so hard their uvula goes into spasm. It reminded me of a time I heard a flock of sheep mustering at dusk on a Lands and Survey block out the back of Stratford: a massed falsetto bouncing off the leaden sky like the sound of the souls of the lost crowded out of the anteroom of heaven.

Praise the Lord the Holy Ghost has descended upon us in Tongues of Flame! the Preacher screeched above the clamour of the Believers, doubling and redoubling their efforts. Then he began to call particular people out of the crowd. Suddenly I heard him say: *There is a young man of sixteen or seventeen years* (I had just turned seventeen) *and he is sitting on the right-hand side of the cinema* (I was) *two thirds of the way towards the back* (exactly!) *and he is wondering whether to come forward now and give his soul to Jesus* (I wasn't, but, hell . . .). *Let us all now raise our voices to the heavens and ask the Lord to give strength to this young man so that he may come and join us . . .*

I looked nervously sideways along the row to see if there were any other suspects who fitted the description; oddly, I didn't think of Graeme. Everyone was too busy chanting *Glory! Hallelujah!* and throwing their hands in the air to notice my dilemma. Graeme was himself hooting along with the rest of them, changing forever the way I thought about him.

And I did feel a powerful force calling me. I was young and uncertain and the exorcism of possible demons from the chaos of my awakening mind did for a moment seem desirable, even seductive. Surely there was no harm in it? It was certainly impressive to see old people getting out of their wheelchairs and tottering forward to lean on the edge of the stage.

In the row in front of us, a couple was caterwauling along with the rest; they had two kids who were not attending. The boy and girl were sporting between the seats. *Glory!* their young Dad shouted, wrapping his horny hand round his son's tender bottom. *You kids shut up!* And *Hallelujah!* as the kid began to howl.

It broke the spell. I had to laugh. Any chance I would go forward to be saved blew away in that poor kid's outraged, helpless sobbing. Thus I missed my shot at salvation. The Preacher switched the beam of his mind to probe other darknesses than mine, and I relaxed.

Though it may be false recall, or wishful thinking, it did seem that the thunder and roar of the crowd reached its crescendo at the point of my imminent involvement and then began to die away again. By now, big instant coffee tins, stripped of their labels and with slits cut by a can opener in their lids, were passing up and down the rows. The Preacher kept the congregation baying until the tins, full of money, reached the back of the theatre. Then we bent our heads in prayer.

There was no buzz of conversation as the sweaty crowd streamed out after the meeting was over. There was no sense of communion that I recall. Nobody seemed to want to meet anyone else's eye. Instead we avoided contact and in little groups dispersed to our cars. It was as if each of us had been alone in there with Jesus or the Preacher or the Blonde or just with ourselves, and whatever the experience, like solitary sex, there was nothing to say about it to anyone else.

I never talked it over with Graeme. I wouldn't have known how to ask him if he'd Praised the Lord because he believed or because his parents did or for some other reason like the collective will of the congregation. I might have told Trevor how crazy it was but then again I might not have. He knew that already. He wouldn't have gone near something like that in a million years.

We went back to work next day as if nothing had happened and pretty soon the summer was over. I went south to rejoin my family with Des Lowe, a horse fancier from Meremere who was also in my class at school. We drove all the way to Wellington in his sister's grape-coloured Isuzu Bellet and fell out soon afterwards; but that's another story.

III

A few years later a farming couple from Pukekawa, just up the road from Naike, were shot with a .22 rifle. Their bodies were wrapped in a candlewick bedspread, weighted with a car axle, and dumped in the Waikato River. Everyone knows the story about how the police contrived a conviction against local farmer Arthur Allan Thomas for the murder of his childhood sweetheart Jeanette Demler and her husband, Harvey Crewe. And how the case later unravelled. Most people remember another suspect, Jeanette's father, Len Demler. There was a third. His name was Mikey Eyre.

Mikey was Graeme's cousin. He was a simpleton who spent a lot of time wandering over the hills with a .22, looking for rabbits. He had no motive, apart from his alleged craziness and his love of killing. I don't see how it's even possible to have an opinion on the matter.

But I was interested enough to go, one day in 1980, up to a room in a tower block near the waterfront in Auckland where they were trying to determine the truth in the case of Arthur Allan Thomas. It was a small room, very crowded. I was standing by the door at the back when someone in the front row got up to leave. A man with red shiny cheeks and jet black hair half stood, waving in my general direction. It was Arthur himself. I walked down the aisle and sat next to him. He beamed and shook my hand.

I was there for a couple of hours. We didn't talk, because the inquiry was in session, but there was a lot of eye contact. Each time a piece of evidence was presented that supported the presumption of his innocence, Arthur nodded and smiled. He seemed a simple soul, utterly without guile. When they broke for lunch, we shook hands again and then I went away.

Was he the murderer? If he didn't kill the Crewes, who did? Some think Jeanette's sister from America hired professionals so she could get her hands on the land. And organised someone to feed the baby, which they did until the crime was discovered four days later. Was that Len's job? Didn't the sister get the baby, Rochelle, as well? What about Mikey Eyre?

I'll never know. There was something backward and hidden and silent about those people. Their religion, too, was inscrutable. They fired off salvos of Hallelujahs as if from a repeating rifle. They Praised the Lord and belted their kids in the same breath. Their ecstatic communion happened only once in a blue moon and they never talked about it afterwards. It was as mysterious as sex.

Theirs is the land that was taken after the wars in the 1860s, when thousands of British imperial troops marched south from Auckland and the 300-ton Australian-built armoured gunboat *Pioneer* paddle steamed up the Waikato to shell the pas at Meremere and Rangiriri. Many of them trace their descent from those soldiers, who were given farms in exchange for fighting the war. Some were recruited by poster off the mean streets of Melbourne and Sydney.

Most of the land on the west bank of the Waikato south of the big bend the river takes at Mercer was confiscated from tribes that did not fight in the war, or fought on the side of the imperial and colonial forces. Perhaps that's where the obscure sense of guilt comes from. It was always said in Huntly that incest was rife on the farms and idiocy a common result.

I never met Mikey Eyre, not that I remember. I imagine him a lot like Graeme, only of a slimmer build. Strolling over the low, rolling hills with his .22 slung in the elbow of his right arm, he has a loose, lazy, limber walk and an eye that seems sleepy and slow until some movement on the opposite hillside flashes across the retina and wakes synapses in the brain. The gun snaps to his shoulder, he aims, fires. A rabbit kicks up dirt as it skids bleeding into the dust.

The echo cracks across distant gullies. The spent cartridge case is ejected into the yellow grass. *Glory, Hallelujah* he murmurs into the faraway blue of the sky. *Praise the Lord.*

Going South

I

When I was nineteen I fell in love with my girlfriend's best friend. It was after I found out R had been making clandestine trysts with an older man, her cousin's husband, who had been her lover before I came along. She used to visit him in the afternoons while I was at work. I'd lived in fear of this fellow's threatened arrival (from England) the whole long sweet year of our young love and it was no help realising, when he did finally turn up, that he was probably one of those closeted gays who have to assert their alleged heterosexuality by seducing younger women. The damage was done. This was the first though not the last time I would react to emotional pressure on a relationship by falling in love with a lover's best friend: a dubious course of action that can be relied upon only to replace one set of complications with another, if it does not simply double the complications.

I didn't tell K I was in love with her. I didn't know how. We were flatmates, the three of us, with a floating fourth who changed unpredictably. I made clandestine moves myself, writing K a love poem that I pushed unsigned under her door one night, a bad idea as it turned out. K, perhaps in ignorance of my authorship – she said she thought it was from another of her admirers – the next evening gave the poem a derisory reading to the whole household around the kitchen table, making it impossible for me to acknowledge it as my own. I never made a copy so I don't know now what it said; but I remember no other humiliation, literary or romantic, as exquisite as this one was, as I sat burning with shame in the face of K's unforced and otherwise infectious merriment at the poem's lovelorn absurdities.

That household, not before time, broke up towards the end of the year and K went back to her home town, Dunedin. I mooned around Auckland, writing more poems to her and even sending one of them along with, bizarrely, the cow bone that inspired it: *This blade bone, shoulder of a gone beast / is white and dry as it was never dry / in the days of the supple shoulder / of the spring in the limb* . . . I was thinking about the use of these particular bones in Chinese divination – they were placed in a fire until cracked and then the cracks were read – but failed to divine the spectacularly bovine nature of my gift. K never answered that letter. Nor did she ever comment upon the bone that went with it.

I no longer recall the mental process by which I came to decide to hitch-hike to Dunedin to see her; nor can I remember exactly when it was: sometime in the summer of 1971–72, either before but more likely after Christmas, which I would have spent with my family in Upper Hutt. I know I didn't tell K I was coming. I was harbouring thoughts of sweeping her off her feet with my unexpected yet longed-for appearance, as crazy as that sounds. On the other hand, I must have been looking for adventure too, because I didn't head straight for the Deep South. I went via the West Coast, with various pauses along the way.

II

The first of these was at a pub in Tahunanui, outside Nelson, where I spent the evening drinking with locals met at the bar . . . under an assumed name. This mild deception simply involved introducing myself as Mike rather than Martin. Of course nobody had any idea I'd changed my name because no one

26

there had ever seen me before, but it did induce in me a frisson of alienation that I found alarming and intoxicating in about equal degrees. There were one or two tricky moments later in the evening when, having forgotten all about it, I failed to respond to the new name as my turn at the pool table was yelled across the room, but I managed to get through without being sprung. I slept that night in the sand dunes behind the beach and, next day, hitched on to Motueka, where I found a job picking tobacco.

The tobacco farmer lent me an old black bicycle to ride back and forth from my pup tent in the camping ground to his farm on the flat, rich land south of the town. He actually owned two farms, about a mile apart from each other, and he had two families, one on each farm. Wife, kids, house, dogs, cats, chooks: two sets of everything. He lived with the younger wife and younger kids on the farm up the back but commuted daily on his tractor to the land nearer town. It was here, where his seemingly amiable older wife and their several grown-up children stayed, that I went to work each morning on my bike.

My companions were itinerant youths who spent the winters grubbing tussock on the Canterbury Plains and the summers in Mot, as it was called, picking fruit or tobacco. They were vague, footloose, hedonistic. The only one I have a distinct memory of now was a lithe, dark, handsome youth called Angel, who one day showed me how, if you threw a clod of earth up into the high blue sky, the big black shapes of otherwise unseen flying insects – bees? blowflies? – dived out of the empyrean after it as it fell. That explained the humming sound that lay over us as we worked.

What I mostly did was pick out the laterals. This was done by hand, you pinched the growing shoots from the forks with your index finger and thumb then discarded them on to the ground, so the plant would turn out tall and straight and strong, with wide, spreading leaves. Picking laterals involved bending and straightening, bending and straightening, and was hell on your back. If you were harvesting the actual leaves, you worked on a machine that drove slowly along among the big-leaved, purple-flowering plants, with a number – four? – of attached, low-slung metal seats that were disposed by means of iron suspension arches between several rows at a time. You sat, just above ground level, on one of these seats, plucked the leaves and put them in a wire basket behind you.

Tobacco stalks, broken, exude a copious white sap that rapidly congeals to a black tarry resin. I used to scrape it off my hands back at the shed and wonder what I was doing, sucking this gunk into my lungs on a daily basis. The shed was where the social life of the farm went on, here we had our lunch and our morning and afternoon smoko, here was where everyone came and went from. It was a big barn with an open area between two kilns in which the picked tobacco leaves were draped, like washing, over wooden racks and left to dry.

Inevitably curious, one day I tried smoking some of this crackly desiccated leaf raw. I managed to get it rolled in cigarette papers and lit up. It burned hot and fast and the smoke I tried to draw in was bitter and harsh and practically impossible to inhale. That day, the farmer told me that what he grew was inferior quality product used only in blended roll-your-own tobaccos, while the tailor-mades I usually smoked were made exclusively of higher quality South African and Rhodesian weed; but that was not why I couldn't smoke it. It was because it hadn't been cured yet.

After work, I'd ride into town to have a beer in the raucous public bar at the Post Office Hotel on High Street. The first time I went in there I was hailed in a plummy accent by an older chap with the high colour and exploded facial veins of an habitual drinker. *Are you into tobacco or into fruit?* he enunciated. *I'm into fruit* . . . His name was James Stuart, known to all as Jimmy, and pinned up on the wall of the caravan where he lived was a great piece of yellowed parchment ornamented with red imperial crowns and heraldic crests, purporting to show his line of descent from the Royal House of Stuart, kings of Scotland and England in the sixteenth and seventeenth century. Bonnie Prince Charlie's lot.

Jimmy co-existed in a paradoxical warp with the aggressively straight males in the public bar. They loved him and he loved them, but no obvious sexual consummation was going to be reached or, if reached, ever admitted: their relationship was of the kind that anthropologists call *joking*. The air was usually blue about Jimmy, blue with hilarity, with innuendo, with downright obscenity. I remember one young bloke pulling his stubbies and his undies down right there in the full view of everyone, while Jimmy's trembling hand forbore attempting that elusive touch. The one time I went back to his caravan with him, he got me drunk on Scotch whisky but didn't insist when I made it clear I wasn't going to have sex with him; I seem to recall melancholy alcoholic weeping as I wobbled away into the night on the farmer's bicycle, but they might have been crocodile tears.

Another night I left the Post Office Hotel in company with some nameless others in a car that we drove way out into the backblocks looking for a rumoured party. I ended up, bizarrely, in some bunkhouse or shearers' quarters in a single bed with a pale, dark-haired Australian girl, while two other couples, likewise in single beds, lay together on either side of us. When the girl adjudged the others to be sleeping, she pushed her two thumbs into the elastic of her panties and rolled them down so we could make brief furtive love under the cold sheets and prickly woollen blanket. I don't know what happened after that. Next morning, hungover, I found myself walking alone down some country road until a car stopped and drove me back to town.

On my day off I took a tab of LSD I'd been saving for a while and lay in my tent reading, of all things, Milton's *Paradise Lost*. I was at the part where Satan hies him off to hell with the other fallen angels when I realised I could not go on: *So stretched out huge in length the arch-fiend lay / Chained on the burning lake . . .* It was that day, a Sunday, that a big red bus bumped into the camping ground and the members of Bruno Lawrence's Electric Revelation and Travelling Apparition set up their tent. One of the women of the troupe was kind enough to come over and ask how I was doing but, rendered all but wordless by the acid, I never took the opportunity to get to know her, or any of BLERTA, better. I didn't see the show either, because this happened right at the end of my stint as a tobacco picker and, next morning, I packed up my tent and headed south to see K.

III

Just out of Hokitika, a big humped American 1940s car, a Ford or a Dodge or a Chevrolet, stopped and offered me a lift. There were two blokes sitting up in the front, one older, one younger, with the older one driving. From Timaru. They didn't talk much but, as evening drew on, mentioned a caravan they used while duck shooting, off the road nearby, and said I could stay the night with them there if I wanted to. I said yes, something I would never do now, and pretty soon we left the highway and wound our way into the swampy land between the main drag and the sea, south of Okarito.

The caravan was in a small clearing in scrubby swampland and the inside was papered over in its entirety with *Playboy* centrefolds. Grinning teeth, breasts and buttocks, golden thighs, everywhere you looked. If you went outside, as you had to do to go to the toilet, the sandflies were so bad you needed to wrap your head in a towel. Even so, they would cluster along the skin of your eyelids, or mass blackly on the backs of your hands. They were the biggest sandflies I have ever seen, juicy as bugs when you squashed them. The two blokes cooked a meal and gave me a bunk to sleep in. Nothing untoward occurred and next morning, after breakfast, we went back out on the road again.

But later that day, as we neared Haast, something did happen. The older bloke, still driving, pulled over to the side of the road at the northern approach to the Haast Bridge. *Come on*, he said, *I'll show you something. What?* I asked. *You'll see*, he said, leering at his mate. The three of us walked down under the bridge. *There*, he said, pointing to an undistinguished spot of waste ground, with weeds and stones and dirt and nothing else to remark upon. *What?* I said again, starting to feel a little faint. He and his mate exchanged another wolfish look. *That's where Jennifer Beard's body was found,* he said.

We walked silently back up to the car, where I said thanks very much but I wouldn't be coming any further with them that day. They were incredulous – they were going all the way to Central after all, maybe even to Dunedin – but I was quite certain I wasn't getting back in that car with those jokers. They shrugged and drove off south and I walked over the Haast Bridge alone and went and had a cup of tea and a bun at a roadside café. I was thinking about Jennifer Beard.

She was a 25-year-old school teacher on a hitch-hiking holiday who, on the last day of 1969, was raped and murdered and her body left under the northern approach to the Haast Bridge. It's thought that she went under the bridge to pee, was there surprised by the man – or men – who had most likely given her a ride, violated and then strangled. Police thought the car in question was a 1950s Vauxhall Velox and even went so far as to identify a possible driver. This man, also from Timaru, was repeatedly and anonymously interviewed over a number of years before eventually going public himself. He said that, although he and his car had been in the area at the time, he was not guilty of the crime. No one was ever arrested for or charged with the murder of Jennifer Beard.

After that, Dunedin was an anticlimax. I pitched my tent in the city camping ground and walked into town to ring K. Her mother told me she was in hospital. I went up to see her. She was lying there on the high white bed, her dark hair cascading around her gaunt, beautiful face, her porcelain skin a startling yellow colour. She had contracted hepatitis from her junkie boyfriend, a notorious dealer and underground identity whose name was once, but no longer, known to me. Rod someone or other. K was still besotted with him and barely had the energy for a wan smile and murmur of surprise at my apparition there at her bedside. I stayed maybe half an hour then went away. Next day, my futile passion undeclared as well as unrequited, I hitched up to Christchurch to stay with my ex-girlfriend's brother and, later, catch the inter-island ferry back to Wellington.

IV

I saw K a few times after that, we remained friends, but nothing ever happened between us and our last meeting was so long ago now I cannot even recall it. She went to London, worked in publishing, married, had children, divorced, is now in another relationship. I think – I hope – she's happy. And yet I know, if ever I were to see her again, I would be beguiled in the same old way. Some things never change, and unrequited love seems to be one of them. Why, I wonder?

Is it because the unrequited lover does not really love the beloved? He or she desires the other, no doubt about that, but does not ask what it is s/he can give, only what can be taken. Let me have your love and then I will be happy. This overweening desire can outlast disappointment and rejection because it does not want a real but a phantom lover, a phantom other. I could go further and suggest that it is also a phantom self who desires the phantom lover. The illusiveness of both self and other makes the 'love' resistant to any reality check. And yet, if, somehow, the rejection of the self by the beloved does transgress into the real, then it is possible, in some people, that the antithetical desire to do the other harm is born.

Is there then a connection between the mental processes of unrequited love and those who kill for sex? It's a scary thought, but maybe so. How? Perhaps in the misapprehension that underlies the nexus of phantom self / phantom other. Perhaps in the desire to possess someone who doesn't want to be possessed, or not by you. It's certain that many, maybe most, men entertain random lusts for women they don't know and can never be with. Few of these are likely to act upon their impulses and, of that few, only a tiny proportion will ever act violently. And even among this moiety, the circumstances probably have to be peculiar and unlikely enough to make the occurrence extremely rare. All men are not rapists; but some can be persuaded by illicit desire and its frustration to take what they cannot otherwise have. And the sequel, as in the case of Jennifer Beard, may be murder: the brutal dispatch of the misapprehended other.

It's probably more common for men to turn the violence rejection can breed against themselves. I had a friend from that time who did just that, coming down to Christchurch from blade shearing in the Alps one cold September day in 1984 to find his house emptied, his flatmates and their things gone, his own packed up and left in a corner of his room. He went to a nearby pub to call his girlfriend and, after this conversation – but what was said? – returned to that desolate house, ran a hot bath and drew his shears along the veins of his wrists. There were other factors but, on the face of it, he died of love gone wrong. He was not the kind who would have hurt another.

What about the blokes from Timaru? There is no way of knowing if I rode to that weird rendezvous in Haast with a couple of gruesome voyeurs who got a thrill out of contemplating one of the dark places of the earth; or something much worse. Two years after the murder, how did they know where the spot was and why did they show it to me? What did they expect me to say? See? These questions are unanswerable, which may be why the strangeness of the encounter has stayed with me: from the caravan with its centrefold wallpaper in the sandfly-infested swamp to the equivocal gloom under the bridge, with cars racketting by overhead, when it did seem for one shuddering moment that the inconsolable ghost of the murdered woman hung in the air before the grimacing spectres of those who had sent her hence. And the silent witness I was.

Prospect Bay

I

Towards the end of the university year in 1972, I took down the name and number of a farmer who was advertising, on the noticeboard in the Quad, for two students to spray the gorse on his land at Takatu. The deal was concluded by telephone and, one October day soon afterwards, I hitch-hiked north out of Auckland with a pack on my back and, no doubt, a wild surmise in my eye. Like so many others in that far-off time, I was consumed by a desire to go back to the land – whatever that meant.

Prospect Bay was on the southern coast of Tawharanui peninsula, a spine of hills running east from Matakana into the Hauraki Gulf. The point, called Tokatu, lies just north of Kawau Island. The nearest town of any size is Warkworth, away to the south. I was let out at the turn-off at Omaha Flats and walked the rest of the way to the farm gate. A few miles. It was a Sunday. Late spring. Warm. Under a blue sky hazed with cirrus, the unsealed road was a dusty white and pink briar roses grew in great banks alongside it. The humming of bees merged with the delicate scent of the roses and the delirious song of unseen skylarks high above. I seemed to be walking into an old story. I couldn't have been happier.

The farmer was a decent chap, vaguely patrician, with one of those displaced English upper-class accents. He drove me from the farm house down the twisting track that led to the bay where I would be living and working for the next couple of months. His land was beautiful: green rolling hill pasture, stands of native bush nestling in the gullies, young tall kauri or round glossy puriri here and there, banks of kanuka flowering in great gulfs of white. Prospect Bay was a small, quiet beach between two rocky headlands with a creek at one end, yellow sand, great gnarled pohutukawa trees leaning over blue water. Old diggings where copper had been prospected for, giving the bay its name. There was a wooden cottage standing on flats just back of the strand. This was where we – me and the other student – would be living.

Wayne was an Engineer. A tall red-headed bloke who rode a black Indian motorbike. He arrived later that evening, belching smoke. There was then, at Auckland University, an absolute division between engineering and arts students. They had a chant: *We are we are we are we are the engineers.* They were bluff and crass and boozy, at least by reputation, while we, in our own minds, were far more sophisticated. We did not play sport. We demonstrated. Against all sorts of things, but particularly the Vietnam War. Most important, we were individuals, not a pack of brute like-minded fellows. So it was perhaps inevitable that Wayne and I would fall out with each other. For the moment, however, we were civil and made, I suppose, some kind of meal together.

The job started next morning. It was fairly straight forward. We'd go to the bridge over the creek just up the track from the cottage and make the mixture to be sprayed on the gorse. The 24D came in round tins; it was a yellowy, viscous, evil-smelling liquid that we poured into the big shiny square steel tank welded on to a trailer. Mixed with water from the creek, it turned into a cloudy, milky white substance that could be sprayed through a nozzle and a hose by a pump connected to the tank. We'd fill up and then bump off on the tractor into the gorse-covered hills. There, one of us would drive and the other spray. The hose was long so you could get down into the gullies and round the other side of the bigger clumps of the gorse. It was not hard work and we could do it at our own pace. When the tank was empty we'd go down to refill and start again. We'd get through maybe four or five tank loads a day, with a single break for lunch.

The herbicide 24D (dichlorophenoxyacetic acid) is, with 245T, the other main constituent of Agent Orange, which the American military had just stopped (1971) deluging over Indochina. Both compounds are chemically similar to the plant hormone, indoleacetic acid, that controls growth and metabolism. 24D and 245T affect the growing points of plants, though their mode of action is still not completely understood. Whatever it is causes the root system and the leaves to flourish uncontrollably. The plant grows itself to death. A few days after we'd sprayed a clump of gorse, it would take on a weirdly fluorescent look, greener than green; but if you went back a week later, those mutant over-sized spurs would already have begun to brown. Two weeks, and the entire plant was dead.

We had no idea. We used no safety equipment whatsoever. No masks, no gloves, no protective overalls. Mostly we just wore shorts and boots. And we were profligate with the stuff. As we drenched the land, we also got it all over our skin and hair and clothes, in our eyes, we breathed it, we even sprayed it on each other sometimes. The farmer never said anything about possible toxicity; perhaps he didn't know. The word *dioxin* wasn't commonly used in those days. There's still dispute in some quarters about whether it occurs as a by-product of 24D, as it certainly does with 245T. I used to wonder if the spray might have shifted my genes around.

II

I was there for other reasons entirely. I'd left university, my degree one ninth uncompleted, to be a Poet. This meant I had to learn many things: the names and orbits and positions of the planets, stars and constellations, for instance; the lore of trees; the nature of the weather and the seasons; most of all, I had to learn about the past. It was necessary to reconnect with what had happened before so that it could, in some meaningful way, inform the present and influence the future. I recall, when my mother stopped her red and white Hillman Imp on a suburban street in Huntly one day and said, *What's it going to be, a doctor or a lawyer?* replying, *Actually, I want to be an archaeologist.* I no longer harboured that ambition but knowledge of archaeology, along with astronomy, was a major part of my desire to be a Poet.

Days off, I would ramble around the coast looking for pa sites. On a small headland to the east, I found what looked like terracing beneath a carpet of fragrant penny royal and tiny wild strawberries, and did some digging. I still have the flakes of obsidian and the brown fragile fish and bird bones I pulled out of the earth there. In a swamp behind the beach I dug up more obsidian, more bones, along with pieces of chert and jasper. The pounamu adzes or pendants I yearned for did not appear but, with a piece of greenstone bought from the museum shop in Auckland, I began to fashion my own hei tiki or hei matau in the old way, sitting out on the back step after work grinding the obdurate jade on sandstone slabs hauled up from the beach.

I had a planisphere – *Showing the Principal Stars Visible for every Hour in the Year from Latitude 35° South* – and used to switch my gaze from its obscure plastic roundel to the no less obscure lights in the sky, trying to map the constellations. I'd copied out of a book the recipe for the spruce beer Captain Cook brewed in Fiordland as an anti-scorbutic for his men; with rimu and manuka leaves gathered from the local bush, and what else I can't remember, I began fermenting my own mess in the washhouse of the cottage. While it hissed and bubbled, I'd read Thomas Hardy novels borrowed from the university library: *Jude the Obscure, The Return of the Native, Far from the Madding Crowd*, also had something – but what? – to do with living in the country and becoming a Poet. At least my book of Gary Snyder poems, *The Back Country*, made a kind of sense, even though I was very far from the kind of Paleolithic Zen he practised.

I don't know if it was the peculiarity of my occupations or something else that put me offside with Wayne. Maybe we were just too different. We worked companionably together for a week or two, then things started getting edgy. While we could keep it more or less together through the day, evenings degenerated into a wordless tension as we skirted each other round the house while the mutton the farmer brought us spat in the oven. It was a classic case of cabin fever I suppose and pretty soon we were just a twitch away from an actual physical fight. This we somehow avoided. Just as well – he would probably have slaughtered me. He was an Engineer after all. But our silent strife soon found a focus that may also have been a cause of it: Dean Buchanan.

Dean lived with Snail, who was a real as opposed to an aspiring Poet, in a small house on the hill behind the town of Leigh, a bit up the coast from where we were. Dean and I were in the first flush of a youthful friendship that was in many respects a romance. Not that we were, or ever would be, lovers; but we were as if in love with each other. Dean was flamboyant, hilarious, an outrageous mimic, and practised in the arts of provocation. He enjoyed antagonising those he could not charm or seduce. In other words, he was as unlike me as anyone could be. Nevertheless, we had a bond, predicated upon the admiration I felt for all those qualities that were not mine. He would lead and I would follow and together we would do unconscionable things.

Dean was quite capable of walking the dozen or so miles cross country from Leigh to Takatu and maybe that's what he did the first time he came there. Or he may have persuaded someone to drive him. Later, and without asking, I would borrow Wayne's Indian and ride it over to Leigh – which seems incredible now, both the helping myself and the riding, since I really didn't know how to do that. Dean embraced Prospect Bay with his usual exuberance and on his visits we would embark on epic walks across the hills, sometimes surprising the flocks of feral turkeys that lived there. These we would try to run down, and if we caught one, as we sometimes did, we'd strangle and then cook it to make a tough but satisfying alternative to the ubiquitous mutton.

Wayne knew Dean already, though only by sight. He and his mates had watched him drinking in the Kiwi, tossing his long golden curls and shouting erotics. To the engineers he was a figure of ridicule. They even had a nickname for him: Flighty. To meet Flighty in person and discover he was a friend of mine was confronting for Wayne. There was no possible common ground between them and, while I can't recall exactly how this happened, it was no surprise when Wayne left the job prematurely and Dean took his place as my mate in the gorse spraying. That didn't last very long either, since Dean was more or less unemployable, but we did work a week or so together before heading off towards other escapades.

III

The farmer must have been a tolerant man. A gentleman, too. He loved his land and he looked after it well. There were a lot of trees on it, which he consciously nurtured, as he protected the stands of remnant bush in the gullies. The farm was plagued, as many farms still are, with opossums, and he fought unremittingly against them and their depredations. One of our jobs, every evening, was to set the traps he'd laid about the bay for them. There were about a dozen and a half of these, mostly in and around the pohutukawa trees the possums were busy destroying. Those jaw traps were fearsome things. Baited with apple, they had a flat metal platform with a hair trigger that, when stepped upon, or even touched, released the two jagged steel claws to snap viciously together. The animal would sometimes be caught by the head, in which case it would probably be dead when you checked the traps in the morning; more often, they were held by a leg and thus still alive. Then you had to kill them.

The farmer had given us a special implement for this. It was a length of native hardwood, perhaps from the root of a pohutukawa itself, perhaps from a piece of knotted kanuka. About two foot long, it had a curve at one end, like a half-size hockey stick. You had to beat the possums to death with the outside of the curved end. Possums are hard to kill. They would see you coming and start to hiss and snarl and twist in the trap. By this time, the clawed leg would be reduced to furless, bloody sinew and bone, but the animal, panic in its lustrous eyes, would still struggle to get away. Occasionally, especially after some practice, I could kill with one blow. Usually I'd have to whack away five or six or more times before it was done.

When the farmer showed us where the traps were, how and when to set and check them, how to kill, I asked him what we were to do with the bodies? *Chuck 'em in the creek*, was the crisp reply. I more or less got used to the killing, but I hated throwing the bodies into the creek. They must have drifted out to sea, becoming fish food, and there probably isn't anything wrong with that; but it seemed as bad a pollution of that lovely place as their living presence there was.

The brute aspect of farming can't be ignored, even by a gentleman. There's always some killing you have to do around a farm. But our farmer showed himself in a different light on election night. Wayne – he was still there then – and I were invited up to the house for the celebration. The farmer belonged to the National Party, he was on the committee for the local electorate of Rodney. They had gathered to see their member, and Jack Marshall's government (Keith Holyoake had retired as leader the previous February), re-elected. Except of course it didn't happen. It was time for a change. Norman Kirk's Labour Party won the poll easily.

I was amused to watch, over the course of the evening, the mood in those elegant rooms, with a portrait of Captain Cook looking doubtfully down over us, darkening. People, mostly other farmers and their wives, began to ignore the delectable food on offer in favour of the brandy bottle. The farmer kept refilling our glasses too. The company was made up of those who believe they are born to rule, that a polity in its natural state would always choose them and their representatives to govern. To learn that it wasn't so, at least not on this occasion, was unacceptable. They were sullenly disbelieving: this could not be happening. Except it was. I never declared my allegiance, it seemed impolite, but I remember chortling happily to Wayne as we stumbled later back down the track to the beach, under stars blazing in a sky that seemed, for once, to belong to us. Or rather, to me: Wayne, it turned out, was a National Party supporter too. Perhaps that's when things started to sour?

IV

I don't know what happened to the greenstone pendant I never finished making. The spruce beer, which Dean and I broached and drank towards the end of our stay, was raw, astringent, with a leafy taste and hardly enough alcohol in it to have an effect, though we pretended to like it, and even to get a little drunk on it. I remember the trees I got to know and love. And the stars. I drew a map of the pa site and sent it to the Auckland Museum, my sole contribution to archaeology. There are a few poems I still feel a fugitive affection for, though fortunately they were never published.

The following year, Dean and I moved into a house together down Pukapuka Road, on the Mahurangi estuary, south of Takatu, and spent the best part of 1973 living there, often in a state of dire penury, frequently hungry, subsisting on porridge, wild turkeys, field mushrooms, and the scant money we sometimes earned cutting scrub with slashers for the local Bohemian farmers round Puhoi. We'd shake down the friends we persuaded to visit for cash and use it to buy tobacco, alcohol and food, in that order. I was still going to be a Poet but the paucity of my efforts had begun to fill me with a despair that, by the end of that drink- and drug-addled year, brought me as close to psychosis as I have been. I was barely *compos mentis* when I set out for Wellington and another career, this time as a Writer.

Yet I had learned something, albeit inadvertently. Dean was and is a painter. Talented, self-taught, confident, he was also supremely dedicated: he lived, forgive the phrase, for his art. And he was generous, in that he often gave paintings away, and in his willingness to open up to others the processes by which he made his works. It was from watching him paint, as he did almost every day, that I discovered how such things are done: not the knowledge of a practitioner, I was still years away from that, but the lesser knowledge of an observer. So it was that, the next year, 1974, I began as an art critic to make my slow way into the still beguiling wonders of print.

Meanwhile, it seems that on that faraway October day I was walking, not into an old story but out of one. I haven't been back, but last time I went to Kawau, it looked from the ferry as if there are now holiday homes where once was just a wooden cottage standing on a quiet shore. Maybe the farmer – was his name Henderson? – subdivided and sold his land. If so, the copper diggings on the hills, worked by Cornishmen, those remnant Celtic people from whom, through my father, I am descended, will have disappeared under the bulldozers. I imagine the possums are still there, though not perhaps the pohutukawa. The obsidian and the chert, the bird bones and fish bones, and maybe the long bones of humans too, remain. In the next-door cove, Millon Bay, popsters the Thompson Twins built a mansion.

The story I was walking out of wasn't even that old, it was just a moment in time; but it's still in my mind. I remember the new growth on the kauri trees flashing silver and gold in the sunlight and the wind. The branch of an old taraire tree, bent like an elbow, we always had to duck under as the tractor jolted along the fenceline at the top of the paddock. The little blue moths that danced above the grasses in the dawn. Gulfs of white on the flowering kanuka. The way purple flowers would fall from the puriri on to the ground round about, and how, underneath a big stand, you could walk between the trunks as if among dark pillars in a temple. The mint smell and the sharp, sweet taste of wild strawberries. Swimming after work in the phosphorescent waters of the bay. Nights on the yellow sand that the moonlight turned to bone while the tide gathered the bodies of possums outward.

Most of all I remember the white road hedged with briar rose, the bees and the skylarks, the sky humming with light; and then I seem to hear my own footsteps scuffing through the dust, no longer walking away but returning to what can't be: down the parabola of years, that paradise found again.

On Trains

Don't say I never warned you
When your train gets lost
— BOB DYLAN

Memory is a palimpsest, recent theory speculates. When we remember, we revisit and in that process revise a site we have been to before. In other words, we don't go back to the unrecoverable original trace, but to our most recent remembrance of it. If this is so, each enactment becomes a re-enactment, each indulgence a re-indulgence, iteration piled upon iteration, past repletion, in a dizzying maze of revisions and reversions that makes a shape as repetitive, redundant and baroque as the Mandelbrot set.

A memory is like a treasure box, then, full of objects that have been handled so often they are as if varnished with age. In the Tanimbar Islands in eastern Indonesia, this image is made literal: treasure boxes are taken, on special occasions, down from the rafters of the house, opened, the precious things within unwrapped and under the sightless eye sockets of the skulls of the ancestors, passed from hand to hand while their stories are re-told; after which both they and those who have handled them are ceremonially oiled before the taonga are re-stowed in the rafters.

My earliest memory is of a bull calf, Sooky; or rather, it is a memory of my solo visit to the bull calf's paddock; but, curiously, this memory includes within it reference to an earlier occasion which, while it surely happened, I do not in fact recall. In this strange concatenation an opening appears, or seems to appear, into the dark backward that is childhood before memory traces are made, as in the testimony of those who claim to recall the unrecallable, their rupture from the womb.

I am walking down a path towards a gate. I am so small, and the grass on either side so tall, that the seed heads bend above me, making an arch. Cocksfoot, brown top, featherhead, rye. I am scared but determined. Scared because Sooky the bull calf lives in the paddock behind the gate and, although I have been this way before with my sisters (this is the recall inside the memory), I have never come alone. To come this way alone is also the root of my determination. I reach the end of the path and climb up the wooden planks of the gate set into a hedge, which is in fact more fence than gate, since I don't know how, or even if, it opened. And I look at Sooky the black bull calf, who looks back at me with drool looping off his muzzle. Exultant and afraid, heart hammering, trembling . . .

That was when we rented the Farm House at Ohakune Junction off Mr McCullough, the headmaster of the District High where my father taught. I must have been about three years old because I was born while we lived in that house and we only stayed three years and a bit before buying and moving into our own place in Burns Street. The Farm House had a long hilly drive down to the road and a cottage on the left near the bottom where another family lived. It was very close to the Main Trunk Line and we must have heard the trains passing daily and nightly, as they did in those days and perhaps still do.

Many years later, or ago, I tried to persuade myself I remembered the pattern on the linoleum floors of the corridors of Raetihi Hospital, where I came into the world, but this was either a recall of subsequent visits or a fiction. As a matter of fact, I was a large baby and in giving birth to me, my mother suffered a tearing of her abdominal muscles that necessitated an operation about six months later to repair the damage. In her autobiography she remarks that when Dr Jordan came to speak with her beforehand, he asked, as if he were God and she Eve, if she wanted a navel? Yes, she said, but ever after her belly was lumpy and wrinkled and on the few occasions I saw it, I felt a pang because I knew I had, albeit inadvertently, done that to her.

We were breastfed babies so I went back to the hospital with her for the op, but that is still too early for memories of linoleum. Nevertheless, when I consider that pre-conscious life, the one we all have and all forget, I sometimes imagine myself at her breast in the dead of night while the Limited Express passes up or down the island, its *chuff-chuff-chuffa* and hiss of steam, its whistle coming into or pulling out of the station – not a memory as such but a pre-memory, something lodged in the senses which would be reprised again and again, through just about every night of my childhood until I was ten years old, becoming a part of me, like mother's milk.

Of course these nightly visitations mostly happened while I was sleeping and so must have been more like dreams; but there were many times when I woke in the Burns Street house and heard the northbound train labouring as it pulled across the face of Te Rangakaika, the range of bush-covered hills before Ruapehu, just a mile or two away across the Mangawhero River and the Waimarino plain from where we lived. The enormous banshee wail of the train whistle would echo off the flank of the mountain and ghost across the dark and otherwise silent land like a loneliness too awful for words, and it would be a comfort to snuggle back down under the covers and listen to the sound of the metal wheels dying along the rails.

I don't know when the books of the Rev. W. Awdry entered my life but it must have been early. I still have some of the old hardback copies from my childhood; the sadly disintegrated one open on the desk beside me as I write is Railway Series No. 1, the very first, published in May 1945 by Edmund Ward of 16 New Street, Leicester, and reprinted twelve times before this impression, from October 1952, when I was just nine months old. It's called *The Three Railway Engines* and has beautiful colour-plate illustrations by C. Reginald Dalby.

The three engines are Gordon the Big Engine, Henry the Green Engine and Edward the Blue Engine and the picture on the first page shows six engines in one railway shed, none of which is Thomas the Tank Engine, with whom the series has since become indelibly associated. I'm not quite sure now who all the six engines in the picture actually are but I do know that, when young, I tended to conflate the children in our family with the Rev. W. Awdry's engines. We were, in descending order of seniority, Gordon, Henry, James, Edward, Percy and Thomas. In this strange simulacrum of myself and my siblings, which transgendered all of my five sisters, I was James the Red Engine, a disagreeable character, vain and self-important, who suffers a calamitous fall. These original stories are in fact all quite disagreeable (one of their favoured words) in themselves, since, like the contemporary Snakes and Ladders, they attempt to narrate virtue rewarded and vice punished in a fairly hamfisted manner.

This didn't bother me as a child because I didn't really rate the morality tale ahead of the actual trials and tribulations of the engines themselves, their humiliations and heroisms, their failures and triumphs. Now when I open the books, it is the pictures that bring back those long-ago emotions, for example the claustrophobic terror I felt and still feel at the sight of Henry the Green Engine being bricked up in a tunnel because he refused to allow his new coat of paint to be wet by the rain. In this instance, the moral failed to bite, since I could never see that anything done or not done by Henry justified such an horrific punishment.

47

Another peculiarity of these stories was that the clean, brightly coloured and personable engines, with their lips and eyes and noses, bore little resemblance to the heaving, black, oily steam-wreathed monsters that pulled the real trains we saw, more or less on a daily basis. The school I went to, Ohakune Primary, had running behind it a branch line connecting Raetihi and the Junction, and it was a favourite sport of ours, during or after school, to go up the back where the macrocarpas grew and watch the train go by.

It was a small engine, with perhaps a couple of trucks and one carriage for passengers, plus guard's van, but tremendous for all that, with its hissing of steam and thundering of wheels. Sometimes we placed pennies on the track and marvelled at the way they returned elongated and skinny and bowed from being squeezed between wheel and rail. Or we indulged a fantasy that too close an encounter with a train would lead to us being sucked under the engine or the carriages, and so, having come as near as we dared, we clutched on to trackside bracken or scrub for support in an ecstasy of pretended fear for our lives.

The fatality of trains was real enough, however, as attested by the Tangiwai Disaster which, while it occurred when I was not quite two years old, loomed balefully over the rest of our lives in that place. For a long time you could see in the river bed the ruined carriages lying alongside the tumbled pillars of the bridge swept away by the combined weight of the northbound train and the lahar flooding out of Ruapehu's crater lake; and everybody in that small community had a tale to tell, usually of loss and grief, though not always: Barry Reynolds, who lived a few doors up from us in Burns Street, coming home for Christmas, caught the train in Taihape and, because he rode in the almost empty first carriage which, with the engine, made it across before the bridge fell, survived the wreck.

And then there was the fatality of the Whangaehu (*wan-guy-hoo*, we said, not *fanga-ehu*) itself, the turbid stream, with its sulphurous smell and cloudy yellow waters, as if it was a river out of hell, whose malignity, it seemed to me, was a cause of the taking of the train and the death, among so many others, of laughing Clare Kennedy who had lived, with her sister Gay and her many Irish brothers, on a farm out at Karioi where we were lucky enough sometimes to go.

I never really understood why the railway station at Greytown, the place we moved to after leaving Ohakune, stood at Woodside, five miles from the town. It seemed unaccountable, given the flatness of the terrain, especially since all the other places on that line – Featherston, Carterton, Masterton, Eketahuna, Pahiatua, Mangatainoka, Woodville – had stations where they belonged, in or at least on the outskirts of town.

On the other hand, that railway line was itself a kind of boy's paradise we would ride to on our bikes at the weekend or in the holidays, to ramble untrammelled through the long dusty afternoons down the hot rails all the way to the river bridge where we swam in deep pools beneath the piles and sometimes heard the thrilling sound of a train going over above, shaking the world to its implacable core. Or perhaps it would be a jigger, those odd engineless vehicles that were worked up and down the rails by men, usually in pairs, operating levers.

Parallel to the train tracks on the further side there was a grassy step about twelve foot high that marked the fault line of the 1855 earthquake, the same one that raised the shelf of land upon which the Hutt Road leading into Wellington runs. It was strange to contemplate the extreme regularity of this upthrust, suggesting as it did that somewhere beneath the chaos of appearances there was another, more arcane, geological order to things.

It was near this prodigy, in one of those mysterious gravel pits you find next to railway lines, that a group of us stripped off one day and compared our rapidly burgeoning private parts, searching out and counting the black pubic hairs just beginning to grow down there: he who had the most somehow thereby gained the highest status among us. I remember my own modest total, seventeen, but little else beyond the peculiarity of Douglas Workman's cock, which, when erect, bent alarmingly to one side like a banana. And that Grant Batty, the future All Black, whom we called Butch, had the smallest one any of us had ever seen.

Further away, up in the wilds of the Rimutakas, were the remains of a railway worked, like the line in Awdry's *Mountain Engines*, by trains that hooked on to a third chain-rail running along the centre between the other two. On a tramp up there one time I saw a stretch of this defunct track culminating in a tunnel that brought to mind the only one of Enid Blyton's Famous Five stories to have left a trace in my memory, about a ghost train that ran ferociously out of just such a derelict tunnel in the black of night towards some fatal destination. I have forgotten the probably mundane explanation for this phenomenon – smuggling perhaps – while retaining the image of the driverless engine hurtling on forever in all its terror and beauty.

If you were going to Wellington from Greytown, you went either by road over the windy Rimutakas or to Woodside to catch the railcar through the tunnel under them, coming out at Maymorn and traversing the evocatively named stations on that route: Brown Owl, Upper Hutt, Trentham, Silverstream, Taita, Naenae, Waterloo, Ava, Petone and then on through Ngauranga and Kaiwharawhara to the vastness of Wellington Railway Station, forever associated in my mind with the rolling stock full of rotting meat and oranges my father remembered seeing there during the Depression.

Woodside is in fact linked for me with my father in his aged state, because he retired to Greytown and sometimes after my visits to him he would drive me out to the station and I would leave by train. At one of these partings, on a bleak winter morning with the grey horizontal rain blowing off the Tararuas, as if negating my youthful priapism just down the line, he confided that he had not had an erection for years and furthermore that

50

it was *a relief*. This was one of the side effects of the pills he took for his depression and his panic attacks.

After that dismal occasion, or another, I remember being at Woodville Station waiting for a train and, to get out of the cold, sheltering in the providentially open waiting room. For some reason I left the room for a moment, perhaps to go to the toilet, and the mean wind slammed the door shut behind me, locking my luggage inside. For those ten minutes or so, alone on the deserted platform, my habitual melancholy took on cosmic proportions and I utterly despaired, until a battered Vauxhall Velox made its uncertain way into the station carpark and a glum railwayman unlocked the waiting room door.

Those waiting rooms, in earlier days and on the Main Trunk Line, stayed open all night long with a coal fire burning in the grate, a radio playing and some cheerful blokes sitting over it with mugs of railway tea and packets of Greys or Park Drive or Pocket Edition tobacco; I recall once at Taihape spending a few feet-warming hours in one of these listening, improbably, to rock 'n' roll records playing on a Sydney, Australia, station they had somehow picked up.

We moved again, to Huntly, where our house at 5 Dudley Avenue on the derisively named Nob Hill overlooked a hillside of clay and gorse, the rugby league ground where Test matches were sometimes played, and the shunting yards that worked through the night as trucks of coal from the mines arrived and were assembled into trains by small diesel engines. By this time – but when did it happen? – steam engines were a curiosity you hardly ever encountered.

Branch lines served the mines both west and east of the town: Kimihia, Rotowaro, Glen Afton, Pukemiro, where little cottages clung to steep hillsides and in winter hardly saw the sun. At Trevor McLeish's Glen Afton house, tiny as it was, the front room was never used unless there was a wedding or a funeral and the furniture in there lay silent and still under white covers while everyone crowded around the coal range in the kitchen, like an engine itself with its hot black iron and red and yellow lights, its hissing, steaming wetback.

Those nights at Dudley Avenue, especially Thursday nights, I would lie awake in my Education Department-built prefabricated room away from the main house, in form not unlike a railway hut, listening to that incessant revving and clanging and crashing, wondering at the infernal energy that drove men to work around the clock; yet never once questioned the utility of the wagons of gleaming black coal because in all the years of my growing up we were never without a fire, sustained by lumps of coal that glowed on long after the wood had gone to powdery grey ash.

Huntly was on the Main Trunk Line as well but the *Limited* came through early in the evening, from Auckland, and then early the next morning, from Wellington, and the line was so busy that it seemed without the enormous significance it had in 'Kune: just another train. Whereas the shunting yard has stayed with me and every time Red Alert, the rock 'n' roll band I went to America with, played their cover of Warren Zevon's 'Nighttime in the Switching Yard' I was back there in the wee small hours hearing that sound like industrial teeth grinding.

Later still, when we had moved from Huntly to Heretaunga, and my father suffered his first breakdown and my mother announced herself as a poet, it came to be time for me to leave home and I did so on the *Limited Express*. Though only notionally together by now, both parents saw me off, with my three younger sisters in tow, at the Wellington Railway Station and I rode the length of the Main Trunk Line to Auckland alone and for the very first time.

It was a memorable trip, not just because I was leaving home: early on, myself and another stray youth teamed up with two girls travelling together and, sitting in pairs opposite each other, with a tartan blanket over our knees (my mother had sewed my surname on one corner of it), we played cards for most of the night. I have forgotten the girl's name but can still remember the delicious feeling of our legs entwined together under the blanket, though it seems strange to me now that that's all we did. She wore tartan as well and was prettier than her friend, or so I thought at the time.

All through my university years we travelled home and away by train, stopping for refreshments at Frankton (Hamilton), Taihape and Palmerston North. You'd go to buy your pie or sandwich or cake and cup of tea in the station cafeteria and take the heavy crockery plate and cup and saucer, with their blue NZR monograms, back to your seat and afterwards leave them on the floor to be collected later by a railwayman with a wheeled wooden trolley that clunked up the aisle. They seemed unbreakable, even when one cut loose and rolled up and down or from side to side in the carriage. You could smoke on the train as well, and drink, though I don't recall doing that.

Mostly you'd try to sleep against the two big white pillows hired on the platform before the journey began, surfacing at each stop to see the blurred shapes of people joining or leaving the train, their breath steaming in the cold night air, huddled into coats as they went to their cars. I always tried to stay awake through the King Country, say from National Park to Taihape if I was going south, because I loved seeing the white or dark outline of Ruapehu on the skyline, the romance of viaducts over bush-filled gorges, the intensely evocative huddle of railway houses at Ohakune Junction where all the loneliness in the world seemed domiciled and where I imagined for years my own estranged soul wandering with the ghosts of trees.

One summer in those university years – it must have been 1971–72 – I spent travelling both islands doing casual agricultural work here and there, and ended up, at the fag end of January, as a farm hand on a Lands and Survey block out the back of Stratford, Taranaki, at a place called Pohokura. Our boss, a genial man with the improbable name of Herbie Blank, supervised half a dozen Borstal boys and me about the daily tasks that are to be done running sheep and cattle on a fairly rugged back country farm.

Fridays, we'd go down to the railway line at the bottom of the drive and catch a ride on a train going to Whangamomona just a few miles east. We'd drink at the pub until closing time, when the same train, consisting of an engine, a couple of carriages and a guard's van, trundled back to – Stratford, I suppose. It'd let us off at the cattle stop on Herbie Blank's drive and we'd roll up the hill to the shearers' quarters and roll ourselves into our single wirewove beds to sleep it off till crack of dawn when the farm work started up again.

The New Plymouth to Taumarunui railcar went through on that line too and you could also hitch a ride on that if you wanted to. One morning I got up at 4 a.m. and went down the drive in a darkness so intense I literally could not see my hand in front of my face. When the faint glow of the railcar's headlight beam appeared in the west, I stood out on the track waving my arms above my head, then leapt clear as the train approached. Somewhat to my surprise, it stopped; even more surprising, there wasn't another passenger aboard, so I rode up front with the driver and the guard, whose sport was counting the possums sitting out on the rails that we squashed as we rocketed through the bush into the dawn.

I don't remember what train I caught to Auckland but do recall in intense lysergic-assisted detail the Rolling Stones concert at Western Springs stadium that was my reason for going there. The moment Mick Jagger stepped to the microphone to sing the words of the old Robert Johnston song 'Love in Vain' –

When the traaaaiiiiiiin come in the staaaaaation . . .

seemed to last forever and I can replay it in my mind whenever

I want. At the end of the concert, the huge black man who'd spent most of his time on stage slowly bouncing a big coloured ball, came forward with a bowl of rose petals with which Mick showered the audience – or at least those few within reach of the stage.

Next day, coming down again, I caught the train back to Pohokura. And not long after that, but I don't know how long, trains ceased to be the first choice of travel among us and we began to go about by road, either hitch-hiking or driving in old cars we had somehow acquired.

When, a few years down the track, in Wellington, I wrote one of the first pieces of work I can still feel the magic of, it was a set of variations on a theme by W. B. Yeats, entitled 'Stations'. The Yeats poem is called 'Hound Voice' and begins: *Because we love bare hills and stunted trees / And were the last to choose the settled ground / . . . Our voices carry*; which for some reason reminded me of growing up in Ohakune. The work is in three parts and each part is named after a railway station: Horopito, The Junction, Tangiwai; all of them attempt to dramatise the moment of departure, a young man leaving on a train from a place he will never forget but won't return to either. Romantic as that but I was young then, just twenty-four.

The work took its theme from Yeats but, formally, it was based upon a poem by Charles Olson, his 'Variations done for Gerald Van De Wiele', which includes three versions of the Rimbaud lyric from *Une Saison en Enfer*, the one that begins: *O saisons, ô châteaux! / Quelle âme est sans défauts! // J'ai fait la magique étude / Du bonheur, qu'aucun n'élude*. Olson translates: *What soul / is without fault // Nobody studies / happiness . . .* in the first of his versions.

'Stations', which has not been published, was dedicated to my father and I sewed the few pieces of paper it consisted of between manila cards and bound them with a red ribbon to give to him.

The booklet returned to me after his death but I don't recall what comment he made about it, if indeed he made any. This was in strict contrast to my mother who, on the rare occasions I showed her any of my writing, usually had too much to say. It's odd in retrospect to think that I hung on every word my father did not utter while largely discounting the admirably enthusiastic and informative commentary my mother lavished upon me. Praise can be harder to bear than silence.

These days, after seven biblical years beside the sea, I am once again living near a railway line – the Western Line, that goes from Sydney's Central Station all the way across the continent to Perth. Sometimes I see the Indian Pacific pass through Summer Hill Station in the mid-afternoon; other times, usually on a Sunday, I hear the unmistakable *chuff-chuff-chuffa* and *whooo-hooo!* of a steam train going by and know it is the 3801, a restored Australian-built 1940s locomotive that does nostalgia runs up to Newcastle and back, one of which I went on, with my sons, for old time's sake a few years ago.

But mostly what I hear, in the early morning hours, is the sound of westbound suburban trains that, by a quirk of architecture, rebound off the brick wall of the next-door apartment building straight in my bedroom window. Then, half asleep, I am as if transported back to my childhood in that wooden villa in Burns Street under the spectral mountain, when our family was all one, unbroken, as we liked to imagine we would always be.

If I wake fully, as I often do, I might think about my parents, sundered in life and also in death, buried as they are on opposite sides of the tracks, as well as either side of the Rimutakas, he at Greytown, she in Akatarawa; but together then, during our King Country years. And this thought somehow leads on to a re-visioning of three images co-mingled and set together: the black bull calf Sooky bawling in the home paddock; the babe I was unconscious, milk-drunk at my mother's breast; and the lonely sound of a train whistle blowing and the great steel wheels rushing by under the dark, bush-covered hills of Te Rangakaika.

In all of this, where is my father? Practically speaking he was probably sleeping the sleep of the just as he prepared for another day teaching English and Physical Education to the pupils of Ohakune District High School. But in truth he is absent, or perhaps dispersed, partaking of both bull calf and steam train yet fully inhabiting neither; while my mother remains the still point and unwobbling pivot of this ideal and quite possibly misbegotten fantasy.

Even so, if it is true that memory is a palimpsest, then this is one I write over again and again in search of the magic combination of letters that will set me free of it; though I know that such freedom is impossible and, even if it were possible, I would not really want it, because those images are me and I them and, like parents and children, without each other we would not exist. This is also a strangeness of memory, that we indefatigably attempt to recapture, time after time, what cannot be recaptured.

Here in Summer Hill, after an early morning train passes, there's always a silence more intense for the racket that has just been. If it's too soon for the magpies to begin their carolling in the jacaranda tree, and there isn't another sound to be heard, then my thought shifts away from birth and towards death, going west into the silence . . . and I wonder why so much melancholy, drama and romance is bound up in trains, why what is just a means of transport continues to have such intense metaphoric resonance for us.

And if I am unable to drop back off to sleep again, I might imagine that this resonance is because a life is indeed like a railway line, with a terminus at either end, and that my birth more than half a century ago among those old cold hills will inevitably, after many stations and much various and variously enjoyed experience, end in death, perhaps in the midst of this thicket of streets and strangers, perhaps somewhere else. I might even remember the concluding lines from 'Stations' and say them over softly, as if talking in my sleep, with a peculiar awareness that words once purporting to describe a young man stepping optimistically forth into the world read now as a kind of *memento mori*:

> *The station master says*
> *the train will be along on time*
> *any minute now*
>
> *He puts some coal on the fire*
> *he turns up the radio*
>
> *The waiting room stays*
> *open till the sun*
> *shines in along the floor.*

On Film

A monkey runs through a desert landscape, pursued by a dozen
or so small, wild pigs. It leaps through the air, clasps the trunk
of one of the tall, cactus-like plants and shimmies upwards. As
it reaches the top, the trunk breaks off, the monkey falls to the
ground, the pigs take up the chase again. The monkey climbs
another cactus, that cactus also breaks, the monkey falls, the
pigs gallop on. I am becoming hysterical, a little boy in a big dark
auditorium, rolling in my seat, laughing so hard it hurts . . .

This was in the Kings Cinema on Goldfinch Street,
Ohakune, sometime in the 1950s. The film, Walt Disney's *The
African Lion* (1955), is a wildlife picture shot over three years on
the high plateaus of Kenya and (then) Tanganyika by Alfred and
Elma Milotte. It is one of series called *True-Life Adventure*: other
programs visited the arctic, the desert, the jungle, the prairie.
It was my first encounter, since television was still years away
then, with the moving image, and made such an impression that
I harassed my parents into taking me back the following week,
this time to the Royal in Raetihi – perhaps solely in order to see
again that burlesque chase of monkey by pigs, in which terror
and absurdity were equally mixed, that is all I retain in memory
of the film.

It is a quintessentially cinematic sequence, with a formal
quality not unlike, say, the Eadweard Muybridge photographs

that anticipate moving pictures, or the great Marcel Duchamp image of the bride descending the staircase: bodies in motion. It is also, if not a car chase, then certainly a chase. I wonder though, now my knowledge of the medium is more sophisticated, if there was some degree of manipulation at work: did that monkey really climb cactus after cactus only to have each one break under it? Or did the editor replay a single event several times over to give the illusion of side-splitting repetition? Were the pigs really even chasing the monkey? Why? Perhaps separate incidents were artfully cut together to make that pursuit, which also resembles one of the classic chases from the silent films of Mack Sennett and his Keystone Kops.

The only way to find out would be to see the film again, which is possible, since all nine *True-Life Adventures* are about to be released on DVD. However, I'm not sure if I want to: along with my fear that the chase will not stand up to scrutiny is another anxiety, that I have remembered an incident from a different film altogether, perhaps *The Living Desert*, which I think I also saw about that time. Are there cactus in Africa? Or monkeys in the south west of the United States? (The answers to these questions are, hopefully, yes and no respectively.) For cinema, while it powerfully evokes memory, is also, and inevitably, an arena where the seemingly authentic is almost always revealed as artifice.

I have another strong association with that theatre, of a completely different kind. The 1961 hit song by Sue Thompson, 'Sad Movies', is for me a film that plays out in the Kings. I am in the audience when I see a teenage girl, resembling my oldest sister, come in and sit down just in front of me, about half way back and to the left in the central bank of seats. They turn down the lights and turn the projector on. The news of the world starts to begin. And then I see, with her, *my darling and my best friend / Walk in* . . .

The most poignant part is not the two kissing right in front of the jilted girl – though that is heart-wrenching enough – nor, in the middle of a colour cartoon, her starting to cry; it is her slow sad walk home alone through the night-time streets of Ohakune, so dark and gloomy, so replete with the presence of the lost forest, overlooked by the ghostly mountain. And then her elegant refusal of both the truth and a lie in what she tells her mother: *Sad movies / make me cry.*

But what was the movie? Absurd as it sounds, I never hear the song without wondering about the film she walked out of. The film, perhaps, that her darling and her best friend didn't really see either, being too busy pashing each other up. I imagine the light from the screen flickering across the faces of the lovers but can never establish what exactly it is they are watching or not watching, as the case may be. Is it, I wonder, the drama of their own infidelity playing out in front of them? Do they see but fail to understand that the story they are watching is their own? And here is another ambiguity of cinema, that its simulacra produce real emotions, its pretend betrayals result in real tears being shed. Even now, although I read far more books than I go to films, I am much more likely to weep in the public darkness of a cinema than I am to splash private tears on to a page.

Some years later, in a different town, one day in the school holidays I told my parents I was going on a bike ride with friends. We wheeled away south down Main Street and out into the de-restricted zone then, at the graveyard where now my father is buried, left our bikes hidden behind the cemetery fence, returning to the highway and hitch-hiking the rest of the ten miles to Featherston. There, we went to the picture theatre in Fitzherbert Street, to meet some girls.

My girlfriend was Gail Sanders and she had come over from Martinborough to stay with her friend Judith Turkington, who was sitting with my friend Grant Batty. I don't recall now who the others were but do remember that the film, bizarrely, was George Pal's 1958 animated feature *Tom Thumb* starring, among others, (the voice of) a villainous Peter Sellers. It too played out almost unwatched as Gail and I inexpertly nuzzled each other.

This memory is also entwined with angst. Not long after our movie date, following an end-of-term school dance during which we spent delirious hours, as I thought, in each other's arms, Gail rode the night bus back to Martinborough sitting on the knee of a second-year fifth and star of the first fifteen, a fellow called Albrecht who liked to walk around with his shirt open just far enough at the collar to show the curl of chest hairs there. Something died in me next morning when, on the football field in Martinborough itself, Grant Thomas helpfully supplied forensic detail of this particular episode. I was devastated that Gail, after all we had felt and done together, would go off with someone else.

My idea of fidelity was no doubt as improbable as a human being two inches tall. Or some of the plot devices that left us, each Saturday afternoon, cliff-hanging until the serial *Ali and his Camel* resumed the next weekend. For the programs in those days were different, they began with 'God Save the Queen', segued into the black and white *Movietone News* or something similar, might include a documentary and, after an episode of the multi-part serial, would conclude, just before half time, with one, two or sometimes three cartoons; the feature, whatever it was, took up the whole of the second half.

In Greytown there wasn't a dedicated theatre, films were shown in the town hall; however, not much else ever seemed to go on there, so it might as well have been a cinema. In winter, after playing football on Saturday morning, we would go to the afternoon matinée, mostly for the serial and the cartoons. It was the usual cliché, trysts in the back row, yelling and screaming and jaffa rolling elsewhere. One of my more louche ambitions, never realised, was to wear my gumboots to one of these matinées.

Curiously, I remember hardly any of the films I saw there, with the single exception of *The Guns of Navarone*, which I went to in an evening session with my father (we sat upstairs); I also recall a poster for Eli Kazan's *Splendor in the Grass* showing a giant Natalie Wood lying on her tummy in a meadow looking straight out at you. The title both excited and alarmed me, suggesting something other than the lines from Wordsworth's 'Intimations of Immortality from Recollections of Early Childhood' – *Though nothing can bring back the hour / Of splendour in the grass, of glory in the flower* – are meant to do.

Perhaps that poster also included this advice, which the American version certainly did: *Whether you live in a small town the way they do, or in a city, maybe this is happening to you right now . . . maybe (if you're older), you remember . . . when suddenly the kissing isn't a kid's game any more, suddenly it's wide-eyed, scary and dangerous.* I was only thirteen but already knew this to be true; Gail Sanders had taught me.

Both of these pictures date from 1961 though it must have been several years later when I saw the one and didn't see the other. *Splendor in the Grass* wouldn't have screened as a matinée and I wouldn't have been allowed to go to an evening session without one or other of my parents; and I can't imagine either of them wanting to see an overwrought teen romance set in 1920s Kansas, even if Natalie Wood and Warren Beatty were in it. Now I wish I'd sneaked out and gone to it rather than the risible *Tom Thumb* – with Gail Sanders, Susan Moynihan, Ngaire Woolcott . . . or anyone, really.

Not long after this, television arrived in our lives. I first saw a set in the window of an appliance shop, stopping in the street along with half a dozen others to stare at the marvel. The family of a boy called Peter Wall bought one and I was invited around to see it. Next Grant Batty's folks acquired one too and I went around to see that as well. Then, somewhat to the chagrin of both Grant and Peter, our own set arrived and was installed in the corner of the sitting room behind the chemist shop at 201 Main Street.

As with cinema, so with television: I have a precise memory of the first program I watched. It was an episode of *Maverick*, set on a paddle steamer travelling down the Mississippi River. The gamblers sat at a table outside under an awning towards the stern, playing cards until a dispute occurred and guns were drawn. *Maverick* was shot on film, in beautiful, crisp black and white that came across brilliantly on our then exclusively monochrome TV sets; now I wish I could remember more about those episodes I saw, because some good people worked on the series. This was the show that made James Garner a star; Roger Moore appeared as an English cousin of the Mavericks in one series; the young Robert Altman wrote and directed an episode; Clint Eastwood, Lee van Cleef and John Carradine – later our very own Scarecrow – all made appearances.

Despite some other wonders – Patrick McGoohan's *The Prisoner*, the first series of *The Avengers*, *Get Smart* – the sad fact is, the advent of television eclipsed the movies for me. From about 1964 until the end of the decade was a lacuna during which, like my contemporaries, I barely went to a film. We just didn't bother. Our lives revolved around the TV and the radio, the one for pictures, the other for music and although we did go to dances at which live bands played, and to the new discotheques that were opening then, we didn't go to the flicks any more. Weekends were otherwise given over to sport, drinking and gambling (we played cards, mostly blackjack or poker) and the largely futile pursuit of sex with sensibly recalcitrant girls. It seems retrospectively bizarre.

All that changed once I went to university. None of the flats I lived in in the early 1970s had a television or a radio, though there was a stereo in every bedroom. You'd hear odd juxtapositions as you walked down the hallway at 6 Margaret Street, Ponsonby:

a Sibelius symphony on the one hand, Leonard Cohen or Van Morrison on the other, the Incredible String Band plunking away somewhere else. Something about being a student seemed to require that you went to films as well, so we did. The Lido, a longish bus trip away down Manukau Road at Epsom, was an institution, you rode out there on a Sunday night to see films that would nowadays be described as art house but were then simply understood as quality cinema. They were invariably European, sub-titled, by masters such as Bergman (*Cries and Whispers*, 1972) or Visconti (*The Damned*, 1969) or Truffaut (*Wild Child*, 1970), as well as lesser known though not necessarily less talented directors. American films would be screened on, or just off, Queen Street: pictures like *Midnight Cowboy* (1969), *Deliverance* (1972) or *The French Connection* (1971), which I saw at the Civic in the aftermath of a mescaline trip: this made the plot more or less impossible to follow, but added a gruesome fascination to the slow-mo images of bullets blasting into human flesh.

You could also see European classics on Queen Street: *Fellini Satyricon* (1969), for example, or Pier Paolo Pasolini's *Trilogy of Life*: *The Decameron* (1970), *The Canterbury Tales* (1971), *The Arabian Nights* (1974). The same director's austere masterpiece, *Theorem* (1968), I saw at the film festival in one of those early 1970s years. The films of Werner Herzog likewise featured in the annual festival – I particularly remember *Fata Morgana* (1971) – along with others that were even more obscure. There was one I saw which, set in the future, was about a monastic order in which some of the monks were inadvertently changing gender. On wide stony paths leading between green lawns, men would meet and, wordless, show each other swollen nipples from which a milky substance oozed. (This has probably stayed in my mind because something similar happened to me when I was younger – about fourteen – causing a panic too extreme to be mentioned to anyone then.)

In those days, young as I was, I tended to think that the

more incomprehensible something was, the more significance it owned. In this way I wilfully misinterpreted some of the films I saw, straining to find in them meanings that were literally beyond me and perhaps beyond them too. This may be why I loved Fellini – because he left so much unexplained, especially in the *Satyricon*. However, there was a corrective to this naïvety at hand; it lay in my introduction to the means of production.

Sometime in 1971 or 1972 I met a budding film maker, Richard Turner. With a sense of entitlement granted by his vaguely patrician background – his father was an admiral, his mother claimed descent from George Grey – Richard was already scripting and shooting his own short films. He enlisted me to work with him as an actor although, apart from a minor role in a Huntly College production of Shakespeare's *Richard III*, I had never acted before.

There was a sequence shot in one of the university lecture theatres in which I played a revolutionary orating from the podium, shouting: *What we need is bombs not books . . . !* I was nervous and got my line wrong, saying *books not bombs*, but it didn't matter because they were filming mute. Another shoot took place on the top level of the Britomart carpark at dawn on a cold Auckland morning, during which I endlessly climbed into or out of a car, why I do not know.

Neither of these films – or were they one film? – was ever screened in my presence and perhaps neither was finished. It's curious now to reflect that the experience was almost without significance: I don't think I learned anything particularly either about acting or film making. As with so much else from that time, I drifted through those sets like a somnambulist, barely aware of who I was or what I was doing, let alone what others were up to.

Towards the end of 1972 another opportunity, as it seemed, came my way. For reasons that now elude me, I determined not to sit the exams for the two stage-three English papers that would have completed my BA. I was one of the favoured students in my class and the announcement led to consternation among my teachers. Meetings were convened in which they tried to persuade me to reverse my decision. (Later, inexplicably, I sat and passed one but not the other paper.)

At one of these meetings, in the Kiwi Hotel, presumably in despair of my academic future, I was offered a job on a film gearing up to be shot in West Auckland. Denis Taylor, then a lecturer in the English department, had written the script and was going to be acting in the film, which was based upon an episode from his own life: a tragic love affair he'd had with a beautiful, doomed young woman who also drifted through those times on her way to an early death by suicide. The job Denis offered me was continuity. Although I did not know what this meant, I accepted it and one weekend went out to the house in Huia which was both the major location for the film and its production office.

A lovely old wooden villa set among kauri trees down near the water's edge, it was empty apart from the odd mattress and sleeping bag on the floor in one or other of the rooms. There were various people in residence but none of them knew who I was or what I was doing there; I didn't really know myself. I spent the best part of a long and lonely day hanging around until, late in the afternoon, the film's director, Geoff Steven, sought me out and told me that someone else had already been hired to do continuity and there wasn't any other job for me on the film either. I made my disconsolate way back to the city.

Sometime during the next year, 1973, I went with a few of my ratbag friends to a raucous outdoor party at the Parnell house of another English department lecturer, Jonathan Lamb. Under huge arc lights hired for the occasion, the event was being filmed for the same movie: *Test Pictures: Eleven Vignettes from a Relationship*. I have never seen it, but someone once told me my fugitive image can be seen, along with so many others, in the swirl of revellers dancing to the Rolling Stones on that faraway and somehow fictitious occasion.

When I ran into Richard Turner again, in Wellington in the mid-1970s, we decided to collaborate upon the writing of a screenplay. It was an adaptation of Maurice Duggan's story 'Along Rideout Road that Summer'. Richard, who had somehow procured an option on the rights, was going to produce and direct; not so long ago, he told me we went within one vote of getting production funding for the film from the QEII Arts Council.

Duggan's story, which takes place almost entirely in the head of the hero, Buster O'Leary, is on the face of it unpromising material for adaptation. The interior monologue only very occasionally breaks into dialogue. We reproduced these breaks verbatim, of course, but the exigencies of story telling in a visual medium also persuaded us to invent scenes that never take place in the text proper. These mostly concern Buster's home life before he goes to work on Puti Hohepa's farm.

I felt weirdly presumptuous, adding to the work of a master like Duggan; that he had just died (1975) only made my temerity seem worse. Now, when I look at the story, I do not understand why we felt we had to extend it in that way. It would be entirely possible to make a film without straying from the Hohepa farm, at which Buster's hideous father in time appears to interrupt his son's idyll with the languorous Fanny. Curiously, no one has yet done so; indeed, I don't think any of Duggan's work has been adapted for the cinema, not even a story as replete with visual and dramatic interest as 'O'Leary's Orchard', which includes in its narrative rehearsals towards a production of *Romeo and Juliet* to be staged in the barn at the orchard.

As to our script – I don't know. I lent my copy, years ago now, to another director and she never gave it back. Sometimes I think I'd like to look at it again, just to see how it reads. On the other hand, as with so much apprentice work, my initial curiosity would probably be replaced by ear-burning embarrassment and I would quite likely lay the document aside before I was many pages in.

Richard and I did get as far as scouting locations, meeting in Paeroa one summer to have a look around; but nothing further was done. However, the experience was not wholly wasted. After that somewhat inadvertent encounter – we had no car so could not in fact look for the farm which would have been the major location of the film – I hitch-hiked away south, getting a ride to Hamilton, improbably, in a hearse. Some years later, this trip formed the basis of *Philosophy*, an eleven-minute-long short I wrote for Geoff Cawthorn, which won him Best Short Film at the 1999 New Zealand Film Awards. Strange to relate, the last line of Duggan's story reads: *I might have hugged him as he drove his hearse through the tail-end of summer.*

My first experience of actual film making took place late in 1977, in Auckland. I was by then a member of Red Mole and we had just begun rehearsals for a season at Phil Warren's Ace of Clubs, above the old Cook Street Markets. We asked film maker, cinematographer and sculptor Leon Narbey to light our brand-new show, a private-eye spoof called *Slaughter on Cockroach Avenue*. Out of that engagement came a plan for Leon to make a short film which we would project as part of the performance.

Someday Morning was shot over the period of a day in the Winter Gardens in the Domain, using a single set, a static camera and a technique called pixilation, which involves exposing the film frame by frame; speeded up it plays like live animation. It's a surreal, Adam and Eve story, during which a couple eat a meal, served them by a malign waiter, who eventually shoots the Adam figure while Eve transforms into a stone woman whose face then disintegrates. I played the waiter, in whiteface, with enormous black panda eyes; after my crime I shimmied, like a fakir, up a rope that uncoiled before me.

An intriguing mix of the avant and the Chaplinesque, *Someday Morning* haunted me for years. After I stopped acting with the troupe, I began doing their lighting and stage management. At various times during my stint, the film resurfaced as part of one show or another, and when, in New York, we put together *Numbered Days in Paradise* for a transcontinental American tour, it was on the program. This meant that for each theatre we played at, I had to find and then operate a projector to screen the film. Something always went wrong, not least because my technical competence, in any area, is somewhat limited.

The worst occasion was at the Odyssey Theatre in Santa Monica, Los Angeles, where we had to perform *Numbered Days* in and around the set for a production of a Brecht play – was it *The Caucasian Chalk Circle*? When it came time for *Someday Morning* to be projected, late in our show, the film jammed in the gate and burned up in full sight of audience and actors, a spectacular *auto-da-fé* I could not expect to repeat or survive. It was in fact the last time I showed it, and when we returned to Auckland early in 1980, I gave the damaged print to Leon, who I think had it restored.

Before I left Auckland again, this time for Sydney, two things happened. One was my employment on the crew of a feature film; the other was the inception of my debut produced screenplay. The first occurred when a guy to whom I used to sell the marijuana I grew in the back yard was retained, in a fairly casual manner, by a production company set up to take advantage of the then generous tax concessions available to film makers in New Zealand. Tim was an American and so were most of the heads of department and lead actors on the film, which was shot using the working title *Shadowlands* and later released under a number of names, including *Strange Behavior*, *Dead Kids* and *Small Town Massacre*.

The job Tim got me was third assistant to the director,

which also required that I drive the make-up van to the set each morning. I hated it from the very first day. The second assistant director, a South African by the name of Mark Jaffee, conceived, quite explicitly, that part of his job was to make mine as miserable as possible. *If you want to get among the big bucks,* he would tell me, *you have to learn to eat shit; later, you can make others eat shit for you.* I spent a lot of time standing somewhere up the road from where the action was taking place, making sure no one disturbed us; and in fact the gig came to a sudden end over a bucket of shit.

For I was also required to empty the dunny in the made-over campervan I drove; and one day I refused. I expected to be fired for this; indeed I wanted to be fired, but for some unknown reason they shifted me instead to the art department. This made a kind of sense: Russell Collins, the art director, was a mate from Red Mole days, and the production designer, Susanna Moore, was herself a writer. She later authored the smart thriller *In the Cut* which Jane Campion adapted, not very well, for her 2003 film of the same title.

Things picked up immediately. Although I wasn't on set as often as I would have liked, I was no longer the victim of a junior sadist either; and the art department was full of laughs. Susanna had a light touch and a wicked sense of humour and she and Russell and I got on well together. The culmination of our adventures was a wonderful absurdity: One day our per diems stopped arriving. We asked for them, and were told they were on the way. They didn't come. We asked again and got the same reply. By the third day we were ropable. We decided to act.

We were working, as usual, ahead of the main crew, preparing a tombstone for its opening. The villain of the movie was a double amputee in a wheelchair who was pretending to be someone else. The real person he was, was allegedly dead and buried. Out of forgotten convolutions in a very silly plot, it was decided to disinter this dead man. The reveal would show that the coffin contained only the bones of the lower leg and the feet, proving that the man in the wheelchair was actually the dead man. Or something.

The scene was going to be shot in a beautiful parklike cemetery out the back of Remuera. We arrived there in the early afternoon, meticulously prepared everything for the opening of the grave . . . then hid the bones in a gully at the bottom of the hill. When the rest of the crew arrived mid-afternoon and began setting up, we announced: no per diems, no bones. Then folded our arms and sat down to watch the fun begin.

It was extraordinary how quickly the bundle of white envelopes arrived. One of the producers, John Barnett, turned up within, oh, half an hour . . . I remember him, red-faced, furious, in his white shoes, picking his way between the gravestones down the green slope towards us. With good grace we took our envelopes and then retrieved the bones. They had the scene in the can before nightfall.

The other event was more significant. One day when Leon Narbey was round at my place in St Mary's Bay he asked, quite casually, if I had any ideas that might make a feature film. I handed him a page of text I'd copied out of *Opium and Gold* (1977). A history of Chinese goldminers in New Zealand, the book reproduces a number of the extraordinary photographs taken by the Reverend Alexander Don, a Presbyterian missionary among miners on the Central Otago goldfields. Much of author Peter Butler's text is excerpted from Don's letters and reports of his yearly journeys through the diggings. My found poem was a transcription of a story Don tells about a miner called Illustrious Energy who went mad.

Leon read the piece and handed it back to me without comment. Several years later, however, when I was living in Sydney, he asked me about it again and the discussions which began then led on to the making of his 1988 film, also called *Illustrious Energy*, the screenplay for which we wrote together. This collaboration, enormously fruitful for me, mostly took place at Leon's house in Mt Eden, Auckland, where the first three of the six or seven drafts were entirely written on a small, durable portable typewriter that had belonged to the father of Leon's wife, Anita.

I had gone to Australia with the specific intention of learning how to write films, which I thought, erroneously, might be a way of supporting myself while I also wrote books; in the event it took fifteen years for my first Australian feature, *Terra Nova*, to be produced. I've now written the screenplays for four produced features (one of which has never been released) and two shorts, as well as half a dozen other scripts that have not gone into production and rather more treatments, outlines, synopses and proposals. Even so, I cannot claim a sure command of the form which, among all the kinds of writing I have attempted, is far and away the most difficult to master. Why this should be is an interesting question, though not one I am sure I can answer.

Perhaps it is because the best cinema is like a dream and dreams – including nightmares – are scripted by the unconscious not the conscious mind; nevertheless, most of the voluminous advice that exists about how to write a successful screenplay stresses the deliberate: structural analysis, craft skills, imitation of proven models, the rigorous application of a methodology derived from exhaustive post mortems. It may be that all this faintly necrophiliac labour is prescribed precisely because a dream does not readily admit of technical explanation; it may also be that the dream, if it is real enough, will survive the grim scaffolding screenplay writing demands. Like the elaborate tracery of wires in the roof of a circus tent, constructed so trapeze artists can be seen to fly through the air with the greatest of ease, the intricate machinery of film, with its manifold technical processes, exists only in order to fashion a *fata morgana*.

Whose dream? Whatever else it may be, a salient quality of

73

good cinema is that it is a collective experience. In this way, film exerts a tyranny far greater than that of literature, which allows you to visualise whatever image you please; while film, because the image is given, allows you to imagine only what it might mean. We sit in the collective dark to watch a film, as we do for the theatre; but we sit there silent and in a world of our own, as we do while reading a book. We are as if dreaming, but if the dream cannot be shared, both in the making and the viewing, it cannot be dreamed at all.

I think now, perhaps irrelevantly, of a film I first saw many years ago in Wellington and again recently. Called *The Night of Counting the Years*, it was the single feature completed, in 1970, by Egyptian director Shadi Abdel Salam. An architect by training, Abdel Salam worked as an art director and costume designer and received his chance to direct through the good offices of Italian producer Roberto Rossellini.

It is a wonderful film. From the first shot – a sepulchral reading from the *Book of the Dead* at a meeting of archaeologists in Cairo – to the last – the hero, Wannis, covering his face and stumbling away up the shores of the Nile at Thebes – it has a gravitas that never falters. Abdel Salam told Rossellini he wanted to make *an undramatic film*, by which he meant he didn't want lots of action or dialogue; there's very little of either in *El Mumia*, as it's also known.

What it has instead is an inexorable fatality as Wannis, the younger son of Selim, the recently deceased chief of his tribe, step by step approaches the only possible course of action open to him: the betrayal to a young archaeologist from Cairo of the whereabouts of a cache of sarcophagi of three dynasties of pharaohs, removed from their tombs in the Valley of the Kings 3000 years before and hidden inside a hill on tribal lands. The tribe has, since time immemorial, plundered these sarcophagi for artefacts to sell on the black market for cash; but as the old generation passes, the young are appalled to learn that their bread comes from the dead, and revolt.

Much of *El Mumia* takes place at night – or rather over two nights, with one day in between – and most of it was filmed among the actual ruins at Thebes. The contemporary (1880s) illiterate Muslim tribespeople do not know who the ancient Egyptians were, even though they are most likely their direct descendants; their writing cannot be read and their names are unknown. This theme of naming runs throughout and is echoed in the old ones' own beliefs: without a name, there is no rebirth and therefore no immortality. The most extraordinary image in *El Mumia* is the progress of the sarcophagi of these old ones along a purple ridge at dawn as they are carried by bearers to river barges and thence down the Nile to another kind of immortality in the museum at Cairo.

Can we then say that the collective dream that is cinema names us as we are and that without it there is no rebirth, no immortality? I think we can. The recent New Zealand film, Roger Donaldson's *The World's Fastest Indian*, is a case in point. A dream of what we were in the 1960s, it suggests that, however gauche or repressed or fundamentally uncommunicative we might have been, our hearts were good and our spirit strong; what's more, there was no problem that could not be overcome using our native ingenuity.

I saw it in Newtown, Sydney, and several times during the picture, almost to my own embarrassment, found myself in tears: not out of pain or sadness, but from a recognition of my affinity with the qualities of the people up there on the screen. I felt empathy not just with the Kiwis, but with the Americans too, and the expatriate Australian who made the movie. In that particular collective, I was lucky enough to be both monkey and pig, heart-breaker and heart-broken, dreamer and dream. Watching the film, I was at the same time in the film. If you have to be in two places at once, and often enough we do, these are good ones to be in.

Diptych

I

Jagtar said something wise as I was leaving but, like so much of the wisdom that has come my way, I have forgotten it. He was a tall, slender young man, the foreman of a gang of Punjabi workers who picked my brother-in-law's apples and pumpkins, but even his natural authority could not make them work on festival days, nor on the days when, for reasons that were obscure, they became spooked. I saw him in the rearview mirror, dressed in white, standing with my sister and her husband as I drove away from the sheds on the rich river flats down by the Tuki Tuki and then on out of the valley.

The back seat of the rental car was full of crisp red apples and my sister had given me some of the strong dope they grew in a favoured spot in the orchard. I was going to Wellington for an art opening, via south Hawke's Bay and the Wairarapa, intending to stop in a town of my youth to visit my father's grave. I was happy to be free and untrammelled on the road, but through the morning and the early afternoon, a troubling image kept surfacing and floating before my mind's eye: the bones of my father's skull coming through the flesh down there in the earth where we'd buried him a couple of years before.

After I left Masterton I smoked a previously rolled joint which, while it did not banish the visage of the skull beneath the skin, did overlay it with intensely nostalgic images from my boyhood: so much so that when I crossed the bridge over the Waiohine, just north of Greytown, and saw kids swimming as I used to do in the swift green waters between the piles, I turned off the road and drove down the short track to the stony river beach where they'd left their heaps of clothes and their towels draped over gorse or broom bushes. Yet soon enough the melancholy realisation came that it was no longer possible for me to join them; I reversed and turned about and bumped back up to the highway and on.

The graveyard is south of the town, with curiously shaped concrete wings over the gate that do not meet to make the arch they suggest. I had never explored it properly before, and was surprised to find it segregated: a small Jewish section and then the Catholics there on the right as you went up the drive, with a row of truncated macrocarpas on the left, behind which my father lay. Over the cattlestop and into the main part of the cemetery. I stopped the car near a small wooden shed built next to the boundary fence, climbed out, stretched. I was feeling strange already, otherworldly, perhaps trepidated, if that's a word.

It was a still, partly cloudy afternoon, alternately bright and shadowed, quiet except for the carolling of magpies from tall pine trees up the back and the seemingly grief-stricken, intermittent bleating of sheep from surrounding paddocks. I walked over to the sexton's shed and peered through the dusty, spider-webbed window. Its floor was uneven, a turmoil of earth, as if someone had tried to excavate within. A broken shovel lay sideways in the dirt and there did not appear to be any back wall to it. That chaos of scumbled filth went forever. It was a vision, not so much of hell, but of some brute vacuum beyond both heaven and hell. I felt myself being pulled into that grim vortex and it took a real effort to drag myself away. The illusion was so strong I went around to check that there was in fact a back wall . . .

A low hedge grew over the fence on that side of the graveyard and from in among its tangled greenery, its twiggy darkness,

I could hear the rustling of some small animal or bird. There was another structure further along. I walked towards it as if impelled through the foreboding atmos around me. More miniature barn than shed, it had double wooden doors, one of which was half open, the other secured with a bolt. The open side held tools and implements, motor mower fuel cans and so forth. I shot the bolt on the other door, it creaked ajar. Inside was a pile of yellow straw and laid on the straw, unaccountably, was the mummified body of a whippet or a small greyhound. The roar building in my ears became louder, I swayed, dizzy, faint. The body of the dog filled me with horror, the persistent rustling in the hedgerow likewise. As if death were, or was about to become, visible. I closed the door and stumbled away.

Up the back, under the huge, raggedy pines, is a rectangular field in which stand a couple of dozen massive, elaborate, nineteenth-century graves all set on a diagonal with respect to the parameters of the enclosure. As I walked into that field, the sun went behind a cloud, with loud cries the magpies flew up out of the pines and away, the roaring in my ears crescendoed and I seemed to hear, above or below or amongst it, the grumbling voices of the dead town fathers and mothers buried here, uttering a stern and heartless rehearsal of the Anglican pieties that ruled the parish. The graves were disposed, I thought, on a ley line that stretched, past the brown hills to the north east, over the manifold ocean, all the way back to some dim, occulted village in England.

No! I said, or shouted, though not out loud. *No!* I would not submit to their dread authority, I was not subject to their haunting, they could not own my soul the way they thought they owned the soul of the town. Their dead hand could fall where it would, but not on my sleeve or shoulder, not on your life. I walked among the old graves, reading the names, muttering my refusals, and, in time, heard the ancient voices diminish to a murmur of discontent then die away into the dark and bright light of the afternoon.

Whatever it was, or had been, was over. I left that baleful field and made my way back through the military section to where my father lay. After we buried him I brought two stones for his grave, one from each of the two rivers that run through the town where I was born. The round one, like a skull, that I found at the bend in the Mangateitei where we used to go swimming, was set in concrete at the head of the grave, but the wide flat footstone I pulled out of the Mangawhero on the slopes of the mountain was missing. I stood where it should have been and spoke a few words out loud to him; then was quiet. The decay of his body no longer worried me. I even felt a kind of peace descend, neither profound nor momentous, but ordinary, mortal. In that silence, that peace, I heard the ticking of his watch on my wrist.

II

The morning after the opening, I hit the road again, driving back to Auckland via Taranaki. I had someone to see, a rich art collector, in New Plymouth. I stayed the night in a motel at Waitara, then continued on up Highway 3, which runs along that wild west coast as far as Mokau. I smoked another joint of my sister's strong dope as I left town, which might explain the experience I was about to have. On the other hand, things like this can happen, unpredictably, when I'm unstoned, or stone-cold sober.

I was barrelling down a wide empty sweep of highway towards a river bridge when I felt a sudden urge to stop. I drove over the bridge and turned off to the right, on to an obscure country dirt road. No, this wasn't it. I turned the car around, went back, re-crossed the bridge and took another road that ran along the side of the river towards the sea. There was a carpark and picnic area about a kilometre along. I left the car here, intending to walk out along the tidal river bed to the sea.

It was mid-morning. A fine day. The tide was out. I took off my shoes, left them where I could easily find them again and set off across mudflats towards a high ridge of black iron sand, glinting with mica. It squeaked as my feet sank into it, leaving behind sighing holes that soon filled up with sand trickles. Past this ridge was a curiously truncated headland made of yellowish-brown sandstone, capped with tough grass. Fragmentary islands of the same rock out in the sea. I thought if I could get around this promontory I might find an ocean beach beyond.

The walk was longer than I expected, and as I neared the head of the headland, I saw that it was riven through by a cave that might or might not go all the way to the other side. The dark aperture of the cave mouth seemed forbidding or forbidden so I plodded on, round the point and out on to a wide beach that stretched away south for kilometres. There before me, at the back of the high-tide line, stood a strange, weather-beaten structure, shiny and white as bones. It resembled one of those platforms that were made to lay out the bodies of the dead until all the flesh had gone from the bones, which would then be cleaned and gathered together and hidden away in some cave.

It even looked, from a distance, as if there might be bones upon it, but as I moved closer I saw that it was not so: just a stage made out of driftwood, about a metre tall and two metres broad. Lashed together with baling twine that was already pale and fraying. What on earth was it for? Who made it? Why? It was as foreboding as it was mysterious. I sat down next to it and wondered; then, since the day was warm and there was no one around, took off my clothes and went down into the surf.

A perfect set, seven waves, rolled in as I walked out, and I caught the last of them and shot shoreward in a hiss and bubble and surge of white water. Beautiful. Out again I went, and in on another perfect wave. Again, and again. I was as if drunk with exaltation and it wasn't until, shivering with cold, I finally, regretfully, left the water and went back up to my clothes that I realised the tide was coming in – fast. The sea was already lapping at the base of the stubby yellow-brown headland where only moments ago, it seemed, I'd walked across crunchy dry black sand.

In a panic now, I dressed and started back. It was too late to return as I had come, the only way was via the cave which did in fact go right through the headland. The premonitory fear I'd felt before was still with me but the urge to reach the other side before the tidal river became impassable was stronger. Sea water was sliding into the cave mouth as I entered, starting to run. So it was that the markings on the cave walls, the ancestral figures with triangular heads and slanted eyes, the chevrons and the double spirals, and, upright along the walls, the many stylised feet, three and four and five and six and seven toed, the toes made of holes drilled in the rock, passed in the blur. And yet I seemed to hear a hiss of voices as I ran, a jostling, archaic, sibilant chorus which might just have been the waves of the sea, advancing.

It was hard to move at speed across that long black reach of glittering sand, and exhausting too, and by the time I was over it, the tidal river was knee deep; when I'd waded back to where my shoes were, under a flax bush on a clod of earthy bank, my rolled-up trousers were wet to the thighs and my heart was going like billy-o. But that was alright; I was safe.

It wasn't until I arrived in Auckland and looked at the catalogue of the art opening I'd attended that I realised where I'd been: Tongaporutu, Tony Fomison writes in a 1980 essay reprinted towards the back of *What shall we tell them?*, is the largest rock art site in Taranaki. Here wayfarers, and war parties, paused on the main Waikato to Taranaki track. Here, perhaps, the ceremony called *uruuruwhenua* was performed. Fomison quotes James Cowan: *If you wish to avoid heavy rain or other obstruction or inconvenience on your day's journey, you must pay due respect to Tokahaere (a 'walking rock' in the King Country) by pulling a handful of fern or manuka and laying it at his foot, reciting as you do an ancient prayer to the spirit of the rock . . .*

I did not of course have time for such a ceremony, even if I'd known how to perform it. All I had was a glimpse of an antique mystery, a once sacred place that is now a curiosity and will soon disappear under the inexorable rise of the ocean, as so many other sites that once existed along that coast already have done. Yet I drove away over the bridge and up the wide sweet highway on the other side with a clean feeling, as if the sea, though not perhaps the cave, had scoured my skin of the accretion of those half-formed, half-unadmitted residues of the flotsam we pick up as we live through our days. As if I had been, momentarily, serendipitously, reborn.

2
MEDITATIONS

Gold Tops

A friend told me there was a mushroom containing psilocybin that grew locally; he described this fungus in detail – small, with a dusty gold skin and, underneath, yellow-green gills tending towards cyan blue; the stems were slender and fragile, and they arched outwards at the bottom to make a characteristic pediment where they entered the earth. These mushrooms, called gold tops, tended to be found after rain where small impromptu streams carried the spores down forest paths; or under trees, also after rain. There was a particular spot in Patonga, the next village to ours, where they grew thickly in the park that runs along the shores of the estuary as the creek broadens among mangroves as it comes down from Patongalonga, before narrowing again to meet the sea.

I was never able to find this place, but I did identify the mushroom itself. My friend only ever ate the stalks, throwing the heads away because he thought there might be too much toxicity in them; but when I came to try them it seemed a waste to do that, so I would eat the whole thing. They had a pleasant taste, slightly nutty, inevitably mixed in with pieces of sandy grit adhering to the stem. I had my first one at the start of the track to the waterfall, where there are the remains of an old saw pit and a deep deposit of yellow clay, on the margins of which the gold tops sometimes grew. This day there were a couple of others I also picked, dropping them into my shirt pocket for later, then carrying on into the bush.

The sky was overcast, full of soft grey clouds moulded by wind currents into smooth creamy swirls. Below, the still, slate-coloured sea was cut through with purple lights like mica glints. Apart from the cries of birds sounding loudly, intermittently in the inert air, it was quiet as I walked up the track, which at this point runs past tennis courts and parallel to the road to a rich man's house. You cannot see house or courts, but the concrete-block fire station could be glimpsed through trees on the left, with a wide patch of burnt ground around it from when the Bush Brigade's last barbecue got away on them. Then all of that, the rutted clay road, the acrid blackened ground, the weeds encroaching from suburban gardens, fell behind as I entered the hushed green shade of the bush.

The track winds along the side of a ridge until it reaches the Ochre Caves, a massive outcrop overhang within which the orange and white sandstone, sculpted by wind and water into filigrees and curlicues like those in the morning's sky, is graffitied with names and dates of otherwise forgotten visits. Here there is a place where you can stand and hear the falling water echo from the rockface, very loud, right next to your ear, sounding much closer than the real waterfall chinking and glinting through the trees. I climbed up the damp slippery rocks to one side of the wide lip of stone over which the water cascades and came out into a broad basin where the stream runs into a shallow pool. Water boatmen sculled the meniscus, their blurred shadows flitting behind them on the rust orange bottom. I crossed over to the other side and climbed up a sandstone shelf to the next level.

Here the stream meanders along a narrow causeway, with bush close on either side, the eucalypts leaning their still leaves over, the wattles dropping golden pollen down. Tiny beaches, miniatures of those on the sea shore, gather at the margins of the flow. I kept on walking up until the track faded to stepping stones in the creek, then went along a low sandy bank flanking a wide, deep pool with a rope swing hanging from the branch of a tree leaning over it. I took off my clothes and slid naked into the brown water, letting the encrusted salt from my last sea swim wash away. Then climbed up over another smooth rock shelf to Pearlie Ponds.

Pebbles of red and yellow ochre lie in the water of the ponds; people use them to draw on the flat or sloping stone faces of the stream bed. There were fish and birds and trees, a rainbow, hearts with arrows, names, initials, dates, spirals, chevrons and random other marks. When it rains, the pigment washes off, leaving vague, faded outlines behind and sending coloured streams down over the rock. Sometimes charcoal from burnt wood is used and then the black too runs down to darken the water. Impromptu fireplaces were scattered about the gallery so it resembled a primitive campsite. Where the water pours over the shelf into the swimming pool below, the soft sandstone has been carved by hands or worn away and then it seems that this place is neither ancient nor modern but one where time has gone so far it curls around and finds itself back at the source.

The track leaves the course of the stream here and follows the contour of the ridge, but I continued in the bed itself, climbing up over massive tumbled boulders to another, smaller pool and then on past two huge rocks with the gap between them dammed by the flood-borne debris of fallen trees. The bush on the banks thinned to scrub and the sandstone outcrops showed pink and white and grey through the sparse tough vegetation. The ubiquitous grey-green was lit here and there with tiny trails of intense purple, or the bright crimson crouch of a hakea or grevillea, or the soft lavender of a small shrub with almond-shaped leaves. I began seeing spiders.

The first one was enormous, at least two hand widths across, poised on the underside of a great rock protruding out over a still black pool. Its reflection – attenuated thorax, bulbous abdomen, great jointed spindly legs – rose to meet it from below, like its

Siamese twin, joined at the tail. A rock spider, I guess. Perhaps they stalk their prey across the quivering meniscus of the water, or perhaps they wait for some unwary creature to come down under on their rock. This one was immobile and anyway on the far side of the pool from where I was; the only way to approach it was through the dark water and, though it was not cold, I could not even imagine doing that.

Further on, as the slopes above get drier and harsher, the slit of the creek bed becomes even lusher and I stepped ankle deep in grasses which released a delicate fragrance as they were crushed beneath my boots; hearing the falsetto creaking of frogs stop as I came near, I began to run into the webs of golden orb weavers. The females are large grey spiders with yellow and black legs, who spin an intricate web out of a tough and elastic thread of golden silk. These are complex, three-dimensional structures around which, when they are established, gather the smaller subsidiary webs of smaller, subsidiary males, poised in their suburban outposts waiting for the opportunity to visit the centre and consummate their longings.

What is remarkable about the female golden weaver is the black and white pattern she bears on her abdomen. As I continued my walk, and found more webs blocking my path, slung between walls of greenery which, by now, almost met across the creek bed, these abdominal patterns seemed like masks. Each one was different, yet each conformed to the primeval pattern of our kind: two eyes, a nose, a mouth, with tattooed or painted chin, cheeks and forehead. I did not feel threatened by these beings grimacing up at me; it did not alarm me to find, as it were, a sprite on the back of every spider: rather it seemed as if the richness of the world had disclosed another detail of itself, beyond, or behind which there were more, as yet hidden revelations to be had.

Deep in the valley, near the cliff face at its head, the big trees returned, with their smooth grey or white trunks, their gouts of red or amber gum oozing from wounds in the bark, their immemorial presence. Here the scrub was so dense on either bank that it literally joined above the surface of the water in a thick mass I had to push apart in order to go on, and there was no place for spiders to spin their webs. The stream was a tiny trickle, a mere thread of liquid in the electric green swampy grass where the sticky-tendrilled red-beaded pods of tiny carnivorous plants lay open.

At length I came to a deep, dark cleft in the rock, full of black water, with a mossy brown shelf at one end and a little stone bud at the other. Ferns and grasses leaned over the still surface. The silence of the afternoon was a deep bass hum under everything. I bent and saw my own face rising towards me. My lips touched the surface and the cold, sweet-tasting water flooded into my mouth. I felt myself falling forward head first into that fissure and disappearing forever . . .

The water dissolved the unspoken words of thought off my tongue, the voices in my head diminished and faded and a profound emptiness, echoed in the stillness of the grey green trees and grey tumbled stones on every side, took their place. It was as if I was myself at the heart of a web made, not out of golden silk or silver thought, but from the silence itself. It was profound, by which I mean depthless; it was endless, by which I mean that everything there was, was underpinned by that silence, even the intermittent birdsong or the returning creak of the frogs; and as I moved it moved with me.

I left the source of the stream, climbing directly up one side of the valley, following the sandstone scarp around until I met the path, going on to the top of Gad's Hill, then walking eastward along the Hope Range, that line of cliffs which defines the northern bank of the Hawkesbury River as it flows into Broken Bay. From there, you can see the whole panorama of the river system, with its humped bush-covered headlands, its long snaky inlets, its wide blue waters crossed by random white lines of boat trails and deeper, more subtle flows of tidal warps or riverine currents.

Here, on a shelf of grey sandstone overlooking the river, I found a place where the outlines of dolphins and turtles and sunfish and whales had been hammered into the rock, along with a man with wild upstanding hair and big genitals. He lay with arms and legs outspread, a spear in one hand, fish in his armpits and another between his thighs, just below the end of his pecked pecker. Long lines emanated from these fish, one pointing up towards the great mangroved and inletted reach of the river, the other out to the rocky shape of Lion Island: surely two very rich fishing grounds.

Coming down from the Hope Range, just past the massive orange overhang where pieces of chert and flint lie in fine sand by a cave mouth, a tree had fallen across the track. It was an old dead grey spike with its roots still clawed into the sandstone, charred black along one side in a bushfire, which probably became waterlogged in a storm and collapsed. The trunk split as it fell, scattering comb from a beehive across the brown-metal and red-clay track. I picked up a piece of it and sniffed the faint honey aroma rising from the waxy hexagonals. In some of the cells there were dead bees; they were the native kind, stingless, with striped conical abdomens. A few live ones were still clinging to the pale golden brown of the newly fractured comb left in the stump, or hovering confusedly above the deep ebony of the old. Someone had been there before me, clearing debris from the track, taking whatever honey there was.

I went on, walking down the fire trail with the piece of comb in my hand, and saw a honeyeater singing on a branch, its neck taut and elongated, its throat swollen to squeeze out the liquid notes, in black silhouette before the yellow atrocity of the sky. Gold tops, I thought, over and over; golden weavers; golden sky: it was as if some veil had drawn back and I saw further than ever before; but whether this veil was in my mind or a distinct quality of the land itself was not clear. It seemed there was a perception behind every perception, the way on a sunny afternoon there is a shadow behind every tree. This regression was infinite in the merest sense of the word. It went forever. The feeling of a moment drew back to reveal a glade from beyond which came the song of a lyre bird imitating a car alarm before the black buzzing of an aeroplane in the depthless blue of the sky. A line from *Illuminations* came: *Arrivée de toujours, qui t'en iras partout.* Arrival of always, which will go everywhere.

Satin Brush Superb

Aesthetics is for artists as ornithology is for the birds.
— BARNETT NEWMAN

I

The house at Onyx had a steep, curving drive up to the flat platform where we parked the car. On the side where the bush began, about two thirds of the way down, there was a big white log lying among the bracken and lantana and other weedy shrubs under a sheoak tree. From here, during our first spring there, daily, loudly, persistently, we would hear the two-note whistle, the trills, the hissing, the buzzing, and the clumsy mimicry of an unidentified bird. Sometimes it sounded like the static of a badly tuned radio; at others, the whirring of a disabled mechanical toy. This bird was difficult to spot. If you approached the log, there was a pause, a scrapple of claws and wings, and it took off on foot through the bracken before shooting out the other side of the thicket. It was a while before I realised that the smallish, portly, glossy blue-black bird flying here and there at great speed and always in a direct line to where it was going was the same one hissing and whirring behind the white log by the drive.

I don't like disturbing wild creatures, especially if they live close by, so it was a long time before I climbed up on the log and walked its length to peer down into the theatre of this one's activity. There, at the edge of a small clearing stamped in the brush, was a twiggy construction like a garden arch, only open at the top. About fifteen centimetres high, and curving inwards as it rose, with a bed of flattened straw at the bottom. On the court in front of this bower lay a profusion of things, almost all of them plastic in the same shade of blue: pegs, lids, straws, biro tops and the like. Among the blue was a scattering of similar bits of puce-coloured plastic and a few natural objects: tiny pale brown hornet's nests like miniature beehives, translucent marine snail shells shading from bone white to indigo, yellow feathers of the sulphur-crested cockatoo. The decoration on this floor was anything but random; it had the repetitive, coherent, stylised aspect of a mosaic.

A path, or rather a tunnel, itself strewn with a sparser collection of things, led away through the bracken: both entrance and escape route. A male satin bower bird sings his curious, broken-toy song in order to attract as many of the shy, plump, speckled, greenish, bosomy females as he can to watch him strutting down the path to the court, there to prance and sport for their pleasure. One day later that summer, I saw four or five of them perched above the floor, intently watching the action going on below. During his dance, the male bird will pick up and throw in the air pieces of his treasure; this has a hypnotic effect on one or other (or one after the other) of the females. In a tranced state she will come down on to the floor, and then into the bower itself, where the male, performing at speed, ravishes her then as quickly evicts her. There are, after all, more waiting. That is the full extent of his involvement in the breeding cycle. The female builds her nest elsewhere – there was one in the bushes below the blueberry ash out the back at Onyx, about fifty metres distant from the bower on the opposite side of the house – and raises the chicks alone.

The males are competitive with each other, and it is not uncommon for a bower to be vandalised by a rival. This happened to ours later on in the second season we were there: one day I climbed the log and found every last stalk of the bower (there must have been over a hundred of them) uprooted and strewn on the ground; while the blue, puce, indigo, white and yellow of the mosaic was as if thrown by a violent hand into the surrounding scrub. A few weeks later, he had rebuilt it, though the court never quite regained the splendour of that first incarnation. By this time the bird had lost some of his shyness and would occasionally pause, perhaps with a bright red berry in his beak, in the branches of the sheoak, to watch me with his strange violet eye. Or was it so that I could admire the Prussian blue of his plumage, black to a casual eye but in the light displaying a depth of colour like that of a clear evening sky just as the first stars prick through?

II

Satin bower birds prefer to live near the pockets of rain forest you find even in the harsh sclerophyll forests of coastal New South Wales. At the bottom of the deep, liana-tangled gully below the cliffs looming over our small neighbourhood of houses, there was an enormous pile of organic stuff, metres high and metres across: the mound of a brush turkey. I first learned about it because the guy who owned the holiday house next door liked to bring his friends up to see it. You would see this line of people crossing the grassy common at the end of the street and disappearing under the palms that grow along the watercourse. They would return, chattering excitedly, ten minutes later. So one day I went to have a look myself. It was a prodigy; but, having gazed upon it, there wasn't much else you could do but come away again, especially since the rain-forested gully was infested with mosquitoes.

It wasn't until we moved round the corner into Cornelian that I had the opportunity to watch brush turkeys at close quarters.

There was a mound, a small one, down the back of the section of the house next door, easily seen from our deck. Brush turkeys are absurd. They have a nearly bald crimson head with a few black feathers like hairs sprouting from it, a vivid collar of yellow at the neck, dull black body and a speckled breast. Their tail, which is a large double fan of dark feathers, extends vertically, not horizontally as in almost all other birds, making them look like one of those early, poorly designed, balsa and chicken-wire aircraft that never flew. They are megapodes – big foots – who scratch a living out of the soil and will eat literally anything, including, for example, Christmas decorations. They have no song, but chuck when feeding, squawk if chased, and, at times, fill their throat cavity with air then let out a deep lugubrious eructation like the belch of someone easing a bad digestion.

It is the male who constructs the mound, brushing up litter from metres around to make a festering pile in which the females lay their eggs. In absolute contrast to the joyous carolling and gambolling of the bower bird, this task seems to fill the brush turkey with anxiety. As the collar round his neck plumps into the loops and folds of a bright yellow wattle which may hang down almost to the ground, he begins desperately to rake up the stuff he needs, sometimes in places so far removed there is no possibility that it will ever actually reach the mound. I remember one scratching the woodchip mulch strewn next to our drive at Onyx down a high retaining wall on to the road, then across the road itself and on to the grassy common. He moved vast quantities of the stuff about fifty metres, but his actual mound was at least twice that far away and our woodchips were never going to make it there. I used to shovel them back up the retaining wall, only to find him, next day, scratching them feverishly back down again. This single-minded wrong-headed obsessive behaviour is the despair of gardeners: once a brush turkey decides to dig up your vegetable or flower patch, nothing but death or a change of season will dissuade him. One local actually had a mound fork-lifted out of his back garden and shifted into the nearby bush;

the turkey came back next day and started brushing up another in the exact same place.

As with the bower birds, so with the brush turkeys: the females make their decision on the credentials of the mound. They go from one to another, inspecting each in turn, before mating with the male (or males) of their choice and laying their eggs in tiers underground at the centre of his pile. There is nothing to prevent a female turkey mating with a series of males and laying in a series of mounds; thus, one mound may have in it the eggs of several, or many, females. Once her eggs are laid, the female abandons them, returning to days of scratching in the earth, nights of roosting in trees. Meanwhile, the male, his wattle now skinny, ragged, streaked with black, his stress levels immeasurable, stays by his mound, monitoring its temperature to ensure it is at exactly the right heat to incubate the eggs. As the air gets cooler, he will add to it; as it warms, he will subtract, testing from time to time with his beak. This labour continues until all eggs have hatched, and then he too goes on his way. Neither parent looks after the chicks: once they burrow out of the mound they are on their own and most of them succumb to snakes, goannas, foxes, feral or domestic cats, dogs or to hunger. Those that manage to survive a hundred days may then join one of the roving bands of turkeys which move up into the bush in the evening, down on to the flats in the morning.

Brush turkeys, related to pheasants, are an ancient order of birds, some of which grew to massive size in prehistoric times. Examples of them were systematically hunted to extinction on most of the smaller islands of the western Pacific and they have survived best on greater land masses like Australia and New Guinea. It is hard to imagine the local variety making much of a meal. Although a large and voracious bird, they are extremely light and carry no extra weight; captured and bred in a cage they might bulk up. They seem to be very stupid, but perhaps that is because we do not know them well enough. Once, up in the bush behind the village, I came across a large group of them, forty or so, walking deliberately, in single file, along the almost horizontal trunk of a fallen angophora. This still living tree had plunged down the slope, so at its leafy end there was a drop of maybe twenty metres to the broken ground below. Each turkey, as it reached that end, leapt off and floated, wings extended, down; then turned and plodded back up the hill again to repeat the exercise, like a group of kids climbing a ladder to a board and then diving off into a pool.

III

At Amethyst one day I heard what sounded like a car alarm coming from the bush behind the Biological Research Station, where no car or alarm would ever be. After listening for a while I realised it was not a car alarm at all, nor even an imitation of one. Rather, it was a highly mannered rendition of the warning cry of the noisy miner aka the soldier bird aka the alarm bird. This was followed by an inexpert version of the currawong's *ka waa ka waa, waaa* and that in its turn by a more skilful, but still not perfect, attempt at the whipbirds' antiphonal *oooooooo-yip! whee-wheeee!* (the male whipbird does the first, whip-like cry, the female *whee-wheeees* in answer; that's how they keep in touch while foraging through the scrub).

This was autumn, and what I was hearing was a young superb lyrebird practising for his first mating season. Although the superb's territorial song does contain a short, species-specific component, it is largely a repertoire of mimicked sounds, including duetting of other bird species and the wingbeats and calls of flying parrot flocks. They have also been known to imitate chainsaws, mobile phones, hydraulic lifters, and hymns sung by forest-dwelling nuns, the tune of one of which, a hundred years lost, was recovered from amongst a community of the birds on the North Coast of New South Wales. Lyrebirds breed in winter; like bower birds, with whom they have a close genetic relationship, the males use a quieter variation of their song to attract females to a small earthy mound in a bush clearing where they dance with the sixteen modified feathers (two lyrates, two medians, twelve filamentaries) of their famous tails thrown forward over the head in a shimmering fan. Like the male bower bird, too, the lyre bird is polygamous and performs no parental duties. His life, apart from time spent raking the forest floor for soil-dwelling invertebrates, consists mostly of song and dance.

This one was an assiduous learner, starting at dawn most days that autumn and carrying on, with a few breaks, until late afternoon. Daily I heard him improve upon the note of almost silent suspense, more like a drawing of breath than anything else, that precedes the whipbird's crack. The melancholy of the currawongs at evening, when they carol a chain of echoes from station to station across the whole valley, he also mastered, along with the delirious lyric effusion of the always vocal noisy miners. There were other cries he never got quite right: although he could do the kookaburra's paroxysmic laugh, it never sounded like the real thing. Nor could he manage the liquid throatiness, reminiscent of a tui, of the butcher bird's song.

His mound was somewhere below the escarpment that rises behind the research station; from the overgrown track running from the top of the waterfall to join the fire trail half way up the Hope Range, you can look down into paradisial glades where ferns, grass trees and the cycads known locally as burrawangs grow among orange-limbed angophoras, and the forest floor is a soft accumulation of bark, gum leaves and fallen fronds. Sometimes I heard him ahead of me on this track, singing his lungs out; but no matter how quietly I crept along the white sandy path twisting through scrub and around grey sandstone outcrops, he always knew I was coming long before I saw him, and would scoot away to the nearest ledge then spread his wings and glide down through the mazy trees. It was better to sit and listen, as I did one of those blue afternoons when the sky's royal and the heat lies on the rocks like some old reptile: he was only a few metres away and the volume of his outpouring hurt my ears, an extravagance of song which seemed preposterous issuing from the throat of what is not a large bird.

So they are difficult, though not impossible, to see. Once I watched one in the Arboretum dexterously climbing a sheoak tree as if the limbs were rungs of a ladder. Another time, up on the Hope Range, I found myself between two duelling males, trying to outsing each other along the border of their adjoining territories: song as bludgeon and threat. They were too crazed to hide themselves like they usually do. The standard description: *dark brown above; grey brown below . . . solid outer feathers patterned chestnut, white and black . . .* doesn't do justice to their subtle, lustrous beauty. Their eyes, particularly, which are large, round, dark and knowing, suggest that the depth and range of song they command is not some instinctual or evolutionary embellishment, but a real intelligence, like the original of thought. I even like their turds: because they often rake over the path to the waterfall, you frequently find there the asymmetrical piles of tubular black and white extrusions, usually covered with a cluster of small bronze blowflies which rise up murmuring as you pass. Meanwhile the author of this offering is already away uphill through the sheoaks, looking for some secret place in which to gather additions to his repertoire: to sing so superbly, how much listening must he do?

Folk Tale

*We are digital archives of the African Pliocene, even of Devonian seas;
walking repositories of wisdom out of the old days. You could spend a lifetime reading in this ancient library* . . . so wrote Richard Dawkins,
who also notes that only about 2 per cent of the human genome
contains information that is actually used in the construction of
our bodies and minds. The rest consists of pseudogenes – faulty
duplicates of functional genes – or multiple copies of sequences
with no known relationship to any purpose: junk, tandem re-
peats, data trash. A gene mutates and the mutation is of no use
to the species, but it stays there on the helix and gets replicated
along with everything else during reproduction.

Does this really mean we carry within the information that
could make an ammonite or a euparkeria, that we could still be,
as Empedocles said he had been, *a bush and a bird / a boy and a girl
/ a mute fish in the sea*? Those reptilian dreams, those delirious
flights in which the landscape unscrolls below, those amoeboid
states before and after sleep . . . are they examples of genetic
memory? Remember Len Lye, who thought he could descend
into the old brain and paint the ancestral information encoded
there?

By the same token, it is commonly believed that we use only
a fraction of our brain power. Is the part we don't access the
unconscious, or not conscious yet, or is it where everything we
have forgotten goes? The brain is a redundant system, there is

a multitude of ways for paths to form, one circuit gets burnt out, another can replace it. Some think that the mechanism by which the body repels disease is as profligate: we do not make a particular antibody to combat a particular virus or bacterium; rather, we make every possible antibody, so that when a micro-predator arrives, it is likely there'll be something there that, in a molecular sense, fits. Another archive is implied, this time of microcosmic warriors and their adversaries, more various and more strange than any sci-fi or horror movie has yet imagined.

Not so long ago I saw a French documentary about Adolf Eichmann. His trial was filmed, and this was a new, complex edit of the material. It's in black and white and there's no commentary, only the words actually spoken by the judges, the prosecutor, witnesses, court officials and Eichmann, who defended himself. And the prosaic sounds of the courtroom: rustling paper, foot-falls, mike noise, clicks, breathings, silence. Eichmann does an impression of a man eager to co-operate: he shares the horror people feel at the crime in which he is accused of having played a part, he wants the trial to go well.

His defence, famously, was that he only followed orders and was never complicit in any crime because he never knew the ul-timate intent of those orders. He even solicits sympathy because he was unwittingly made to participate in this terrible event. If only he had known! He might have killed himself. When asked if he believes those who gave him his orders knew what they were doing, he will not answer. *I choose not to reveal my innermost self*, he says primly and you are asked to imagine it for yourself. In fact, his recall of what he observed on the few visits he made to the actual camps is forensic. He savours the *fountains of blood* – apparently a phenomenon associated with mass graves – he had heard about but never before seen, and shows the same ob-session with detail which made him such an efficient manager of train transport.

I had a vertiginous sense part way through the two hours of the film that the trial was somehow superfluous, that there was no charge equivalent to the crime, no way a whole people could interrogate a single individual. One of the implications of Eichmann's defence is that the same thing will happen again in much the same way somewhere else: as if we are all under instruction from a higher power, all incompetent to reckon the intent of the orders we obey. Almost the last thing he says, when those around him are being wiped one by one from the screen – as, most poignantly, earlier in the film, a succession of survivor-witnesses appeared and spoke and disappeared – is the proud boast that he was never once rebuked by his superiors for dereliction of duty, never once accused of a want of assiduousness in the carrying out of his allotted tasks.

Recently there was a local sighting of a tiger-striped quoll, the largest marsupial carnivore left on the mainland. No quoll has been seen in these parts for many years; if they are back, it must be because the 1080 poison National Parks and Reserves has been laying for foxes is starting to work. You don't have to destroy the fox population, only reduce it to about 20 per cent of its current level and keep it there. Then the native animals can outbreed them.

The sighting of the quoll is a cause of great satisfaction for many who live in the village and will be featured in the next issue of the local news sheet. Nature, with all its profligate wonders, is coming back, at least to this neck of the woods. The closeness of wild creatures to our lives, independent of any particular use they are to us, seems to confirm that an harmonious accommodation can be reached. We with our machines, our prophylactics, our distant cultivars, our nearby abattoirs, imagine a simulacrum of the archaic wilderness forming around us. We know there are limits upon it, that the valley where the quoll hunts is bounded by a paved highway, and the wilderness beyond, enormous though it is, is bifurcated by a busy freeway; but that does not stop us wanting it. It's the yearning for extension bred into us through prehistory, when we could never look at a horizon without wondering what lay beyond it.

Perhaps wilderness is equivalent to that area of the brain we do not use, where whatever electrical impulses jump the synapses go unregistered by consciousness. And equivalent to the dark matter in space, the 90 per cent of stuff (they say) we cannot detect but which must be there in order to balance our grandiose equations. Dark matter in space, darkness in our heads, dark deeds . . . is darkness the procreant quality of the innermost selves we choose or choose not to reveal? A void that, by being kept secret, remains void and by being revealed, becomes something other than void, some thing? What are those never before seen shapes glistening as they move forward into the equivocal light of the mind?

In the reptile park they are throwing de-feathered battery hens from one of the nearby chicken farms to the alligators. Alligators don't eat all year round; this mid-April feed is the last most of them will have until Christmas. The keeper tries to get them interested by playing the old Stealers Wheel song: . . . *clowns to the left of me / jokers to the right / I'm stuck in the middle with you* . . . then beating on the jetty with a stick.

Later this same keeper, a thin, greying man with the face of a tired vaudevillian, will have better success provoking a female funnel-web spider into rearing up at his dancing hands and expressing drops of venom on the tips of her fangs. The people assembled around the low tin fence of the enclosure in which she performs cannot actually see the venom, but, if they wish, in Spider World they can watch glassed-in women only a few feet away milking male funnel-web spiders of their far more lethal poison, which will then be used to make antivenin.

Today the larger laboratory where venomous snakes are likewise milked is deserted; but in the lighted cases nearby and the open walled enclosures outside, those same snakes can be viewed in all their slender elegance, drowsing on the hot stones or curled and knotted in the shade of a dusty bush or clump of grass: tiger snakes, red-bellied blacks, eastern browns, death adders, taipans and the rest. The Lost World of Reptiles, where the tropical and desert snakes, along with various iguana and other lizards, are kept, has an Egyptian theme, with wrapped mummies in alcoves in the walls, hieroglyphs on the roof and an enormous statue of Sebek, the crocodile god, presiding.

In the United States, a group of lapsed Protestants spend their time round a Ouija board channelling messages from people they call the Cassiopaeans. Though the transmissions are ostensibly received from that part of the northern sky in which the constellation Cassiopeia is, they believe the Cassiopaeans are actually themselves in a future state of being; their purpose in manifesting is to alter the past so that the recipients of their messages will, in time, become them. In other words they are being instructed by their enlightened future selves, who are teaching them the difference between STS (service to self) and STO (service to others). The human race was genetically altered, the Cassiopaeans say, 309,000 years ago by aliens called the Lizard People. This is why 98 per cent of our DNA is junk. The Lizard People changed us and then set us against each other because that way they could draw off our energy for their own detestable purposes.

Sometimes this group hears from another people, the Nommo, an amphibious race from the star Sirius whom the Dogon of central Saharan Africa call bringers of water. The Nommo tell the group that they are themselves the so-called Lizard People of the Cassiopaeans but it is the Cassiopaeans, not the Nommo, who are feeding psychically upon us. Further, the Nommo deny we have been genetically altered; our afflictions date from the latest transposition of the earth's magnetic poles, when we lost both our telepathic powers and our ability to discriminate between good and evil. There are arguments in the group between those who believe the Cassiopaeans and those who believe the Nommo and it seems that a split is developing.

The last reversal of the poles occurred about 780,000 years ago. During the changeover, which can take 5000 years, earth's magnetic field weakens and the planet and its inhabitants become much more vulnerable to forces from space like the solar wind . . . or the Cassiopaeans. What this meant for *Homo erectus*, whose era that was, we cannot say. Did it help them become us? And was the cost the loss of telepathy and a functional ethical sense? Len Lye was among those who believe that transposition causes genetic changes.

The magnetic poles reverse on a usual interval of a quarter of a million years, but there have been periods of stability as long as 35 million years. Now some French and Danish scientists think they have found evidence that the next one has begun: the earth's magnetic field is weakening and, if the trend continues at the current rate, will disappear in about 2000 years. They have discovered this from a study of variations or anomalies in the rotation of columns of liquid iron in the core of the planet.

Darkness is rising over the reptile park. Eastern grey kangaroos move out to graze on the lawn where earlier picnickers lunched. Beside the owl enclosure, the wild tawny frogmouths, who like to sleep in the trees near their caged fellows, will be stirring ready for the night's hunting. The barrier between the captive and the free, unusually pervious in this practical and relatively humane zoo, is further dissolving. The dingos are going home for the night to the house of the tired vaudevillian, whose pets they are; but the rest – the turtles and tortoises, the cassowaries, the flying foxes, the echidnas, and all the other birds, reptiles, marsupials and monotremes, most of them nocturnal – will remain in their cages, wide awake and perhaps telepathic beneath the unquestionable stars, seeking ways into or out of the nightmares of humans on this planet which must seem to them both dunghill and Elysium.

The documentary's walk-out tune and only music was the instrumental 'Russian Dance' from *The Black Rider*, the album of songs written by Tom Waits for the dramatisation of a German folk tale Robert Wilson, in collaboration with William Burroughs, did with the Thalia Theatre of Hamburg: a doomed carousel riding gaudily to oblivion: *Da da da da da-da . . . da da-da-da-da-da . . .*

Rosetta

we set out now in the boat of millions of years

In March 2004, the fifteen nations of the European Space Agency launch, from Kourou in French Guiana, a probe called *Rosetta*. *Rosetta* carries a television-sized robot which it is to land on the surface of comet 67P/Churyumov-Gerasimenko, one of the very few orbiting within the solar system. Churyumov-Gerasimenko ellipses the sun every 6.6 years without going beyond Jupiter. An Ariane 5 rockets *Rosetta* in the direction of Mars, which it passes in February 2007. Mars' gravity accelerates *Rosetta* on its loop back towards Earth as, in November 2007, it makes its second fly-by; later, in September 2008, it will pass close to asteroid 2876 Šteins. In November 2009, on its third solar orbit, *Rosetta* makes another pass of the Earth, so that our gravity can slingshot it almost as far as Jupiter. On the way to Churyumov-Gerasimenko, in July 2010, it flies by asteroid 21 Lutetia.

your love in my flesh like a reed in the arms of the wind

Rosetta is in deep space hibernation from May 2010 until January 2014, when it begins approaching the comet, tracking it from behind at a speed of 90 km/h. It continues to close until it glides past about 35 km out at a speed of 7 km/h. From the control centre in Germany, the probe is slowed to let the comet overtake; then it repasses. This manoeuvre is repeated maybe ten times, with the probe coming closer on each pass until it is a kilometre above the surface, at which point it goes into orbit and then, in November 2014, lets go the 100-kilogram, three-legged lander called Philae, after an island in the Nile where a temple to Isis once stood. In the comet's gravity, 100,000 times weaker than Earth's, Philae weighs just one gram. It drops straight down to the surface, anchors itself with screws, harpoons and wires, and begins three weeks of surface experiments. Ten cameras take panoramas and close-ups. Microphones listen for echoes of pips emitted by speakers fitted to each leg. A drill digs 25 cm under the surface for samples which are analysed and photographed on board. Radio waves beam from the lander, through the comet and on to *Rosetta*, scanning Churyumov-Gerasimenko's interior. Philae falls silent when its battery dies. But, a year later, as the comet, escorted by *Rosetta*, nears the sun, light falling on solar panels revives the probe. Unlike previous vessels sent to the outer solar system – NASA's *Pioneer*, *Voyager*, *Galileo* and *Cassini* missions – *Rosetta* is not nuclear powered. Instead, it is fitted with 70 square metres of solar panels covered in tiny glass pyramids to catch as much of the sun as possible.

our hearts as light as the feather of truth on the scales

Comets are the oldest things in the solar system. They are rubble left over from the accretion of the other bodies that orbit our sun, fragments of what the planets are made from. On their surfaces are water-ice, carbon dioxide, carbon monoxide and methane, covered in a black tar produced by intergalactic dust and carbon raining down for billions of years. Halley's Comet turned out to be the blackest object ever seen in space, blacker than coal dust. As a comet approaches the sun, ice inside of it starts to vaporise, gas and dust jet out through holes and envelop it in a cloud, or coma, of water vapour, hydrogen, and cyanide;

then the action of the solar wind on the coma makes the gas and dust stream out for millions of kilometres in the blazing white tail that so troubled the ancients.

our names stars on the arching belly of night

The Rosetta Stone is a basalt slab 114 x 72 x 28 cm found in the summer of 1799 in the small Egyptian village of Raschid in the western delta of the Nile. It has been re-used in a structure being demolished by a group of Napoleon's soldiers so that they can build a barracks. The actual discoverer of the piece is a man by the name of Bouchard or Boussard. The Stone, cut in 196 BC, presents a single text in three different scripts; it is a decree of the priests of Memphis in honour of Ptolemy V Epiphanes, written originally in Greek and then translated into hieroglyphs and demotic script. The final, strangely prescient words are: *this decree shall be inscribed on a stela of hard stone in sacred and native and Greek characters and set up in each of the first, second and third temples beside the image of the ever-living king.* Publication of the trilingual inscriptions in Bonaparte's scholars' *Description de l'Egypt* (1809) enables, by 1822, Frenchman Jean François Champollion to decipher the Stone. Further, with his knowledge of Coptic, the language of Christian descendants of the ancient Egyptians, Champollion construes the phonetic value of some hieroglyphs, showing that they do not simply have symbolic meaning, but represent a spoken language as well. It is an obelisk found on Philae, with a bilingual inscription including the names of Cleopatra and Ptolemy in hieroglyphs, that gives Champollion the last clues towards decipherment.

crossing the water we speak the hieroglyph of darkness

The European Space Agency's decision to call their probe *Rosetta* declares an intent to decipher the hieroglyph comet but are we equal to the task? Our civilisation believes understanding is reached when we can a) describe an object, b) identify its origin and c) find a use for it. We cannot escape the preconceptions of this method: current orthodoxy believes the universe originated in a Big Bang, like a nuclear bomb: we are living in the debris of an explosion. There are other models. Those who think the earth's biosphere is a living organism see comets not as black snowballs but cosmic sperm looking for planets to fertilise with hydrocarbons. There are millions of them in the Kuiper Belt and the Oort Cloud. Most scientists do not admit that they practise cosmogony, which makes it hard for them to understand the immensely long tradition they are heir to. Rather, they are obsessed with the notion that there is one explanation which covers all cases – a Theory of Everything. Since Stephen Hawking's audience with the Pope last century, when it was decided that what is at issue is not who created the universe but how he went about doing it, even the most extravagant notions of the astrophysicists have been reckoned compatible with the teachings of the Catholic Church.

on the far horizon of our eyes the ancient sun rises

What might *Rosetta* find that would astonish us? Every time a probe goes out and sends back information for analysis, the scientists announce their incredulity. This is almost always be-cause the particulars do not precisely answer their predictions. Then they beaver away at their equations again to make room for errant data. There is nothing surprising about this process: it is the empirical method, confirming its own veracity via revi-sion of theory in accord with observation. At the same time, all other explanations are explicitly or implicitly cancelled. There is no other way of understanding. Curiously, those who hunt down heretics call themselves skeptics.

together we place our hands on the greeting stone

What about the Stone? Recent research suggests it may have been one of many identical stelae set up all over Egypt in a propaganda exercise designed to boost the fading fortunes of the Ptolemaic dynasty. Fascinating as the decree is in its detail of Ptolemy V's reign – his endowment of temples with corn and money and their adornment with gold and jewels, his remission of taxes on the people, the freeing of prisoners, the damming of the Nile during victorious wars, care for old soldiers, gifts to the sacred animals of Egypt, honouring of the dead – we believe it to be essentially misconceived: *Ptolemy, the ever-living, beloved of Ptah, the God Epiphanes Eucharis, the son of the Gods Soteres, and the Gods Adelphoi, and the Gods Euergetai, and the Gods Philopatores* was not divine, nor were his ancestors, and nor were the archaic deities he represented in himself. In the same way, all of the sacred writing of the Egyptians, which Rosetta taught us to read, is wrong about the big things, because they had no science. And what does science say of the big things? God, process, technology, end. As it gathers sunlight on its glass pyramids and, over the next few years, swings away, back, away, back, away and back again towards the black comet, what could *Rosetta* possibly find there but the elemental dust?

our souls will be birds on the distant road of the sky

an.aesthetic

I

'*Aint No Aesthetics Here Man*' Phil Clairmont wrote across the top of a 1976 drawing of some French doors. I don't know if he was quoting someone else or not. Like modernist poets and vernacular letter writers, he was in the habit of putting quotation marks around all sorts of things, 'for emphasis', so it could just have been an example of that. Or it might have been a line rewritten from a Grateful Dead song. The painting from the drawing is called *To Give Blazing Light*, referencing (perhaps) what Colin McCahon said about not being interested in the sun but wanting to spread a little light around. It did blaze, too, for a while, though I understand it's faded now.

Much earlier, I recall some serious discussion of aesthetics with Vic Filmer while we were stacking condiments at the Cerebos warehouse in Newton, Auckland, in the summer of 1970–71. The aesthetic emotion came from a sense of completeness in the work, we decided beside the immaculately finished chow-chow stand. Vic was a philosophy student who became a founder member and candidate of the Alpha Party, which took Ayn Rand's vision to the New Zealand people in the 1975 election, was it? Now he lives in the Blue Mountains, writes plays and studies Ancient Greek.

Along with completeness, it was that expressionist urgency I wanted to bring to my writing but it doesn't come easy. For a long time what I thought and what I did were in massive contradiction. The half-examined aesthetic behind my prolonged, failed enterprise as a lyric poet no longer detains me, or only insofar as it relates to an interest in the pathology of that quest. Likewise, an attempt to act in the theatre left me with a deep suspicion of the 'I' I could not seem to mask or body forth. 'I' was okay at lighting theatre though, and sometimes bands. No surprise, then, that much of my writing since has been in the almost anonymous and allegedly egoless zone of the screenplay.

There I've experienced the joys and humiliations that are a screenwriter's lot. I've been paid; I've been fired. The credit for my work has been taken by others and I've been praised for what wasn't mine. Screenplays have been butchered by producers, and given meticulous and generous treatment by directors. Films have been written and not made, made and not released, or made, released and then disappeared. Some have been seen around the world, though not by millions. I'm lucky: about a third of what I've written has gone to screen. This is a good ratio, although I still live for the day when everything I write is made.

All of what I do in film is collaborative or commissioned or both. It's better that way; there's always company, and you can toss around the question of what works and what doesn't. Is this a different question from what's beautiful? I don't know. Aesthetic inquiry may best be left in abeyance until someone else comes along and looks at the work. A by-product, then? Fellow screenwriter Billy MacKinnon said to me once that writing screenplays is first a technical procedure, then a matter of doing business (does it entertain?), and only then, and only perhaps, a work of art. It's not my decision, it's yours; my decisions were all made previously, at the nano-level.

I remember trying to justify to another friend the effort that had gone into a conspicuous dud of mine by repeating the nostrum that we learn more from our failures than our successes. *Yes*, she said, *but did you need to know that?* One screenplay I wrote was described as *too well written*. A certain level of illiteracy is seen by some as a guarantee of integrity: we can tell the guy has vision, he can't spell or punctuate. On the other hand, a screenplay has to be a plan for a film, not a literary artefact. All that lovely language is worth nothing if the actors can't say it or the cinematographer can't see it.

It's a syntax of emotion I'm after. In film, as in prose, I'm trying to map the wasteland within, those places where we go wordless with joy or grief or anger or ecstasy or fear or love or pain. It would be idle to pretend I know how to do this; all I know is how to try. It isn't language itself I want to interrogate, although I'm aware of, and sometimes sympathetic to, the attempts others make to do that. When it comes to words, I just want to use them; but a few thoughts on the subject might still be in order.

II

Aesthetics, from the Greek, *aisthanomai*, to perceive. Not to perceive beauty, just to perceive. A whole is implied: how strange would that be, to see things whole? A mystic might then say, it is beautiful. The Gnostics trawled the darkness within for the spark of light that reunites us with the cosmos. Theirs was an urgent desire for a totality. They were inheritors of an older, pre-literate tradition, one in which words had the value of real things that acted on the world.

Some words are very old: *Mano, Kuna, Mako, K'olo, Puti, Tik, Aq'wa.* Man, Woman, Child, Hole, Vulva, Finger, Water. Seven root words from Nostratic, 'our' language, aka Proto-Global, and found all over the world in many different language groups. We are older than our words, but not by much. Every child names the world anew, using the ancient syllables. Even a very young child will gasp in wonder when shown the clear night sky. They say *star* with a hush of the voice and prattle walking by the sea.

Do they also hear the stones talking? There are humanly deserted places where a cacophony of voices does rise up to greet or warn a passer-by. The silence over the bush on a blue day, or the sigh that rises from a great body of water, have been listened to again and again until they too have become part of our endless conversation: like birdsong, what we say to each other is eternally other and always the same. An irreducible social act, partaking of archaic verities. The exact same words, over and over again.

What is the connection between speech and writing? The tax records from Uruk are not the original writ. Sumerian is preceded by other Artificial Memory Systems: Palaeolithic tally sticks, the La Manche antler, the Vinca signs and more. The Old European script, with its probable descendant, the undeciphered Cretan Linear A, has not yet found its Rosetta stone: it could be about cosmogony, not economics. The correspondences between this set of signs and those from beyond the Mediterranean – Africa, the Indus Valley, China, Siberia, the Americas, the Pacific, Australia, South East Asia – have hardly been investigated. Some think graphics of sexual difference lie behind writing systems, others that they result from the calendrical obsessions of astronomical time keepers.

Fascination with prehistoric and aboriginal cultures arises from the proposition that they had/have intact a grammar of emotion. We do and we don't. There's a vast hinterland here. Early European explorers in the Pacific were amazed at the way mourners at a death could be passionately weeping one minute then laughing the next. This was clear evidence of savage insincerity, they thought. Their own axis of stern repression and appropriate expression is still with us: how to get out of these clutches?

We often don't know how to say what we feel. Incredible, we say. Unbelievable. The aesthetic quest, with its implicit or explicit *look at me*, has drained our emotions. It restrains us the same as any pathology. We still haven't realised that to exhibit the plumage of a self is a derisory undertaking. The recovery of the repressed may require wholesale demolition of the I. The ego on its rampage through the world causes endless sorrow.

The other day a neighbour's daughter, home from play-group, went running down the drive with glad cries to greet her dad. He, a builder, swung around, nearly hitting her with the machine tool he was using, then walked off around the side of the house without a word. She hugged the dog instead. This wasn't because he doesn't love her, but because he was being watched. He'd rather be seen as a brute than a loving father.

If you can show people how their behaviour looks to others, is that going to change it? Feeling makes us vulnerable and vulnerability may provoke change. Or, equally, violence. Why should we assume that change is always progress? Is this what history means? It seems more likely we are reverting, but to what? The truth of our time is difficult to tell and unlikely to be beautiful. You have to include everything you can.

Writing is best in response to a demand: to redress a balance or illuminate something obscure. To throw rocks in the pond. The received version of things is mostly bad burlesque. It's more important to get something said and understood than it is to make an aesthetic object. Take it as a given that the other voices coming through are always more compelling than your own; increasingly mine or yours or ours is made up of others anyway.

The far past is flashing before our eyes as we expire. Will we see what we are before we cease to be? Writing is a way of intervening, of de-railing and re-routing the trains of thought we are on. Another voice interleaved in the interior monologue. It remains a memory system, but are we adding items or subtracting them? Writing and memory are inextricably entwined: you remember in order to write but you write to forget. It's a way of giving things away.

And thus of retrieving what has been lost. Words as a tool to excavate and reconstruct the past: that's a project, a representation of a misrepresentation no one is wholly responsible for, though you have to take responsibility. The least we can do for the dead inside us is bring them up to date. As an archaeo-astronomist once said, the span of forgotten time is so vast we have only the constellations and some parallax of response in our brains to navigate by.

Language is infinite, our means are limited, the tasks at hand are onerous, time is short and words are many, who said that? If you can make a whole, and people perceive a whole, you've kept the conversation going. That singularity can be a sentence or it can be the full story. The paradox is, if it is complete, it'll have the clue, the radical of the next, embedded in it. And so on until you reach an end.

. . . *among the ruins with the poor*

Alan Brunton was someone I knew and worked with on and off, but mostly on, for nearly thirty years. I have been reading his writings for longer than that, he is among those few whose works are constantly by my side and available anyway, either voluntarily or involuntarily, in memory. In the weeks before he died we were just beginning to launch Bumper Books in Australia, but what I had in mind during that period was 'Living in the Real World', the penultimate poem in his 1991 collection, *Slow Passes* . . . lines kept coming back from that great resolution of the quest for right living. Why? Because they were a clue to solving a problem in my own life.

Then, coincidentally, and in all ignorance, on the day he had a heart attack in Amsterdam and went into unconsciousness, I found a back issue of *brief* magazine mislaid when we shifted house two years before and looked for many times since. In it is Alan's explication of his poem 'Don't Shoot the Piano Player' from the epochal first *Freed*. Characteristically, the exegesis is as mysterious as the poem as he plumbs the 77 levels of meaning he once (jokingly?) said were to be found in his work. By then I had begun to resolve my life problem, so it was for pure pleasure that, over the next few days, I read and re-read and wondered over the concatenation of allusion and perception in that piece, which ends by quoting Keats' epitaph: *Here lies one whose name was writ in water.*

So it was not unusual for me to be reading Alan; why I mention it here is because in those two readings both the man and the poet may be found. The ability to be of genuine help to others in writing and in life is as rare as the capacity to give deep and lasting pleasure in made work, but he could do both and did so, all his life, unstintingly, with an energy and commitment and grace and generosity of spirit which were with him to the end.

When I first met Alan, at a function at Downstage in Wellington in the winter of 1974, I already knew who he was. I'd been at a delirious performance by the *Freed* poets at the Auckland Technical Institute in 1970, in a packed hall with an audience who behaved more like a crowd at a rock concert. And, later that same year, at a party in Hargreaves Street in Freemans Bay, I watched, incredulous, as 'Brunton' misbehaved outrageously amongst his peers. After that he went overseas, and when we met at Downstage, courtesy of his partner, Sally Rodwell, whom I knew from staying for a few months at the Living Theatre house in Sentinel Road, Herne Bay, they had just returned from the East.

He was wearing a cloth cap. I was over-awed. He asked who a woman across the crowded room was, I told him, he came straight back with a joke, and instantly I was at ease – and, apart from the odd disquieted moment, we were easy with each other from then on in. I had been writing art reviews for *Salient*, and Alan, who read everything, thought well enough of them to suggest I might contribute to the paper he was starting with Ian Wedde and Russell Haley. They were going to call it *Stool* but settled on *Spleen* instead. It was just what I needed to grow: an enterprise I could devote myself to without having to formulate policy or make executive decisions.

At the same time, my then partner, Jan Preston, was invited to compose the music for the first Red Mole shows; thus I came to participate in the genesis, rehearsal and performance of most of the many shows there were over the next seven years. They were the cabaret years, at Carmen's Balcony and the Ace of Clubs and the Sweet Factory and the Easter Show, on the road up and down New Zealand and then in New York, London, Sheffield and cities and towns all over the USA, meeting and working with many different people and playing some wonderful rooms along the way: His Majesty's, the Kimo Theatre in Albuquerque, the State Opera House.

Unusually, Red Mole used to invite groupies, roadies and assorted hangers-on to make a contribution on as well as off stage and so, without ever really wanting to, I briefly came to act in, and later, with more aptitude, light the shows. My real interest was in writing and the enduring gift of those seven years was the opportunity to live and work in the presence of a master. I learned from Alan what makes good writing, and I also learned, more slowly, what it means to live an ethical life; the two are not distinct from each other, I believe. Any accomplishment there is in my own writing owes an immense debt to him; he was my mentor, my *experienced and trusted adviser*. I know he performed this role, in different ways, for many different people.

Sally and Alan and Deborah Hunt and John Davies went back to New York a year after Red Mole's 1980 return to New Zealand; I moved to Sydney, and I didn't see him again until 1988. I think now I needed those second seven years to absorb the lessons and rearrange myself. When contact resumed, I set up a season for Red Mole at the Belvoir Street Theatre in Surry Hills and a reading for Alan at the Harold Park Hotel in Glebe; I remember particularly his rendition of 'Their Diet Consists of Carrion' and my friend Johnny Bear, soon to die of AIDS, saying to him afterwards that he hoped he would not be buried, as criminals in Tibet were, in the ground. Like Alan, he was cremated.

Sometimes in Red Mole shows, a presence would fill the auditorium and you would remember that the theatre of the Greeks was designed to give voice to the god(s). There were some every night at the Belvoir Street, for instance when puppet boats crossed the stage on their way to Johnston Island with a cargo of nuclear waste. Like the more extravagant illusions Red Mole constructed, this one was created to music: among his other achievements, Alan found ways to expand theatre to include all kinds of music, most of which was played live.

My mind is full now of evanescent memories of theatrical moments, many of them very funny, some tragic, and I wish I had seen more shows after *The Book of Life* at the Belvoir. Instead, literary collaboration resumed. It was Alan who suggested I give the manuscript of *The Autobiography of My Father* to Michele Leggott, who forwarded it to Auckland University Press, who published it. Later, among much else, Bumper Books published two other books of mine. Working with Alan as editor and publisher was a joy: he was meticulous, inventive, swift and had a way of imagining futures that sustained an often equivocal present. There were plans: a book on the history of the Indian Ocean, republishing Harry Foster's 1927 *A Vagabond in Fiji*, various other unwritten and perhaps unwriteable books. Near the end his mind was turning towards the Pacific.

When I heard he had gone I remembered his voice: deep and rich, it always sounded as if it came from the heart of his being. He said some hard things to me over the years, including the intimation, in two cryptic remarks made seven years apart, that I was a prose writer not a poet; but there was never any malice in it, only the hope that what he said would be taken as what he meant . . . which sounds simple but, for Alan, who was frequently misunderstood, wasn't. I can't help thinking that he did it harder than he might have, even though the difficulty was partly self-imposed: he dined with bankers and smoked with tribal leaders and, in New York, got to know one man who had flown over Nagasaki on the *Great Artiste* and another who had worked as a scientist on the Manhattan Project; but he really did spend his days among the ruins with the poor. Even so, as he said, in his mind he lived in luxury. That luxury was in no sense exclusive, it was, rather, his gift, and given equally to us all. I doubt he ever met a person he could not have empathy with, though he did not always choose to.

Not long before he left on his last trip, he fixed the bilge pump on the canoe at the Island Bay Surf Club, which he and Sally and others used as a space to work in. We performed *Towards Bethlehem*, a Christmas pageant, to seven people there in 1976, and Alan was not one to forget something like that. An ethical sense of community was what he dedicated his life towards and we will, I hope, honour that commitment in the days to come.

Then there are the writings: I do not expect to get to the end of them in my lifetime and believe there will be others of like inclination to follow. What I know of them is an enduring astonishment, and in saying this I'm mindful that I'm not acquainted with most of the theatre work Red Mole did after 1981. The prose is lucid, resonant and crackles with ideas and the poetry books – *Messengers in Blackface, Black & White Anthology, Oh, Ravachol, Day for a Daughter, Slow Passes, Romaunt of Glossa: A Saga, Moonshine, Ecstasy, Fq* – ineffable delights, containing thought that goes into the atoms and beyond the solar system, before time and after the end. A unique cast of characters, among whom you are always glimpsing a man, a woman and a child journeying, enact primal dramas in landscapes and cities both paradisial and apocalyptic but also, weirdly, recognisable as our world. Not so long ago Alan said to me that the essence of his book *Ecstasy* was what James K. Baxter used to say: *love, man; aroha*. I also remember him saying that poetry did not have to mean so much as be: the fecundity and recombinant power of his use of language sings before it signs, which is why it is, practically speaking, inexhaustible.

Last night as I wrote this, it was cold and clear outside, with big stars and a wild surf cracking on the beach as some obscure storm from the Tasman played itself out along our shore. This morning I woke from a dream in which I drove the Falcon recklessly out on to the sand and then, thinking better of it, reversing, saw a pride of lions lounging under the paperbark trees in the reserve. As I started back down Coral Crescent, one of the lions put its head through the car window and licked the side of my face with a broad, rough tongue. Though he was a Libran, there always was something leonine about Alan. Already I miss him more than I can say, and yet he is in some way still with us. He will not mind if I use his own words to hail him:

Yo Papa

Yama   Yo

3 JULY 2002

Lighting Out for the Territory

I

Poetry is always written within a cosmogony. But the meaning of the universe and where it stops and starts are still matters of conjecture.

Alan Brunton's book-length poem, *Moonshine* (Bumper Books, 1998), is a hermetic text, which does not mean it is inscrutable, only that you have to follow certain paths of knowledge to understanding. It can be read as writing floating in a dark pool of unknowing which it serves to bring into the light. So densely referential is it that any cybertext would be almost entirely blue; annotated it will make a book twice as long as its 82 pages. Unlike much of the hermetica, however, it is not backward looking, it does not attempt elucidation of the lost wisdom of the past. What it proposes instead is a tracing of the ways in which the transformative power coded in the hermetica was misused, and what the consequences of this are. Alan Brunton was a poet of large ambition – those quoted or evoked in the three introductory verses alone include Plato (in Dr Dee's translation), Horace, Chaucer, Spenser, Milton and Baudelaire – and this is his epic: a cosmic love story ending in apocalypse.

The narrative of the poem begins in the age of amphibians and ends with *the slow HaHa of charming quarks*: life on earth. Its three major parts are a history in eight numbered sections, a dramatic monologue which is also a biography of Ernest Rutherford, and a post-apocalyptic vision written in free verse. These are preceded by a Dedication, a Preface and an Invocation, and followed by four short, almost mute, pieces framed decisively in our misused present; the work concludes with Notes and Omitted Verses. The armature of genuine scholarship which informs *Moonshine* is astonishing, more so the speculative power of its imagining of past, present and future. As an account of how the quest for the philosopher's stone, with its ability to transform matter and confer immortality, was fulfilled in the disastrous experiments of late nineteenth- and twentieth-century scientists, it proposes an alternative canon – philosophic, artistic, scientific – which amounts to a major revision of the thought of the West. If, as quantum physicist J. A. Wheeler believes, *most of the universe consists of huge clouds of uncertainty that have not yet interacted with a conscious observer . . . a vast arena containing realms where the past is not yet fixed . . .* such revision is not simply of interest but crucial for our future.

The first indication of a biographical impulse in Alan Brunton's published work is the short poem 'For Petrus van der Velden' in *The Young New Zealand Poets* (1973). A collage of factual information and direct quotation, it encapsulates a whole life and its artistic legacy in seven short stanzas, which end:

> 'colour is light – light is love
> love is God & when you understand
> this you are an artist'

Van der Velden's trajectory was from nineteenth-century Europe to the antipodes, his illumination came at the end of his life at the end of the world; Ernest Rutherford moved in precisely the opposite direction, from the obscurity of Brightwater, south of

Nelson, to Trinity College in Cambridge and world fame as the man who split the atom. His life, however, in this telling, like van der Velden's, is the life of an artist.

An epic intent in Alan Brunton's work manifested in the 1978 Red Mole production *Ghost Rite*, an intensely theatrical, almost wordless universal history which began with creation out of the primordial waters and ended in a song of longing as a group of cargo cultists implored themselves off planet. As the pageant moved from prehistoric times through Egypt, the Dark Ages, plague-infested medieval Europe, the early Renaissance, to a surreal modern age afflicted by demagoguery and war, two figures recurred: the Fool and the Magus, sometimes paired, as in the sequence where an evil Svengali manipulated the oracular utterances of an innocent called Hans Bones. These presentiments – *there are no fences on the sun . . . why should I pay for light?* – so excited the crowd they set upon the Svengali, tearing him to pieces before chairing the Fool from the stage. The scryer thus defeated his magus but then the wheel turned again, literally – an aluminium wheel was built for *Ghost Rite* and, with an actor spread-eagled star-shaped within, passed across the stage to mark the transitions between periods.

A third, and immediate, precursor to *Moonshine* was a Red Mole show mounted in New York in 1982. *The Excursion* took its dramatic structure from the progress of the Boat of a Million Years on its nightly journey through the Egyptian Land of the Dead. John Davies, who lit it, writes: *There were the long grey coats with mud smeared on them and round masks that opened to reveal other masks . . . berimbau music on the soundtrack. Backdrops up close to the audience which would be pulled aside to reveal set ups behind. There were suitcases (these re-occurring motifs). There was a tree of people and the scattering of corn. Just the three actors and something was burnt in flame.*

Alan Brunton wrote about *The Excursion* in a poem published in his 1991 collection *Slow Passes*. 'Their Diet Consists of Carrion' answers New York drama critic Eileen Blumenthal's rhetorical question as to *why Flaubert was in the play in the first place* by way of a simultaneously hilarious and chilling account of a mugging on the Lower East Side of Manhattan. This during the writing of:

> *my mask-and-gallanty show*
> *based on the proceedings of Ra, the archaic deity,*
> *through the Underworld.*

It is from these perspectives, then, that *Moonshine* would be written: the documentary and the quotation, vatic speech and its contrarieties, the nightly progress through the land of the dead. Masks would open to reveal other masks, screens would slide back to reveal other scenes. *Moonshine*'s writing takes us from a prophetic fragment inscribed on a piece of clay in ancient Iraq, via the Egyptian mysteries of Hermes Trismegistus, to the site of Trinity in New Mexico where the prophecy was fulfilled.

II

Moonshine proposes that history was directed, not in any Hegelian sense, from the first fish to get up onto the Silurian beach towards the birth of Rutherford, in Brightwater.

Hermetic philosophy began in Alexandria under the Ptolemys as a fusion of Greek and Egyptian thought with each other and with the wisdom of the East – the Levant, Mesopotamia, Persia, India, Sunda and China – along with what those traditions retained of humanity's single pan-belief system, shamanism. The Hermetics practised breathing techniques, meditation and sexual magic in which the lovers joined the continuum of the earth and the stars: as above, so below. The union of lover and beloved enabled them to perfect themselves, transcend ordinary reality and enter into bliss, which means both to see and be part of the universal web of connectedness; this ecstasy is (still) available to us all.

The Hermetics believed there were nodal points in the web where force was concentrated that could be used to make change. These nodes were sometimes expressed as symbols (words, hieroglyphs) but were also in the actual sounds of speech, which are thus storage cells charged with power the way a battery is charged with electricity:

> *Known about batteries since the Dynasties*
> *Memm*
> *the Arrows of Ra, aha!*

At the most basic level, *Moonshine* proposes A and O as the primordial sounds, the Alpha being, perhaps, the Ah! of understanding, the Omega the Oh! of wonder: that is, an indrawn breath and an expelled breath, in turn related to the systole/diastole, the contraction and expansion of the heart. O incarnates as a woman through the ages and sometimes takes on the attributes of A. When she does, paradise is on earth; when not, we are in hell. A's primary manifestation is Whoosh, the HaHa Man, who, in the mysterious crime which initiates the (black) comedy, violates O in the Idalian Grove, where Persephone was raped by Pluto. She flees, and thereafter his crew of alchemists and proto-scientists, philosophers and prelates, chase her down the centuries of the last two millennia.

The account of this pursuit is the matter of the first part of the poem. We meet Ovid, Zosimus, St Bernard (founder of the Knights Templar), Cola de Rienzi, the washerwoman's son who rose against the Pope in fourteenth-century Italy, the early Portuguese navigators to Africa, Pico Mirandole and his patron, Lorenzo de Medici, before going with Columbus to America and Magellan round the world. From Elizabethan England, with its magus-poets and holy fools, comes a brief life of Sir Philip Sidney, then we speed up past the wooden O at Bankside, Galileo's heresy, Newton at Trinity College, Omai's visit to London, Coleridge's agony in the Greyhound, until we arrive (breathless) in New Zealand:

Silver eyes walked on the beach
of a cloud inside a hand
during the virgin hours of
A Forever & A Day
Belonging to Strangers gone
there to establish a State

O returns, reversing the roles: it's the hell of the alchemists and she's coming for the man who wronged her. Whoosh is now a scientist, Joe Wurtz, stuck in some dread limbo with other damned immortals, and O an avenging angel cum interplanetary cardsharp cum bar girl. With a wicked pack of cards, she wins the game hands down – they are playing baccarat – and claims her prize. In a delirious consummation framed by the Angelology of Aquinas, early modernism (Mallarmé, Ravel, Duchamp, Joyce), the A and B of molecular ascent and decay as defined by Einstein, and the poet's own initials, the product of their union is Ernest Rutherford.

This picaresque chronicle is written, with great brio, mostly in a metre that derives ultimately from François Villon. Part I is an archaic text, something transcribed from a stone, full of ellipses, illegibilities, reconstructions; part II, in Chaucerian Ynglish, initiates the three-accent, seven-syllable line into which most of the rest is cast. Along the way, a marvellous ear for language puts the canon through its paces. When Whoosh disguises himself as the Kalif of Rum (Sufi poet Rumi):

With fiery looks he courted
Miss Universe and Miss World
those blushing theodoras
who figged their full figuras
in moonlight flits and startles
through palazzo publicos
where venture capitalists
sifted the erst for clues . . .

In the esoteric tradition of alchemy, the manipulation of physical elements is a metaphor for the chemical wedding of the lovers. Renaissance alchemists thought of themselves as botanists as much as chemists, nurturing metals as love is nurtured, and making them grow. But a parallel tradition *Moonshine* charts is more problematic: the earliest surviving alchemical text from Alexandria contains recipes for imitating the gold and jewels encrusting sarcophagi of the Egyptian great dead, and for fabricating the purple dyes used in the pharaohs' grave cloth. The intrinsic, intimate relationship between alchemy, forgery, and the issuance of currency, as strange in its way as the mania for gold itself, and the related obsession with measurement, are shown to be behind the drive to weigh the elements and thus the splitting of the atom: by dealing exclusively with reality considered only as material facts, we not only lost the ecstatic potential in alchemy, but also, calamitously, started unpicking the fabric of the web itself. Insofar as this first section is a history of ideas, it is also a history of misunderstanding, cupidity, foolishness and misapprehension. False gold is always being taken for true, currency is not value, Isaac Newton, physicist, alchemist, ends up Master of the Mint.

III

The universe we live in is a work of art. The authentic poet knows this. Science is the way we imagine today, but that changes every day. For a while everything looks like Jurassic Park, *then it's something else.*

In the second section of the poem, 'Waves', the life of Ernest Rutherford (ER) is told, with many asides, by an unnamed immortal in conversation with a mysterious interlocutor called Memm. They are in some kind of dread limbo, two ancient Egyptians, perhaps Hermes Trismegistus in congress with his

Other, his Soul, who, because of the atomisation of the structure of reality, are at the end of their ability to reincarnate. Memm could also be an avatar of the Roman poet Gaius Memmius, the contemporary of Lucretius and Catullus, and/or an acronym for the Maximum Entropy Markov Model, a powerful algorithm for processing the large amounts of text on the World Wide Web: these superannuated reincarnates may be stranded somewhere out on the Net. Markov was a Russian mathematician and poet whose work, in 1923, was taken up by Norbert Weiner. The Markov assumption states that the next state depends only on the current state:

> *it stands to reason*
> *Memm*
> *you don't need the Band of Hope*
> *to tell you*
> *if you know the question,*
> *that the world's all a continuity*
> *along parameters set centuries ago,*
> *you need no glazed*
> *optic tube*
> *Memm, to tell you that*

The unnamed narrator is grumpy, world weary, incredulous, outraged and ultimately resigned: one of Alan Brunton's funniest incarnations. His narration of the life of Rutherford is at once intellectual biography, mock-heroic colonial saga, portrait of the artist and hallucinatory account of that essential step towards the fission technology which so haunts us today, the splitting of the atom – actually the transformation of nitrogen into isotopes of oxygen and hydrogen by bombarding it with nuclei of helium.

Floddy, Geiger, Giesel, J. J. Thompson, Wien, Wittgenstein – radium for the epochal experiments at Cambridge was surreptitiously obtained from one of Wittgenstein's father's Austrian mines – make appearances, but the heroine of 'Waves' is Marie Curie, née Sklodowska, Polish wife of Pierre and divine bride of the unique ER. She is the inheritor of that other alchemical tradition, the female line that goes back to Cleopatra of Alexandria and Maria the Prophetess, who made many of the early technical and instrumental innovations in alchemy and also stand at the head of traditions in healing, aromatherapy, perfumery and cosmetics. Marie is Rutherford's *Other*, his *rebel soul*:

> *waltzing in a black*
> *grenadine dress bordered with rouches*
> *on a foundation of faille*
> *while on her neck flashed rhinestone*
> *clocks and amber beads on golden threads*
> *clasped with a Bohemian*
> *garnet, the seal of Seals.*

Together, after the strange death of her husband (*sideswiped by a cart / in Rue Dauphine . . . 16 pits in his head . . .*) they embark on a motoring trip to the south of France, troubadour country, to consummate their mission: the collection of radioactive matter with which to unlock creation. Their chemical wedding takes place to the sound of the 144,000 virgins out of Revelations singing *new songs*. Whether there is an historic basis for this adventure is not the point: they are lover and beloved incarnate, legendary in this recension of time, our own.

Despite the auguries which gather at his birth:

> *a kaka went in flight between the window*
> *and the golden moon,*
> *the Earthly Guest was born,*
> *his mother 'beautiful as a wreck of paradise'*
> *dreamed him in her skirt of dust,*
> *dreamed him beneath the open sky*
> *dreamed her little anomaly on a mallow eating fire*

Rutherford himself emerges as something of a buffoon: full of brag and bluster, a hearty boomer from the sticks of Nelson who makes his mark initially through tremendous feats of counting scintillations on a screen. He is a man unconscious of everything except his destiny, a recognisable colonial-antipodean type who excels primarily by effort and doesn't question what it is he is doing. The commentary by the eternity-weary Egyptian magus on the doings of this calamitous fool is exquisitely wry and ultimately intensely moving:

> time is heavy and hot
> and slides us towards catastrophe,
> the harvest will be lost,
> G-men blast the sun with ghosts,
> there is no god to pacify the gods,
> the sum of perfections is the perfect mystery,
> we've made a mess
> and why should the micrococci repair the
> damage?

The heart of the poem, 'Waves' is a fine piece of biographical writing as well as a cogent summary of some difficult science expressed in such a way that you can still read it for the information even when you don't get the detail: we will have to await the annotated edition for that and even then it will likely prove to be a chapter in an infinite book, spinning off into places no library or search engine will take you. As an account of the genesis of one of the major insights of our time, 'Waves' is poised between authentic wonder at the beauty and strangeness of the sub-atomic world thereby revealed and a deep, unassuageable disquiet at the consequences of the discovery.

IV

The last section is a myth-version of three month's travel with Sally and Ruby in south France and Spain in 1988.

'Sleepwalker', the third part of the narrative, is a future in which the wanderings of atomised and profoundly uprooted tribes is narrated by another nameless being, this time a woman, a shadow version of O. She is much changed:

> *I lay naked in the sun, sweat running down my*
> *breast, not caring whose hands caressed me*
> *nor caring who I was*

She recounts encounters with the Milk-drinkers, the Gossipers, the Manahunes, the Sames, the Sandramblers, the Cow Riders, the Stilt People and more. Although there are early appearances of a mysterious figure, perhaps the contemporary geneticist, Fontdevila, who steals the tribe's yafeen (children? dope?), and of Italian socialist Vacca (aka *the great bell*), this section of the poem is less densely referential or, rather, its references are to myth and folk tale as remote fragments of the ungathered memory of the entire race after catastrophe.

Alan Brunton wrote many accounts of journeys of nameless people through landscapes blasted by unexplained calamity; the eerie quality of these projections is that, in amongst their genuine strangeness, there are sudden glimpses of the quotidian:

> *Then we met the Manahunes who are famous for*
> *their carved walking sticks and are so jealous*
> *of that skill that any Manahune who leaves*
> *the village is brought back by force if necessary*
> *and tried under the Police Offences Act*
> *for violating the privilege of being*
> *from that village*

The tone of these dystopic narratives is often that of explorer's journals, say, Marco Polo and Rustichello of Pisa's *A Description of the World* or the *Ethiopian Itineraries* of fifteenth-century Italian monks. Frequently they lack a conclusion, simply ending in an unexplained silence or passing via a narrative voice which does not miss a beat into some other part of the territory; but 'Sleepwalker' differs in that, like Fukuyama's history, it does come to an end. At a place called Lake Ti the people divide, the dissidents following Commander Zero into the hills while the rest await the arrival ashore of *a respectable person . . . masculine and feminine / undivided.*

This time-lapsed Tiresias, as diminished in his way as O, is carried, Gulliver-like, to *a stadium with hundreds and thousands of us attached / to him by strings* and there interrogated by a representative of the people. His cross examination proceeds while Zero's armies haul ashore artillery for the final battle, but he seems terminally confused in the face of the anguished tribal search for meaning and quite unable to answer, or even understand, the questions put to him: *Is the origin of life significant?* brings the reply: *Yes yes, what will we know when we know that?*

It is the arraignment by Humanity of Science in the person of the 'perfected' Rutherford, held under the gun, with the old man's speech cut through by equal parts extravagant foolishness and elegiac disenchantment:

> *We left pions where the midnight lessens,*
> *Pushing ourselves closer to the Unrevealed;*
> *We were a cloud, stupid and immense,*
> *What we wanted most was always concealed*

Meanwhile, armed destruction proceeds, there is no longer any communication possible between those directing this plot of doom and those doomed by it. The perfected man is executed and interred in a culvert while for the rest:

There will be an answer if not now then
before when we sail into the black bindoos
in our black ship

The four short pieces following 'Sleepwalker' – 'What Shape Now', 'Common Thing', 'Principle Undertaking' and 'Ci Falt La Geste' – are deeply disconcerting in their bleak assumption that what began as a chemical reaction in the primordial soup will end in a chemical dump so toxic it threatens our genetic integrity and that of every other living thing on the planet. In the light of these bitter koan, the Notes and Omitted Verses which finish the book are an absurdist joke returning us gracefully to the present. While the Omitted Verses suggest a multitude of paths that could have been, or were, taken up, the Notes do not so much illuminate as obfuscate: the last informs us *Pharos was the name of a bookshop on Highway 1* but apropos of what else in the poem is not immediately apparent.

V

In science, it would be called a groove, or a vibration. At the centre of the book, there are atomic 'scintillations' – the Logos comes and it is 'PSSSSSSSSSSST', white lightning . . .

In 1933, four years before his death, Ernest Rutherford said that people who thought his discoveries would lead to nuclear power were *talking moonshine*. Subsequently, when Alan Brunton found a still in the museum at Brightwater, his intuition that the gimcrackery and naïvety of colonial New Zealanders had played their part on the world stage was confirmed. For moonshine is also alcohol: those Benedictine monks who distilled the liqueur that bears their name were practising alchemists, as were Renaissance herbalists and, latterly, the chemist Albert Hofmann, the discoverer of LSD. And, of course, Alan Brunton himself, transforming the dross of history into a made work at the same time as he codes the letters of his own name throughout the poem.

Yet *Moonshine* was received almost in silence. There was a single review which, while enthusiastic, failed to articulate its author's excitement in the poem; and that was it. Brunton commented: *My epic-construction* Moonshine *is probably better known on Alpha Centauri than it is here, one big medicine ball I threw into the air that never came back.* It is a remark of the magus as fool, and anticipates a different fate for the poem at some time yet to come. In fact, the first edition of *Moonshine* sold out and the book is presently unavailable.

Just as he could be both magus and fool, Alan Brunton united in himself goliard and troubadour. If the *trobar clu*, the hermetic style, was something to which he was strongly attracted, at the same time he did literally, like the goliards, go from town to town chanting verses against the venality of the powerful. Early drafts of *Moonshine* invoke the troubadour Marcabru in the introductory verses, although this invocation later sank back into the unconscious of the poem. But Marcabru's distinction between true and false love holds, not just in *Moonshine* but in all of Brunton's work: true love is joyful, intense, in harmony with itself and the welfare of a community; false love is bitter, dissolute, self regarding and destructive. One thing every reader of *Moonshine* has to decide is the status of the love affair which is at its centre.

If much of the entertainment in the poem comes from its mock heroics and satiric grotesqueries, on a deeper level it is the story of a man and a woman playing out a mythic comedy in which they pursue each other down the ages. The lovers are Alpha and Omega, earth and sky, oxygen and hydrogen: chemical elements dropped by passing comets to transmute under sunlight in shallow seas. O as oxygen and Whoosh, the HaHa man, as a double of hydrogen, together make H_2O, the water of life. It is this limpid simplicity which our scientific heritage threatens.

What's water but the generated soul? wrote W. B. Yeats. We might as well ask what fire is: just as water has a memory, so there is a mathematics of fire; these elemental actualities are the ground zero of *Moonshine*. Alan Brunton shared with Isaac Newton a belief that words inscribed on clay in ancient Sumer were a kind of prophecy. Newton never divulged the secret, but Brunton did offer a translation of the ur-text: *An Bar*, sky on fire. At the end of *Moonshine*, O, who is beloved as world and, literally, the atmosphere, ignites: *the welkin burns.* Leaving behind the question: is this really our fate?

While we meditate upon this possibility, there is plenty to divert us. One of *Moonshine's* fascinations is that it takes you, in the same way the scientists went inside the atom, inside the language. The U apostrophised at the beginning is simultaneously Urania, the universe, the urafangs and you. The letters which stand for elements in the periodic table are conjured in the manner the Hermetics conjured with sounds:

> *masked revellers sprawl on the floor*
> *as the ship nears the ice they hear*
> *the sounds of the h̲, the constant h̲*
> *the voiceless h̲ of the universe*

The poem plays with the alphabet as it does with sound, finding meaning in the plainness of signs: ER, in conjunction with O's various incarnations, makes EROS. This play with language as sign and/or sound, intertwined with an intricate, arcane numerology, incalculable here, and supported by enigmatic illustrations drawn from the arcana of early twentieth-century experimental physics laboratories, renders *Moonshine* inexhaustible.

And it retains its mysteries: the vein of moth and butterfly imagery running through it, culminating in Rutherford on his deathbed *stretched / out, salient and strange / like a kind of cinnabar* – not simply the alchemical staple mercuric sulphide but also a red-winged moth – renders the Big Man suddenly as Egyptian as Thoth. Then there is the enigma of the full-page quote (the third of three; the others are from Revelations and Alfred Jarry) that ends 'Waves' and initiates 'Sleepwalker': *'I have stolen the golden secret of the EGYPTIANS and will now divulge my sacred fury,' was something he said,* which turns out to be Kepler rewritten by Edgar Allan Poe rewritten by Alan Brunton; but what is the secret and who is 'he'?

The greatest of mysteries is how mind arises out of matter. The hermetic solution, which, if we take it to be a survival of shamanic tradition, is the original answer, imagines a descent of spirit into matter at birth and its ascent after death. Adepts attempt to comprehend the fullness of this process in their own consciousness, and to hand on the secret of how to do it. Rutherford's descent into matter went further than anyone had ever gone before, and the account of it in the poem is appropriately estranged:

> *he feels more within the mass than outside*
> *absolutely alone, weighing*
> *the weight of a paperweight,*
> *or a zombie*
> *lost in the hyperbola of Emptiness*

That hyperbola of Emptiness, inhabited by another mutating binary pair, would be the territory of Alan Brunton's next investigation, *Fq*, begun in the year of *Moonshine*'s publication. It is where we all live now, amidst a cacophony of signs which mostly go undeciphered. In a world such as this, anyone who can manage to occupy some of that emptiness with meaning, to enter *that vast arena . . . where the past is not yet fixed*, gives a great gift to the rest of us. *Moonshine* discovers in the fell history of our science an order which, if it does not provide us with a pro-phylactic against its fallout, at least tells us the way it came to be, what is likely happening as a result, and how, perhaps, to live with it: like a great dark jewel, it refracts the black light to multi-tudinous facets of illumination.

The Oblate of Unknowing

a note on Fq

Alan Brunton's *Fq* (2002) is a long poem in twelve books, each of which is introduced with an argument, in the way that chapters in nineteenth-century travel books were summarised at their beginning; or like older, narrative poems, with a précis of the action and themes at the head of each canto. The whole is prefaced by a Pro Luego, also in twelve parts, each with a relationship to one of the twelve books that follow.

The first line of the Pro Luego – *From Zero, any start is arbitrary* – signals the continuity of *Fq* with the author's previously published long poem *Moonshine*, whose heroine, O, now appears vertically oblated to 0; but it is also an evocation of the zero that is the beginning of all work and hence a sign of the prospective: dark though the poem cycle is, it is also structured towards a hard-won optimism for a future.

The argument of Book I includes these lines:

> *Ahead: the Oblate of Unknowing,*
> *the last thing on his mind.*

Oblate is a heteronym in the grammatical sense: the same word with two different meanings. An oblate is a person dedicated to monastic or religious life or work; and a geometrical figure *flattened at the poles*, as in a compressed spheroid. What is *the*

Oblate of Unknowing? Is it one dedicated to the task of decoding the world? Or is it rather the world itself, spheroid, flattened at the poles, unknowing? Given the linguistic pyrotechnics set off throughout *Fq*, the only possible answer is both. We might go further and speculate that the Oblate of Unknowing is not only congruent with the numberless number *(. . . zenero, the Not-here, / the vacant Is, the end of This,* as it is put in *Moonshine*), but with Empedocles' sphere, the planet itself, and perhaps the universe too.

The following line, *the last thing on his mind,* while it probably also refers to the Tom Paxton song made famous by Peter, Paul and Mary, gains an eerie force when we realise *Fq* drives inexorably towards an exit – typographically expressed as **.** – and the fact of the poem's posthumous publication. For what is death if not the last thing on anyone's mind?

The poem proper begins with the introduction *in lights* of a character, Shoe, the protagonist of the action that follows. Shoe is on a mission, *the Op,* the nature of which is unclear to him, and unclear to us, the readers, too, though some clues are given as to what it might be. He is a kind of gumshoe, a quest figure, and *the Op* seems partly to be about his progress through a place called *Down* in search of the aforementioned *Exit*; but it also involves Shoe's relations with various women, including a certain Lola International™, who is herself implicated in the geopolitical imbroglio currently imploding in Iraq.

In the early passages of the poem, we might assume, as readers, that the voice in which Shoe's adventures are narrated is that of the poet. But then, in number 6, only a few pages in, these lines occur:

> *The Casino glares*
> *like NebuchadneZZar's palace of faiences beside the*
> *smoky river*
> *where Shoe wanders for the love of saintgod*
> quando will beings be free of Babylon with

the waters thereof unfit to drink?
Each step is more delirious than even a line by
Alan Brunton,
life's supreme uranic poet,
Overseer of the Scribes of the Great Records.

Suddenly our perhaps complacent assumption that because Alan Brunton's name is on the cover of the book, the poems are written in his voice, becomes unstable. If he is a character in the poem, can he also be the narrative voice of it? He turns up several more times in *Fq*, once as *Mr Brunton / the Unknown's closest friend*, once explicitly paired with and distinguished from his alter ego (*That's, I don't know, true / for Al, but not Shoe . . .*) and finally, and enigmatically, in these lines towards the end of the sequence:

Say
where's Brunton 'sum. tot. whatsoever can be said of
sharpe invention & schollership'?

Where indeed? The effect of these interpolations is that the authorial voice floats disconcertingly free of its references. Disembodied, autonomous, indeed orthonymic, it can seem, on the one hand, in some poems entirely autobiographical and in others like the voice of god – except that god, or rather saintgod, is also a character in the poem. For another of the multifarious aspects to Shoe's quest is his desire to clarify his relationship with saintgod, which has the effect of relativising saintgod himself, and his presumed voice (he never speaks) in the hall of mirror voices that *Fq* is. It is a kind of religious poem, but what kind? *Our century is saintgod's obituary* one line says. A poem, then, about the death of god?

In interview, Alan Brunton once speculated upon the rival claims of the immanent and the transcendent: *Can words be tactile? Some sort of phenomenology needed here, I guess. Although I have always preferred notions of transcendence to those of immanence.* Whether it is better to leave the world than to live without the continuous presence of the divine is another of the arguments set running in *Fq*; it is one of the many binary oppositions the work is constructed around, the most important of which is, as in *Moonshine*, the primary human pair, male/female. This pair is the Poet and his Beloved, but not only. For Shoe does not remain Shoe, he morphs into others: Roadman, Road Knight, Rooster, the Roadster, The Road Man . . . Likewise, his fugitive Beloved refuses to remain single: is she Nadia, BIJOU, Polly Pop, Lola International™? Are all of these aspects of the same woman, just as Shoe's aliases (or allomorphs) seem to be aspects of him? Is the difference between man and woman analogous to that between zero and one and if so which is 1 and which 0?

Probably the answer is that woman is the generative zero, man, the upright integer. The dramatic structure of *Fq* reinforces this notion, especially towards the end, when the various characters say farewell or are farewelled. This is an incident during Nadia's departure downriver:

> *Above her, men*
> *clutch the rail, call: who are you?*
> *Don't they know?*
> *She is the last of the binary series,*
> *unavailable after today . . .*

This is not the place to explore in detail the multiple voices and manifold echoes set up in the course of *Fq*; the particular point to grasp is technical and paradoxical: as the identification of the author as a character in the poem confounds the autobiographical, so the unstoppable mutation of the characters generates a wealth of forms adapted to the vast and disparate accumulation of content *Fq* examines as it attempts, like Walter Benjamin before Paris, to decipher the indecipherable enigma of the world.

Throughout *Fq* there is in fact an ultimate deferral of names: in the end, anyone's real name is spoken not by the self but an other; this may be what *True Love*, evoked several times in the poem, means. Nor is the binary opposition confined to a heterosexual pair. Through a variety of re-gendering exercises the poem offers M/F, F/M, F/F, M/M, or any other combination (e.g. F/Q, which itself signifies Edmund Spenser's *The Faerie Queene*) that can be constituted out of the anima/animus bits of ourselves. We can travel into the other, voice the other, become the other, traduce the other.

Fq is thus a black comedy, calling forth painful laughter; at the same time, out of its darkness comes a clairvoyance, the poem anticipates futures, with possible dimensions in stellar travel, the refashioning of the body, mutation into birds, animals, insects or microbes, angelology, reincarnation as beings made out of thought and desire, or simply out of words. From the Oblate of Unknowing, then, arise multitudinous worlds.

The Abandoned House
as a Refuge for the Imagination

I

Driving in New Zealand you pass through countryside littered with empty, wooden, decaying houses, many of them overlooked by their replacements, brand-new brick and tile homes with immaculate gardens, well-cut lawns, TV aerials, satellite dishes. These new houses look like something out of a David Lynch movie and it's hard to believe there are not scary things going on in some of them just like in, say, *Twin Peaks*. In the double spectre of these differently haunted houses, the colonial dream reaches apotheosis yet leaves behind a nightmare, a paradise lost. At the new house, where people sleep, eat and watch TV, imagination seems like an optional extra no one subscribes to any more while down below, as the old house rots back into the soil, it is monstrously alive, conjuring ghosts, dramas, mysteries. Out of these two kinds of horror, it was always the old house I was drawn to explore and, from quite a young age, I used to do so whenever I could.

Some of these incursions were memorable. One was into a house on the opposite corner from ours in Spring Street, Freemans Bay, in 1971. An old man lived there, he'd gone to hospital and never come back. His house was so plain and bare it looked like the set for a Beckett play. Mug. Sink. Table. Chair. Bed. Rug. Outside, his garden, a sunken yard with sheds along the back, was overgrown with a kind of melon, carpeted on the concrete, canopied opulently over the sheds, festooning the buildings with innumerable big green hanging fruit inedible as raw chokos.

Another was in Herne Bay, a big old villa near the top of Ardmore Road, just back from the Jervois Road shops. In 1972, friends of ours were thinking of buying it, which is why we felt able to break in. It was a family home, then the children moved out, leaving the parents, one of whom, the father, died first; now the mother had gone as well. All red plush and dark wood, with glass-fronted cabinets full of china and a line of ivory-tusked ebony elephants on the mantelpiece, it was pristine the way old ladies' houses sometimes are. Everything was in place, but dust had begun to fall and was not being swept up any more. We were there at dusk, and didn't dare open the curtains or see if the power was connected; we tiptoed round in the half-dark, disturbing nothing. I felt as if I'd breached my paternal grand-parents' suite in Methodist heaven.

Up north, the following year, out the back of Puhoi, I remem-ber walking across flat fields and under pine trees to a grand old farmhouse set back a kilometre from the road, in which there was a collection of austere and majestic kauri furniture too mas-sive to be moved; all the bric-à-brac had already been poozled but Cameron Thompson, whose gun we used for hunting goats and turkeys to eat, took the stag's head with twelve points on the antlers down from over the mantelpiece and staggered across the rutted ground back to the van with it in his arms.

All of these episodes were exciting in a creepy kind of way. We call this experience gothic, but what do we mean by that word? The Goths were a Christianised Germanic tribe from the banks of the Vistula – the ostro from the east and the visi from the west – who swept out of the north and sacked Imperial Rome. Gothic cathedrals were built in the Middle Ages with arches soaring skywards, steepling steeples, and a mind-numbing profusion of detail in their ornament, as if grace could be found only through exhaustion.

Gothic no longer meant an irruption of chaos, it now signified an instinct for transcendence; by the eighteenth century, while still linked to a theory of the sublime, it referred to stories, often in a medieval setting, with supernatural or horrifying events. What rationalism could not explain or wanted to deny was exiled into the realms of art where, two centuries later, in our half-ignorant, post-modern way, we continue to 'sample' it.

If one of the post-Enlightenment projects is re-colonisation of the unconscious, who are our shock troops? Who will enter the haunted house and bring back news of what is to be found there? And if the instinct for psychic re-colonisation is a gothic impulse, what is its relationship to the historical process? Are fantasies of terror and horror in these obsolete locations an evasion of the real terror and horror abroad in the house on the hill? Or are they an aid to seeing what is going on, not only in the house on the hill, but under our own roof as well? Is it the case that the gothic imagination, suspecting the quest for paradise has led us into hell, wants to know how to live in the hell we have made?

II

I grew up in a large wooden villa in Burns Street, Ohakune. Burns Street was named after the Scots poet Robert Burns but I didn't know this at the time. I thought the name came from the fact that the old business district of the town had stood in our street until destroyed by a fire in 1917. The original street names in Ohakune, given in 1908, were all Maori, but as early as 1914 the citizenry were advocating that the main ones be changed – *on the grounds that the present . . . names are meaningless, lacking in euphony and conducive to confusion in pronunciation* – for the names of British poets and rivers: Milton, Burns, Moore, Clyde,

Shannon, Wye. Burns Street had no name of its own previously, it was simply called Pipiriki Road because that's the way you went then to get to Pipiriki on the Whanganui River.

Our part of the street was over the bridge, and our house amongst a raggle-taggle of about a dozen built on one side of the road only. Mrs Clancy. The house of my eldest sister's friend Thelma Magee. The Rochforts, a resonant name, for it was surveyor John Rochfort who in the 1880s mapped out the track the Main Trunk Line would follow, during which task he was several times fired at with guns and once held prisoner for three days by Maori at Papatupu, near Ohakune. The Reynolds, who had the garage. Another school teacher's family, the Jenkins, who, when they moved, were replaced by some people whose name was Strange. In the house next door but one to us lived two ancient brothers called Williams who drove an original Model T Ford with the number plate 000 011 and kept a couple of magpies in a cage by their letter box. They would peck you through the wire netting if you got too close.

On the far side was Mrs Aubrey and her children: Tut and Pet, grown-up daughters who were training to be a primary school teacher and a nurse, respectively; Alfie, a cheerful teenage delinquent; and Denise, a quiet girl my younger sister's age. There were rumours that Denise was the child of another older daughter, and thus actually Mrs Aubrey's granddaughter. The Aubreys lived in the grey unpainted falling-down whare without electricity or running water along with Charlie Herkt, an old German man who was the college caretaker and a guide on Ruapehu, which he had climbed countless times. They cooked outside and got their water from the river which ran behind us.

Then there were the Jamiesons, unruly, freckled Convent kids who used to tough us up on our way home from school; the stone crusher; the Maori bush; the Morrises, another large Catholic family among whose sons were Jock, who rode an Indian motorbike, and Johnny who, I found out later while interviewing a cousin of Philip Clairmont's in Palmerston North, became a country and western guitar player and singer acclaimed throughout Taranaki, Whanganui and the Horowhenua; and, finally, a pig farmer whose daughter, Valerie Pram, was another contemporary of my sister's.

On the other side of the road in all that stretch there was just one place, and that was Miss Seth-Smith's. Her house was built up on a hill, with such a thick growth of trees around it you could not see it from the road. You walked up a curving drive lined with massive rhododendron trees which met over your head to make a gloomy tunnel carpeted with fantastic gleams of colour if it was flowering time, then came out on a lawn beneath a ramshackle house with dormer windows and stained glass and finials and wooden lace, literally rotting back into the ground. A classic piece of carpenter's gothic, and a classic haunted house too. Miss Seth-Smith wasn't there much and when she was she just added to the spookiness.

She was the only child of the remittance man who built the crumbling mansion. Who this man was and what happened to him I do not know, but there is a suggestion that his farm, of which the house and the land it stood upon was the sole remnant, was always a folly, and he the most impractical of men. The name Seth-Smith is uncommon, but one H. G. Seth-Smith was a judge of the Native Land Court in the late nineteenth century, and heard claims in the Horowhenua. Another, Basil, from Surrey in England, farmed and bred livestock in Canterbury in the early twentieth century; but what connection, if any, there was between either of these men and our neighbour is unclear. Remittance men, unless they do something unforgettable, tend not to figure in historical records.

In the 1950s, Miss Seth-Smith was an old woman with white hair, rarely seen, and so absolutely singular you never thought of her as having relatives or friends of any kind. The reason for her absences and the place, or places, she went were mysterious and fearful. *The madhouse*, people whispered. Later I found out that she did indeed suffer from some kind of mental illness and spent long periods in hospital. How many of the mad are mad from loneliness? When at home, she was a disturbing presence, like a witch up there in the lonely house on the hill. Dogs roamed in numbers unrestrained through her rooms; when they had puppies, she would leave them on other people's doorsteps in the hope they would be looked after. The four she left on ours we took back.

Miss Seth-Smith also kept stock which she let wander to graze beside the road. One day my mother, about to go with the children to pick up my father from school, found a bull in the vegetable garden, eating cabbages. She rang my father, he called the local cop and the cop came down on a bicycle with a .303 rifle, shot the bull then rode away again. That night, in the rain, there came a knock on the door. I imagine a flash of lightning and a crack of thunder as my father goes out into the porch to see who it is: Miss Seth-Smith, with bloody knife. She'd come to get some meat for her dogs and was butchering the bull herself, by storm light. The council had the remains dragged away a couple of days later.

My most vivid personal memory of Miss Seth-Smith is the time, on the road outside our place, she gave packets of seeds to us kids. She had a lined face below her white hair, vacant, not unkindly eyes, and was dressed in a faded print frock and worn tennis shoes; she spoke in an educated voice and seemed like someone out of an old tale. My seeds were coleus, those delicate plants with variegated leaves, often grown indoors. Some varieties are psychedelic, though I have never tried them. I don't remember planting them, and perhaps I wasn't allowed to: my mother wrote later that the seeds had been stolen from a shop in town, so she probably took them back. Miss Seth-Smith sometimes also stole food to eat. The only other thing I know about her is that she was writing a children's opera for the BBC; many years later when I revisited, I found some notes and drawings for a set design among the detritus out the back of the long-demolished house.

Her place was scary but we still used to go up there when she was away. I smoked my first cigarette with my older sister beneath the rhododendrons on the lawn at Seth-Smith's, gagging into the browning blossoms afterwards. I sometimes played with Robert Chamberlain, who lived with his mother, Iris, and his sister Patricia in a small two-room cottage behind the mansion, hard up against the fence line of the paddock where my sisters kept their horses. Mrs Chamberlain had a pet magpie too, it would *quardle oodle* on command at four fifteen in the afternoon, summoning the children home for tea. Robert would go pale when he heard it, and turn and run: he was beaten if he was late.

Iris Chamberlain was the local prostitute, hence the need to have her children fed and bedded so early in the evening. She was a buxom, perfumed woman with tall hair, like Elsie Tanner from Coronation Street; the men who came to see her (including a regular, Claude) either went up the gloomy drive and round the back of the crumbling mansion or, like Robert, climbed the fence and walked up the grass of the steep, terraced, cloddish horse paddock.

The Chamberlains had moved away by the time we broke in to Miss Seth-Smith's place. It was a torpid day as Bobby Hammond, whose family farm started at the back of our horse paddock, and I walked up the drive, across the rank lawn and climbed the stairs to the veranda. The steps were rotten so we clambered up the banisters, jamming our feet sideways through the rails; then pushed open the door.

Inside, torn curtains hung crazily in front of the dusty light; there was an antlered stag's head with its eyes eaten out hanging on the wall, couches and armchairs with springs and horse hair protruding through great rents in their fabric, stuff all over the floor and, on a dressing table before a mirror, an open casket with jewellery spilling out of it: necklaces, beads, brooches, rings, bracelets. Maybe it was paste, maybe not: to us it was real so we didn't touch it, that would have been thieving. But when we found, amid the debris on the floor, sheets of transfers of characters from Mother Goose, we took them and fled back down the driveway, pursued by phantoms of guilt and excitement.

I have no doubt that a primary source of the affinity I felt for the paintings of Philip Clairmont when I first saw them was that furtive, wondrous glimpse into the ruined world of the remittance man's daughter. The paste jewellery, the rotting gowns, the mouldering furniture of her mansion were a premonition of Clairmont's paintings of doomed, luxe interiors. The two things literally looked alike: the overflowing casket of jewellery before a dusty mirror, in particular, had an uncanny resemblance to the 1974 Clairmont paintings of butterfly mirrors which were the first works of his I saw. Even the discovery of the transfers out of Mother Goose has an ironic parallel in those slightly earlier Clairmonts which sample bits of Disney comics. And the theme of the psychopathology of the artist which the Clairmont oeuvre explores was also present in the recurrent madness of Miss Seth-Smith.

The remittance man's exile, his impractical dream, his daughter's wreck, were part of the debris of empire, scattered through our lives the way her things were strewn through those rooms. And yet to me, as a kid, the place looked fabulous, something superb belonging not to empire but to someone who lived right opposite where we did. This is a deeper resemblance to Philip Clairmont's work, which comes not so much out of empire as from the experience of being one of the marginal (the word then was *deprived*) people in post-World War Two post-colonial society.

Like many people from the wrong side of the tracks, Clairmont had a special need for the magic that makes each moment supreme. His paintings are rites which transform the painter, his house and family, out of the mundane into resplendence; the audience too, if you want to go along. But for him the way to summon the resplendent turned out to be via an investigation of the occult properties of the mundane. His work constructs a dream house in which an obsessive compulsively rearranges a set of everyday images looking for that magic combination that will free him from the spell of the past.

An assumption of this method is that a house is a repository for the emotions of those who live there. Objects are stained by residues of human presence even after those people have passed on, perhaps to other houses, perhaps into death. Abandoned houses are primary material for the imagination because there we may restore to existence something which has been lost. Clairmont, by painting the hell the loss of paradise leaves, attempts the resurrection of every dream of paradise ever dreamed.

This strategy is intrinsically gothic, by which I mean its primary mode is an exaggeration of emotional effect for the sake of some kind of release. Frequently the emotions that are dramatised are the complex to which fear, dread, awe and astonishment belong. This complex can be released as much by horror as by beauty and its release leads to a kind of ecstasy.

III

To get to town from our place, you had to cross a bridge made of roughly trimmed lengths of timber like railway sleepers and with no sides to speak of; it rumbled as the bits of wood moved up and down when you drove over it. On the other side, to the left, across a similar bridge, was what we called *the pa*, actually Maungarongo Marae, very neat and tidy, with its own white-painted school and church, which had been founded by Catholic Maori after a vision in 1925. This was the stretch of road where the old town had been, on river flats at the junction of two streams; after the fire, Ohakune was reconstructed further up the hill on slightly raised ground overlooking the former site. In the 1950s, nothing remained of that original town except a sense of desolation among the sheds and machinery and, perhaps, the two-storey, double-fronted wooden building near the corner of Burns Street and the Tohunga Road. This building had a metal-pole-supported rolled corrugated iron awning beneath which it was always dark, and big plate-glass windows painted that opaque, greeny-cream colour disused shop windows used to be painted so you couldn't see inside. The front doors were flush with the footpath in the old style, but no one used them any more; to get upstairs, you went down the side of the building, through a gate into a yard and then up some outside stairs. I knew this because a boy in my class lived there and I sometimes walked home from school with him.

Richard Morton was a freckled, plump kid with sandy hair who kept to himself most of the time. The only thing I knew about his family situation was that he lived upstairs in that otherwise empty building just with his father. What did his father do? I don't think I ever knew. A working man of some kind, probably. I can't recall ever seeing him either, though I sometimes had a sense of a face upstairs in the building, looking out through tightly closed sash windows at the almost complete absence of traffic, vehicular or pedestrian, in that quiet town.

In her autobiography, my mother mentions a place on the outskirts of Ohakune, supposedly a furniture shop, but actually a sly-groggers. In those days the King Country was a dry area and if you wanted to drink you went either to one of the three licensed clubs – the Sunbeam, the Pioneer or the RSA – or else to a dropper, as they were known. It may be fanciful to suggest that's what really went on after hours at Richard Morton's place, but it would explain the mixture of excitement and foreboding I always felt when I went past there. Or perhaps it was simply the titillation the child of respectable parents experiences in proximity to the marginal.

I never went inside, so I have to imagine what it might have been like: tall gloomy rooms with brown wallpaper sucking in and out in the wind through the scrim, narrow, fraying rugs down the middle of creaking wooden floors, dark varnished wardrobes, sagging wirewove beds, bare light bulbs you turned on and off using a hanging cord with a bakelite knob on the end, cracked linoleum on the kitchen floor – did they have a kitchen? What did they eat? Who cooked? Who did the dishes? Richard was always neatly dressed but he wore old-fashioned clothes, sometimes a waistcoat buttoned tightly over his checked shirt, sometimes braces holding up his shorts. It was as if he came to school out of the past and went back there afterwards.

By the time we moved away from Ohakune, Richard Morton and his father had gone already, catching a taxi to the station one day to take the train to parts unknown. Curiously, their some-time dwelling is the last thing I remember seeing when we left town ourselves. We had packed up the house and the Hillman, and were making that final drive up the dirt road with grass growing along the middle, over the clunking bridge, past the pa, the market gardeners, the truck depots, along that desolate stretch of rusty machinery and decaying sheds where the old town had been.

As we turned right past that big two-storey building, I looked out the car window and saw another boy from my class, my name-sake, Martin Miller, with his blond hair and big teeth, strolling along in a green striped t-shirt and grey shorts. I watched him walk out of the blinding sun of the summer Saturday morning and disappear into the cool, dark shadow of the empty shop veranda, like my own image passing from the memory of the town. *I'll never be really happy again*, I remember thinking, melodramatically, to myself. I was ten years old.

I have always associated the old shops where Richard Morton lived with Dabney's funeral parlour in Ronald Hugh Morrieson's first book, *The Scarecrow*. This is where Hubert Salter, the Sensational, hides out. I think it was the way the cavernous empty spaces downstairs and in the flat next door to the Morton's seemed inhabited by sorrow and loss. You look at those old buildings in remote places and think: what went wrong? Whose dream died here? This small town melancholy is a constant presence in Morrieson's work.

Salter the Sensational is a conjurer, an alcoholic, a drug addict and a necrophiliac. Though he appears only rarely in the novel, his nightmarish shadow looms over the action with increasing foreboding until, in the penultimate chapter, he dies from a blow on the temple sustained when he falls against the corner of an empty coffin during a fight over a bottle of brandy in the funeral parlour. By this time he has violated the corpse of the local music teacher, murdered the village idiot and killed and raped a sixteen-year-old girl.

All of Morrieson's books are lurid, and what makes them so is their preoccupation with three areas of human experience: sex, money and death. How much of what he wrote is invention and how much observation? I think his inventions are mostly in his plots; even so, his plots are based on the kind of yarning that goes on in bars and after gigs. With this, and the pulp fiction he read, the movies he went to and the newspapers he read, he made up stories to encompass the characters he met and the language they spoke. *Truth* is a source for Morrieson's fiction, as well as the place where he first showed up in print – as a hit and run driver.

Morrieson's sexual imagination is prurient and adolescent and revolves almost exclusively around fantasy, just like the sexual imaginations of almost all the boys I grew up with in small-town New Zealand. Some of them will not have changed as men. And his books are shocking, not least for the way that he is able to make vile crimes and wicked people both everyday and of the essence as well. He writes about blackmail, arson, rape and murder, and his tales are narrated, with a strange mixture of cupidity and alarm, by an innocent stumbling into this nexus of evil and desire. As in Clairmont's work, the emotional complex revealed includes fear, anxiety, astonishment, awe – and the blackest of humour.

One way to look at his work is as spiritual autobiography told as low comedy. It was his honesty about his alter egos that allowed Morrieson to be truthful about his other characters – and also the reason some of the people he wrote about objected to his works. Real individuals were recognised in Morrieson's books – for instance the dipsomaniacal undertaker, Dabney, in *The Scarecrow*, was a portrait of the Hawera town jeweller. Not all of Morrieson's people appreciated being plucked from obscurity to perform, in gorgeous caricature, on a stage as big as his dreams. Instead, they acknowledged the veracity of his portraiture by trying to destroy his memory after he died. They succeeded in destroying his house.

IV

At some point in my childhood in Ohakune, a friend of my parents tried to give us a farm. The land was around the western side of Ruapehu, but I no longer remember exactly where. We turned left at the end of Burns Street one day and drove out along the Tohunga Road to Tohunga Junction, then through Horopito up Highway 4 towards Taumarunui, to look at it. It was off the main road, in a landscape of sagging fences, weedy paddocks full of burnt or broken stumps, pools of standing water, rusty machinery, bracken and willow, dark hills in the distance . . . we bumped along the unsealed road, found the place, went through a gate and up a drive full of potholes and puddles to a house on top of a small hill.

It was a weatherboard cottage, painted white, with a flat roof. We parked and got out and walked in the back door to a small kitchen and then through that into a sitting room, the floor of which was covered with half-packed tea chests containing household items; out of these tea chests poured a sleek stream of squeaking rats, so fast and fluid they seemed liquid as they slid down the sides of the tea chests and away – where? I don't know. We didn't stick around. There was nothing to see, unless you wanted to cross the rising paddocks to the dark bush line beyond. Needless to say, we never moved there or took it on in any serious way.

My father sometimes said he wanted to be a farmer, and I think it was from him that I inherited a counter-image to that forsaken place – a storybook farm, with white picket fences, a red barn, tidy fields of crops and stock, a blue David Brown tractor, beds of English flowers massed around the house and bordering the neatly mowed lawns. To me, this is an image of claustrophobia and silent death, not felicity; while the rat-infested shack full of someone's abandoned gear falling down on its weedy patch of alienated land still has a frisson of excitement about it.

It wasn't just the rats. I was impressed that someone had walked off leaving all their things behind. At the time, and for many years after, I thought the owner had gone, like some kind of anti-remittance man, back to England; recently I learned he actually went to South America. Gilbert imagined himself to be in love with my mother – despite (or perhaps because of) the fact she was married to someone else and with an ever-increasing number of children.

Anyway, in a fit of hopelessness, Gilbert, who had money and was not dependent on the farm for a living, decided to leave the country. The offer of the land was a gesture he made on going, only half serious, an ironic token of his thwarted hopes and, perhaps, his need for some acknowledgement of this from my parents. He turned up again after my mother died, speaking of her as one would a lover of one's youth, even though there had never been anything between them; the intervening years, forty or more, he had spent entirely in South America. He never married.

When I read John Mulgan's *Man Alone*, the King Country farm the hero, Johnson, lives and works on in the middle part of the book instantly fused in my mind with Gilbert's decaying patch out the back of beyond. I thought the farm's mysterious owner might well have been murdered by someone who then went off, like Johnson, to fight in Spain, even though it was the wrong decade and after the wrong war. In fact, Johnson is one of the Johnsons celebrated by, among others, William Burroughs: stateless working men whose community is global, mobile, without possessions or commitments, except to a shared humanity. He is someone passing through who thought, wrongly, he might be able to make a life for himself here.

Mulgan's book, often praised for its realism, can be seen as closet gothic: while living on Stenning's farm, Johnson has a casual affair with Rua, Stenning's Maori wife, which, in turn, leads to the violent death of Stenning. The sequence following the murder, as Johnson ranges across the country from Waimarino to Rangipo and on through the Kaimanawas, is fantastical in the way of gothic novels; I always see Johnson crouched beneath those enigmatic peaks and dark forests like a figure out of a Tony Fomison painting.

Meanwhile Rua goes home to her people and Stenning's farm, presumably, goes back to bush, rejoining the hills rising to the distant mountains, as the heart of the lost kingdom of the King Country expands in a great gulf of green. This image is make-believe; yet I think we all recognise its pull. It is the other side of Mulgan's disappointed idealism, the atavistic romanticism which makes us long for the country to return to the pristine state we imagine it to have been in before our interventions – a fantasy perilously close to the impulse to total destruction.

Mulgan's book gives a brilliant portrait of the externals of a community that has lost its dream, but his attempt at some kind of interior drama stumbles over his own inhibitions. The repressed matter of *Man Alone* is a love affair, not between Johnson and Rua, but between Johnson and Stenning, and it is this repression which makes the book inadvertently gothic. Yet *Man Alone*'s deconstruction of the putative rural paradise of New Zealand between the wars is definitive.

V

Apart from our old villa in Burns Street, now a back-packer's lodge, none of these houses is there any more. Like the splendidly baroque Ruapehu Hotel which used to stand not far away in Dreadnought Road, Richard Morton's sometime domicile has gone the way of the rest of the old town. Gilbert's house, wherever it was, could not have survived the forty years since I saw it. Miss Seth-Smith's fell down or was demolished years ago, the land bought by a wealthy businessman from Wellington. The drive and the trees are still there, shrunken with the years, and an army hut now stands, long and low, where the lawn used to be.

The house, built by his Shetland Islander grandfather, in which Ronald Hugh Morrieson lived his entire fifty years, is also gone. Its creepiness was legendary while he was alive, it was dark and gloomy and had a strange musty smell; people shuddered at the thought of eating anything inside. But it was also a house of wonders: one day in the late 1960s, while attempting some re-pairs, Morrieson found dangling from a string in the attic near the chimney one of the bottles of blackberry wine he had made as an eleven-year-old boy back in 1933. This wine was broached and ceremonially drunk with friends, who thought it *better than might be expected*.

The demolition of this house was the revenge of the locals: when the high school art teacher got up a petition advocating it be preserved as a museum, the townsfolk of Hawera, still ran-kled over Morrieson's portrayal of them in his books, responded with a petition of their own; the figures are instructive. Sixty-odd people gave their names to try to save 1 Regent Street; over 1300 signed for its destruction. It was pulled down in 1993 and a Kentucky Fried Chicken restaurant stands there now.

Most of the houses Philip Clairmont lived and painted in are still standing, including the one he owned and died in, which is also the only one that still looks anything like it did when he was alive. The rest of them are just normal dwellings – or offices. In some essential way it is probably true that this return to normality began the moment he moved out: if there is a Clairmont ghost, it is haunting his art not his houses. And yet, if his art is the house he made for himself, it's a house always in need of renovation and always threatened with demolition.

Whatever the fate of Clairmont's work, his example remains. Like Morrieson's, it suggests that the way to negotiate self and world is not evasion, circumvention or repression. Instead, it is by taking both fallen world and corrupted self as the raw material of what you do. This conviction explains the grunginess of both men's work – the stickiness of real life, its fluid and chaotic tactility, its resistance to imposed order – as well as its fearful fearlessness.

Morrieson was an interior writer the way Clairmont was an interior painter. They were both rigorously mothered boys who grew up fatherless and asthmatic. Both took as their subject the psychic underbelly of the community as a whole, which they represent via their account of what they saw on their own self-abusive, self-destructive ricochets through it. Both rejoice in the revelation of the monstrous masquerading as the norm: creatures of horror are always ourselves in another guise. No couch will ever look the same once you have looked at a Clairmont painting of a couch. None of your neighbours will ever seem normal again after you have read a Ronald Hugh Morrieson book.

If the paradise of the settlers has become the hell we live in, that is because of our exclusions. It is in this context that the gothic imagination attempts its representations of evil abroad in the community and in the psyche. It is immensely difficult to descry, in words or paint, the lineaments of a hell. Then, when you show or say what you have managed to see, you risk being accused of degeneracy and perversion, as Clairmont and Morrieson each were. They were both also suicides, as was John Mulgan. But the act of descrying hell is not antithetical to paradise, it is preparatory to a view of it. The heresy of the gothic is its suggestion that paradise is to be found only by going through hell.

Demolition of the abandoned house is not the answer, that will only leave our ghosts to wander abroad; what we have to do is re-inhabit it, recollect the lives buried there so that the poor, the lost, the forsaken, the insane, come back to join us. When this happens, we find that the ruinous images of the gothic generate, paradoxically, hope: riches born out of squalor, madness which is the other side of sanity, alienated land once again belonging to us all. The gothic, then, is prospective, restorative, a redemption of the botched past.

Entoptics

I

In rock art all over the world you find odd pieces of abstract, usually geometric, patterning – chevrons, spirals, lattices, zigzags, dots, wave forms and so on. Perhaps significantly, at the Aurignacian and Magdalenian caves of southern France and northern Spain, these abstractions are commoner at the entrances to the caves than they are further in, where the animal portraits we are more familiar with usually appear: they may mark a stage in a process of shamanic intoxication. In his book *The Mind in the Cave*, David Lewis-Williams suggests these marks can be understood as entoptic phenomena.

Entoptic = within vision. In other words, this imagery *may originate . . . between the eye itself and the cortex of the brain.* Lewis-Williams distinguishes two types of entoptic imagery: *phosphenes*, induced by physical stimulation such as pressure on the eyeball itself; and *form constants* which derive from the optic system beyond the eye. There is a spatial relationship between the retina and the visual cortex which means that points close together on the retina, if stimulated, lead to the firing of equivalently placed neurons in the cortex. He suggests that, when psychotropic substances are taken, as he believes they were by most ancient artists, the usual order of this process is, or can be, reversed so that *the pattern in the cortex is perceived as the visual percept*. People in this state may see the structure of their own brains.

I was reminded of this recently while looking at a copy of a small pamphlet with a reproduction of a Colin McCahon drawing on the front. This was going to be the cover of a statement on aesthetics, called *On the Nature of Art*, written by McCahon and his friend and collaborator John Caselberg in the early 1950s but not published until 1999. The drawing has a lighted candle on a table in the foreground, behind which, and to one side, is a kerosene lamp, also lit; the beams of this lamp open out across the drawing to illuminate a piece of rectangular lattice work which looks just like a piece of entoptic imagery derived from laboratory experiments in human neurology/perception, and also one of those grids you find in rock art.

I very much like the idea that those who make art are looking both ways at once, into the brain/mind and out at the world of appearances as well; and that, when we look at the things they have made, we are as it were looking both ways twice: into and out of the artist's brain/mind and simultaneously into and out of our own.

II

In a section of *The Mind in the Cave* titled *Construing universals* Lewis-Williams introduces a neurological concept called the *navicular entoptic phenomenon* aka the *fortification illusion*. Its form has, he says, been established by laboratory research. Further: *This is a scotoma frequently experienced by migraine sufferers.* There are some wonderful colour illustrations of the phenomenon in Oliver Sacks's book *Migraine*. This is how Lewis-Williams describes it: *In its more elaborate form, this percept comprises two elements: an outer arc characterized by iridescent flickering bars of light or zigzags, and, within the arc, a lunate area of invisibility – a 'black hole' that obliterates veridical imagery. Beyond the area of invisibility is the centre of vision* . . .

The navicular entoptic phenomenon appears again and again in the rock art of the San of southern Africa, particularly in rock engravings; it is less common in the paintings. For a long time it was not recognised for what it is: people thought the crescent-shaped figures were boats and wondered why a desert people should draw them over and over. The phenomenon is often represented as a beehive, perhaps because those entering trance states frequently experience aural hallucinations reminiscent of the buzzing of bees: *it seems that some San link this aural experience to their simultaneous, shimmering visual hallucinations* . . . *and believed they were both seeing and hearing bees swarming over honeycombs.* The flickering outer curve may be construed as the flashing of antelope legs; these animals, or others, are shown emerging from 'behind' the navicule in the same way that so many of the animals painted in the caves of France and Spain are painted coming out of the rock upon which they seem to float.

Another class of these images as painted by the San depict therianthropic beings rising from the inner curve of the navicule, out of *the area of invisibility in the centre of vision.* Lewis-Williams continues: *It seems that some painters took the area of invisibility within the arc* . . . *to be an entrance into the spirit world and a gateway to transformation; in this way the area of invisibility paralleled the vortex.* San shamans, who could be either men or women, do not use psychotropic drugs to have their visions, rather they enter trance states by *intense concentration, audio-driving, prolonged rhythmic movement and hyperventilation;* i.e. through music, dance and chanting. Sometimes a shaman will fall down trembling violently in a cataleptic fit; sometimes they suffer nosebleeds, and then, since they are healers, the blood is smeared on those they wish to cure. In a deep trance their spirits are thought to leave their bodies through the tops of their heads. It is not known if in their culture there is a relationship between migraine and the navicular entoptic phenomenon.

III

One May or June day like this – sunny and cold and very clear, the air blue and sharp with distance – more than thirty years ago, Dean and Kepa and I each swallowed a tab of California Sunshine and set off from Snail's house at Leigh to climb the Pakiri Hill and then go down the other side to the beach. While Dean strode on ahead and I tried to keep up with him, Kepa, who lost a lung to tuberculosis and wheezed constantly through the other, hung back and complained: *when do we get to THE beach?* he would say. This was funny rather than annoying and helped keep us cheerful as we climbed, and the acid started to work, and the world began to fragment into geometrics and entoptics and other rhythm grids which were probably physiologically rather than neurologically based. When we got to *THE* beach, standing on that amazed reach of glittery white sand and looking out to sea, I saw how the air itself triangulated in ghostly shining chevrons all connected to each other, which seemed constantly to recede into the blue beyond. It helped me understand why Dean, even then, when he was just twenty or so, always used to lay out his canvases with a similar kind of triangulated grid before painting his cubistic kauri trees or nikau palms or seascapes.

After we'd had a swim and been at *THE* beach for a while we decided to go around the coast to Goat Island, a rocky bay enclosed by an island, with water so clear a Marine Research Laboratory has been built there to study the plants and animals living in the sea and on the littoral. It was on that clamber back over slick wet black rocks and across tiny beaches made entirely out of fragments of sea shells, that I freaked out: we came to a place where the only way to cross a chasm of deep green rocking water was to leap over it. Dean leapt, and made it; Kepa tried, nearly fell, but Dean grabbed and pulled him up to safety. Then it was my turn; and I couldn't do it.

It was a failure of nerve, some kind of excess of imagination that meant I had already thought what it would be like to fail and fall and so felt unable to take the risk. Dean and Kepa stood on the other side of the chasm, encouraging, exhorting, finally abusing me, as if shame might accomplish what gentler means could not; but still I would not jump. It was only when Kepa pointed out, reasonably enough, that I had the pipe and the tobacco and it wasn't really fair that he and Dean should have to continue on without anything to smoke, that my anxiety left me and I found the courage to leap.

Later, as evening gathered in the cold trees under the hill, we stopped in at Quentin Lush's for a cup of tea with honey but no milk, then walked on in the dark up the unsealed road and down the other side to Snail's lighted house set up on the hill above the old sawmill and the town. Always when I think of that trip, it is the triangulated air swarming above the lines of surf at Pakiri I remember, the fear and then the overcoming of fear at the chasm and, perhaps incongruously, some words of Keats that came into my head at one of the tiny coves with beaches made only of shell fragments hissing and rustling and sighing as the sea sifted in and out:

> *Charm'd magic casements, opening on the foam*
> *Of perilous seas, in faery lands forlorn . . .*

IV

These lines from 'Ode to a Nightingale' are a response to sound not vision; yet the birdsong nevertheless evokes *a vision, or a waking dream* that finds its own music in the verse. Language so used is sound and vision at once, heard in the inner ear, seen in the inner eye: *on the viewless wings of Poesy.* This remains so even when the lines are spoken aloud into the air, just as when something seen – *tiny coves with beaches made of shell fragments* – initiates a mental recall of the lines. At the head of the ode Keats suggests his state of mind resembles opiate intoxication or the onset of hemlock poisoning; later he calls for wine and later still evokes an *embalmed darkness* he navigates by scent alone. At poem's end he is no longer sure if he wakes or sleeps . . .

His report on experience is congruent with analysis of San and prehistoric cave art as evidence of entoptic phenomena, the bodying forth in the world of images that originate in our own mental or psychic structures. It is an easy and obvious step from here to posit that so-called imaginative writing is itself entoptic – within vision – using the perceived world to construct or reconstruct the psyche while at the same time, in the same act, configuring or reconfiguring the world in terms of structures of the mind. This doubling and redoubling of mind/world relation is both dynamic and open-ended and its results, if it has results, can never be anything but provisional. Is then the light of eternity in which art is said to repose the very thing that lets us see at all – this transformative stream of photons pouring from the sun?

The Inconsolable Song

Sometime in the early 1980s I wrote down this sentence: *Mysterious and eerie are the immense areas of the northern Pacific, carpeted with a soft red sediment, in which there are no organic remains but shark's teeth and the ear bones of whales.* It came from Rachel Carson's *The Sea* but its ultimate origin is perhaps a lecture delivered by Archibald Geikie of Edinburgh at the evening meeting of the Royal Geographical Society, 24 March 1879. Geikie, citing the dredging work of a Mr Murray at an unspecified location, said:

On the tracts farthest removed from any land the sediment seems to settle scarcely so rapidly as the dust that gathers over the floor of a deserted hall . . . from these remote depths large numbers of shark's teeth and ear bones of whales were dredged up . . . some were comparatively fresh, others had greatly decayed, and were incrusted with or even completely buried in a deposit of earthy manganese. Yet the same cast of the dredge brought up these different stages of decay from the same surface of the sea floor . . . the remains which sink today may lie side by side with the mouldered and incrusted bones that found their way to the bottom hundreds of years ago.

Another striking indication of the very slow rate at which sedimentation takes place in these abysses has also been brought to notice . . . In the clay from the bottom [are] found numerous minute spherical granules of native iron . . . almost certainly of meteoric origin, fragments of those falling stars which, coming to us from planetary space, burst . . . when they rush into the denser layers of our atmosphere . . . in this case, again, it is not needful to suppose that meteorites have disappeared over these ocean depths more numerously than over other parts of the earth's surface . . . mud . . . gathers so slowly, that the very star dust which falls from outer space forms an appreciable part of it.

One of Geikie's intentions was to review *evidence whereby we establish the fundamental fact that the present surface of any country or continent is not that which it has always borne, and the data by which we may trace backward the origin of the land.* My intent in recording the quote was different. During the early 1980s there was an upsurge of anti-war, specifically anti-nuclear, protests. Ronald Reagan had recently been elected, and before him Margaret Thatcher, and their cold warriors were busy installing nuclear-armed Pershing and cruise missiles in West Germany, to which the then Soviet Union was expected to respond by adding similarly armed ss-22s and -23s to the massive, nuclear-tipped ss-20s already deployed in East Germany and Czechoslovakia.

It looked like the endgame it turned out to be, though fortunately without the fireworks, and the demonstrations, in Sydney at least, were as large as any of the anti-Vietnam War protests in the previous decade. They were also, though we didn't know it at the time, the last marches of that scale for twenty years and perhaps for much longer. We felt then that extinction in a nuclear war was not just possible but likely and it was in this context that I picked up the shark's teeth and the whale ear bones, to use in something I was writing.

It was a lyrical piece that never came to fruition. I was trying to evoke the annual celebration of Cracker Night – since discontinued for safety reasons – which was held in mid-winter, having been displaced earlier from Guy Fawkes Night because you simply can't go firing off rockets and bangers and so forth in southeastern Australia on 5 November without causing major fires. There was an explicit and obvious analogy between one set of explosives (fireworks) and the other (missiles), with the over-arching metaphor of the cosmos itself as the mute inheritor of our failed dream. The bones and teeth were ciphers of the longevity that would not be ours if we wiped ourselves out.

I'd been anxious about nuclear war for a long time. I can remember the Cuban missile crisis, specifically the worrying effect it had on my parents. Perhaps that was what provoked a nine- or ten-year old's fantasy – that I would bring Kennedy and Khrushchev together, they'd shake hands and the whole thing would be sorted out. I recalled this improbable dream the other day when my son, who's the same age now as I was then, said he wishes the whole world would become one nation, under one leader, and that leader would save the planet – from environmental degradation, which is his fear, as mine was nuclear war. Yet I don't worry about it any more, not because I think it won't happen, but because I have very little agency in whether it does or not. The consolations of eternity/infinity . . . I still reach for those.

Geikie probably thought he was practising science when he gave his talk, which now reads very much like literature: *In the quaint preface to his* Navigations and Voyages of the English Nation, *Hakluyt calls geography and chronology 'the sunne and moone, the right eye and the left of all history . . .'* he begins and shows throughout a fine awareness of the uses of language towards the precise articulation of thought. If science seeks an explanation, a handle on the world, that doesn't remove it from the consolations we might reach for when faced with a death, either of an individual or a species.

I heard a scientist say on television the other night that we are presently living through a mass extinction equal to any previous, which is drawing a long bow when you consider that the Permian extinction (*The Great Dying*) wiped out 90 per cent of marine species and 70 per cent of land-based vertebrates; in the aftermath, the land was colonised by funguses. The Cretaceous extinction that killed the non-avian dinosaurs was a milder event; only about 50 per cent of creatures disappeared. Catastrophes punctuate the far reaches of Terran time: the Cambrian extinction, the Ordovician, the Triassic-Jurassic, the Late Devonian . . . we proceed, it seems, from extinction to extinction and maybe it matters less how these mass dyings are caused or engineered than how we console ourselves against them. But how do we?

De consolatione philosophiae, written in 523–4 by Anicius Manlius Severinus Boethius in a prison in Pavia where he awaited execution for treason, was for a millennium the book most widely read in Christendom after the Bible, even though it makes no mention of Christ or the Christian God. Boethius, who was *magister officiorum* of Rome under the Ostrogoth Emperor Theodoric the Great, was accused of conspiring with the Emperor's rival in Byzantium but himself said he was brought down by the slander of enemies.

The central argument of his discourse is the brevity and unreality of all earthly greatness and the superior value of things of the mind. Elsewhere, in his commentary on the *Isagoge* of Porphyry, Boethius discusses the nature of species: whether they are entities that would exist if anyone thought of them or not, or whether they subsist as ideas alone. Science has answered that one for us, hasn't it? And even those thousand years during which Boethius consoled so many of the literate is a speck in the context of geological time, as the literate themselves were then a tiny proportion of humanity.

What consoles us now when we consider the end? Are these the last days? Will we too be succeeded by fungoids? How will the great Catherine wheel of the solar system turn without us? What is the solace in contemplating those vast reaches of time and space? Or, for that matter, *things of the mind*? Those questions were perhaps easier to answer when most people believed in the immortality of the soul: not many of us now think we'll persist in some form or other after our physical body dies.

I read recently a statement of belief of an African people who distinguish three orders of being: the living; the recently dead;

the long dead or ancestors. The distinction between the two kinds of dead is: if you persist as a memory trace in the mind of anyone living, you are among the recent dead; once the last person who has known you dies, you join the ancestors. Our function, in this redaction, is to remember even the unremembered, because it turns out the ancestors are closer and more powerful than the recently dead, who may haunt us but do not exert an ethical force upon the way life is lived, as the ancestors do.

Sometimes it seems that even the notion of consolation is as redundant as the ancestors: as if anyone these days could imagine such a thing to be really possible, as if the consolations are themselves about to be swept away by catastrophe, or have already been swept away; as if memory itself were about to be disremembered. On the other hand, Jorge Luis Borges, in a 1978 lecture called 'Immortality', said: *My opinions do not matter, nor my judgement; the names of the past do not matter as long as we are continually helping the future of the world, our immortality. That immortality has no reason to be personal, it can do without the accident of names, it can ignore our memory.*

In the Cracker Night piece, with its evocation of the green flare of Emerald Fires, the scarlet-pink of Bengal Lights, the squat, cylindrical Mt Vesuviuses and Mt Egmonts, the slender Golden Rains and tall Roman Candles we used to push into the earth then light to watch their brief efflorescence of stars, I wrote: *From the far reaches, from outside the negative curve of space, beyond all deconstructionist urges, comes a music unlike any we have heard, composed of falling sediments, grains of matter whirling round magnetic poles, valent fires inside the atoms and whatever through eternity vibrates the ear bones of whales.*

This sounds merely rhetorical now; the conceit that the otoliths of defunct whales vibrate to anything at all seems nugatory as the idea that moribund shark's teeth might still taste fresh fish blood. Still, it's a peculiarity of thought that we can imagine things that are not, like absence or death. During those same years in the early 1980s I also wanted to write something called

The Inconsolable Song but what it was or how to do it I did not know; now I suspect that even if I had known I still would not have been able to write anything truly consoling under that title. But perhaps I didn't need to, perhaps the words with which Borges concludes his essay are enough: . . . *beyond our memory will remain our actions, our circumstances, our attitudes, all that marvelous part of universal history, although we won't know, and it is better that we won't know it.*

Strangers in the House of the Mind

To see something new, we must make something new.

— LICHTENBERG

I

In the sixty-odd years since the publication of his poems, the story of Ern Malley has assumed increasing complexity. What seemed at first to be a simple case of an obscure poet submitting his work to an editor, and that editor accepting the work, has developed layer upon layer of meaning in such a way as to call into question any and all of the certainties with which such processes were previously and perhaps still sometimes are understood. The recent discovery in Sydney of what purports to be an autobiographical manuscript from the hand of Ern Malley – someone who presumably did not exist – has added another twist to the tale.

The obvious conclusion to be drawn from this is that the said memoir is, like the poems themselves, a hoax – yet this raises further questions. If it is another hoax, who perpetrated it? And if it is not, what then is it? I'm not in a position to solve these problems at this time, but have been fortunate enough, through someone who was once a friend, to read a transcription of the alleged memoir. (It was a disagreement over the status of the document that led to our falling out; of which more later.) What I want to do now is summarise it as if it were true. However, I would ask you to remember that it may not be. What you are about to read is, most likely, the summary of an autobiography of a fiction.

II

Ernest Lalor Malley was born on 14 March 1918, in Liverpool, England. His father, Albert George Malley, an Englishman and a coachbuilder by trade, was gassed and wounded in the neck at Ypres in 1917 and died in 1920 from complications from his war injuries; he never really recovered from the horrors of the trenches and may have spent time in the immediate post war period in an institution of some kind. The circumstances of the poet's conception are thus obscure but it is probable this event occurred before his father went – or returned – to the Front in time for the beginning of the Third Battle of Ypres on 31 July 1917. It may also be the case that Ern's history of ill health had its inception in the blighted fate of his father.

The memoir does not give much more information about Albert George Malley. Ern Malley acknowledges his birth in Liverpool but states he has no memory of his father. Indeed, he relates only one childhood memory of that time, a memory, moreover, he explicitly denies, saying it is not his own recall, but a piece of family history he learned from its constant rehearsal by his mother and his sister. It is the kind of thing a family would not easily forget: as a child in his cradle, the young Ern was once bitten by a rat.

Emma Millicent Malley, called Milly, the poet's mother, maiden name Lalor (pronounced Lawler), was an Irishwoman from the south of the country who had come, like so many of the Irish, to Liverpool in search of work. Little is said of her immediate family either, apart from the fact that they were poor relations. We do not know under what circumstances she met and married her husband, nor if the union was happy or otherwise. Her daughter, Ethel, three years older than Ern, must have been conceived pre-war or early in the war and, we surmise, raised mostly by her mother alone. After the death of her husband, Milly Malley emigrated with her two children, Ethel and Ernest, to Australia, where she had a brother, Francis, called Frank. Reference is made in the memoir to a unique photograph of Frank and Ernest Malley but no actual print is reproduced therein.

Lalor is a famous Australian name: Peter Lalor, an Irishman from County Laois, south and west of Dublin, was one of the leaders of the rebellion at the Eureka Stockade, during which he lost an arm. Lalor subsequently represented Ballarat in the Victorian parliament, of which he was for many years the Speaker. He was not, as has sometimes been claimed, a radical left winger. In an 1856 speech to the parliament, he clarified his lifelong position: *I would ask these gentlemen what they mean by the term 'democracy'. Do they mean Chartism or Communism or Republicanism? If so, I never was, I am not now, nor do I ever intend to be a democrat. But if a democrat means opposition to a tyrannical press, a tyrannical people, or a tyrannical government, then I have been, I am still, and will ever remain a democrat.* This is still a political position many Australians take, even if their overt behaviour contradicts it. Peter's grandson, Joseph, who'd been in the French Foreign Legion, was one of the heroes of Gallipoli, carrying the family sword ashore at Anzac Cove on the 25th and, later that day, dying somewhere beyond the hill called Baby 700. His memorial there carries the inscription: *Lord Thou Knowest Best.* The precise relationship between the Malleys and these Lalors is unknown, if indeed there was any direct family connection.

Upon their arrival by ship in Sydney, the Malley family moved into Frank Lalor's place at 20 Terminus Street, Petersham, near the railway station. When Frank died about a year later, of malaria contracted during wartime service in New Guinea, they inherited the house, freehold. Terminus Street which, oddly, has in it no odd numbers (the houses on the south side of the road were apparently demolished to make way for the train line) runs parallel to the tracks from Crystal Street west to Palace Street. The house, which is still there, is a small one-storey terrace with, like so many in the inner west, an asymmetrically placed miniaturised Italianate tower, with battlements, over the front door.

Milly initially supported herself and her two young children by taking in washing; later, after the children were both in school, she was employed at Sunlight Laundries in nearby Summer Hill; later still, ill health forced her retirement. She is a grotesque figure in the memory of her son: alcoholic, choleric, diabetic, she dominates her daughter and conducts an incessant guerilla war against Ern, beating him with a belt at the least excuse. Ern never gives in to her but he never openly confronts her either, preferring a secretive – and characteristic – passive resistance.

It cannot have been an easy life for a solo mother with two young children. Ern relates the bare facts about the circumstances in which he grew up in a tone of oblique yearning and incipient shame that passes over the detail of what must have been an exacting childhood. He does, however, describe a series of mildly incestuous pre-pubescent episodes with his sister, initiated on an occasion when she rescued him from one of the violent persecutions he suffered daily at the hands of his schoolmates. He would put this experience to good use later on.

The memoir consists of a number of intensely written vignettes, as the poet, looking back towards the end of his short life, records impressionistically those events that most shaped him. Among these was his mother's habit of going out to Rookwood Necropolis every Sunday to visit her brother Frank's grave. Ern writes vividly and nostalgically about the graveyard itself which was, to him, an enormous playground. Not surprisingly, it was here that he first conceived his vocation as a poet.

This was a specific occasion. He was, he writes, about eight years old. It was spring, a hot blue day. Bored, he wandered off to look for lizards in the long brown grass growing over the stones in the old part of the graveyard. He found a beehive in a crack in an old tree and describes how, as he peered into the dark aperture, returning workers banged into the back of his head. He set a hare running from nearly under his feet. Instead of lizards, he startled a fully grown red-bellied black snake that hissed at him before sliding away among the bones. And then, after crossing a small creek via a stone bridge and entering another part of that vast city of the dead, he came upon a woman.

She was, he wrote, beautiful and distraught, tear-stained, carrying an arm-load of freshly picked daisies. At first he did not know what she was doing and simply watched, a small boy half hidden in the dappled light of gum trees, as she placed the flowers one by one on the bare red cemetery earth near a fresh grave, evidently that of a child. It was the understanding that the daisies made a pattern that drew the boy out from under the gums. He realised the flowers on the ground spelt out a word. That word began with the letters C – H – R – I – S – T . . . but we should not attach too much significance to this, since it is clear from Ern's account that he interrupted the young woman and there was more to come.

They sat together in the shade of the gums and talked. He does not say much about this conversation, only that it was the seminal event in his young life, determining all that came after. The elements are clear: grief, its commemoration, words standing in for that which is lost, the making over of enduring sorrow into something evanescent which will yet outlast the dead. And so on. When the young woman surrendered Ern to his family she said: *Look after this boy. He is one who can remember paradise* before limping away to resume her memorial.

Time and space may be infinitely malleable, but there isn't enough of either right now for me to go into as much detail about other episodes of Ern's growing up. I can't linger over his sustained, hilarious polemic against the game of cricket, which he hated, inspired by a chance encounter with the young Don Bradman at Petersham Oval, on the occasion of the great man's first century in club cricket, made on that ground in the summer of 1926. I can't explore his fascination with birds, particularly the pet magpie he kept in a coop out the back of the house at 20 Terminus Street, which he taught to speak and which in many ways became the friend and confidante he never really had. There isn't time to talk about the loss of his virginity to his childhood sweetheart, Lizzie Sedgewick, on a flowery bank above Hawthorne Canal in Summer Hill, and how she betrayed him for another, his best friend, Tan Dann.

No, for now I'm stuck with a bare recital of the facts. Ern Malley attended Petersham Public School and Summer Hill Intermediate High. He was an average student, but with a degree of mechanical aptitude rare in a poet and, when not reading, spent a great deal of his spare time dismantling and re-assembling various devices. A neighbour, a Mr Saxon, procured for him some watch-making tools and by the time he was twelve he could take apart and put back together in less than two hours the pocket watch that was his only inheritance from his father.

When his mother died in August 1933, of complications attendant upon her diabetes, Ern, aged fifteen and against his sister's advice, left school. He found himself a job at Harry Palmer's garage on Taverner's Hill, where he worked for two years; it was during this period that another chance meeting occurred, one that decided the shape of the rest of his life. It was with a young woman who gave him a ticket to the gala opening of the new Luna Park at Milsons Point.

The young poet describes in detail his visit to Luna Park with his sweetheart Lizzie who is, he finds out on the night, pregnant with Tan Dann's baby. On the rebound, he meets again the young woman, Lois Lidden, who is, it turns out, married to a rich young man with shares in two Luna Parks, both the one in Sydney and the one at St Kilda in Melbourne. Ern and Lois smoke cigarettes – Craven A – together down by the water and she confesses that her marriage is unhappy. In the aftermath, Ern determines to follow her to Melbourne, where she lives.

Ern Malley's time in Melbourne is poorly documented and the memoir does not add much to the story in terms of objective fact. In this final third of the manuscript, the poet's reminiscences are almost entirely interior: he meditates upon his own experiences without necessarily describing what those experiences were. Many of them are not real-world encounters at all, but the fruit of his reading, of his thought, of his struggles within his own intellect.

This was a period of almost appalling solitude for the poet – I say *almost* because nowhere in it do we find the accents of self pity – during which he attempted to educate himself so as to make himself worthy of the woman with whom he had fallen in love. Meanwhile, he lived in a single room in a boarding house in South Melbourne, employed by his landlady as a cleaner in lieu of rent. Lamentably, he fell into the habit of visiting the prostitutes in Fitzroy Street in St Kilda; and also became adept at winning small amounts of money from gambling, mostly, it seems, at cards.

These were of course the immediate pre-war and war years and Ern Malley, like every other young man of his generation, faced the call-up. He refers only in passing to his exemption on grounds of ill-health – it was not Graves Disease he suffered from, but the then fatal auto-immune condition, Goodpasture's Syndrome – and does not have a great deal to say about the war itself or his attitude to it. He seems to have viewed the hostilities in Europe and, later, the Pacific, as a development that should surprise no one. It is almost as if he believed war were a natural state of man.

To take the point a little further, it may be that he largely ignores the war raging in the world because he knows that same war is also going on, not just within his own psyche but literally within his own body. By now, Ern Malley, under a sentence of death, was deeply involved in the experiences that would lead to the composition of *The Darkening Ecliptic* and he probably thought the only place he could now make a difference was in the verse itself.

This brings us to a question that has exercised many critics: how did an unremarkable motor mechanic, insurance salesman, watch-repairer, petty gambler – albeit one who was very well read and of independent mind – make the leap into the incomparable poetry of *The Darkening Ecliptic?* The answer is clear in the memoir: at some time during his Melbourne sojourn, just about the time war broke out in September 1939, Ern's long period of solitude came to an end: he won the woman of his dreams, the love of his life; and his poetic flowering is consequent upon this relationship. Or, more precisely, upon its demise.

This woman remains a shadowy figure. Her name – Lois Lidden – is soon revealed to be a pseudonym. The surname was her husband's and the Christian name assumed; at one point she tells Ern her real name but we have only his word for that. Their relationship was obsessive, fugitive, clandestine; it took place while her husband, Ralph Lidden, was away at war. At first they would meet out, in some pub, dance hall, movie theatre, coffee shop or tearooms. They often walked together in the park. Later, Lois would take Ern back to her place, at the famous Kia Ora Flats in St Kilda Road, pretending to the neighbours that he was her long-lost half-brother.

Their relationship was passionately sexual, but that was not all it was. Lois was an experienced woman, an intelligent woman, a woman of great sensitivity. She was older than Ern. And she was not free – given that she had come off the streets herself, her circumstances simply did not allow her to contemplate abandoning herself to life with an itinerant and indigent poet. In his poems, Ern suggests that it was he who ended the affair, the better to devote himself to his work; but in the memoir it is clear that the situation was more complex than this. The choice of work over love was in fact forced upon the poet, and he subsequently made a version of it that, poetically, dignified the choice as his own.

Nevertheless, this affair of the heart was certainly the inspiration for the poems, as the memoir makes clear. And it may also have had one other unexpected consequence. Almost at the very end of his account, the author mentions receiving a postcard from Lois, with a cryptic message on the back. He does not quote this message nor say what it means but he does, soon afterwards, speculate thus: *It's possible*, he writes, *that she was with child when we parted; it's possible that she has given birth to a son or daughter of ours, and that my peculiar trace is repeated, modified by its entanglement with hers, in another . . .*

It is of course fascinating to think there might be, however occluded, a Malley dynasty. On the other hand, this possibility should not obscure the verifiable progeny of the union of Ern and Lois: the poems. We cannot derive from the memoir, alas, a precise chronology for them. Nor do we have, beyond tantalising glimpses here and there, any idea of the work that must have preceded them: Ern destroyed his juvenilia, and the work of his middle period, before he left Melbourne for Sydney. What we do now know is that this return home was for a specific purpose. Ern had decided to attempt publication of his poems.

I've come now to the portion of the story that is well known, and will not rehearse its details here, beyond observing that the memoir confirms that Ern secured, by blackmail, the complicity of his sister in the successful attempt to publish the allegedly posthumous poems: he threatened to reveal their youthful follies to a certain Reverend Tooke, of whom she was fond, if Ethel did not do what he wanted. It is curious to think of Ern Malley as a silent witness to all that followed: Max Harris's delirious acceptance of the work, its publication in *Angry Penguins*, the exposure of the hoax, the obscenity trial that followed . . . and yet it seems these public events were not Ern's primary focus at this time. He hardly mentions them.

I've written about the memoir mostly in literary terms, because that is the context in which we know Ern Malley. However, a unique feature of it, what makes it so poignant, is how little concerned it is with literariness. It is something else: a sustained, philosophical reflection upon identity, made in the person of one who felt he had none. To put it another way, Ern Malley found that publication of his poems, rather than confirming in him the sense of who he was, in fact leached him of his sense of self. He had, as it were, disappeared into the work and yet some kind of entity remained behind. It is this entity he interrogates in his memoir.

His remark in the preface to *The Darkening Ecliptic – There is no biographical data* – clearly came back to haunt him once the poems were on their way into the world. Thus the memoir is not so much the creation of a poet *per se* as it is of someone who was once a poet – there are analogies here with Rimbaud – but, at the end of his life discovered himself to be something completely different: a human being. The paradoxical force of the memoir arises from the fact that it delivers an anonymous voice out of the past, whose concerns are not with literature, or literariness, but with life itself.

Nothing is known of the circumstances of Ern Malley's second death, beyond a fugitive date – 11/11/44 – inscribed on the last sheet of the copy I read. The memoir concludes with a poem – the finished version of the unfinished draft, called 'So Long', that Ethel had sent to Max Harris, but which Harris did not publish. This unique and unexpected addition to the Malley corpus, his seventeenth and last poem, is immediately followed by these last, enigmatic words: *And now, I'm going back to Rookwood.* Given that two of the three previous sections of the memoir also end at the Necropolis, the repetition suggests that the narrator of this strange work has been, like the figure of Fernando Pessoa in José Saramago's *The Year of the Death of Ricardo Reis*, on leave from the graveyard for the duration. In other words, that Ern Malley was dead all along.

III

After reading the copy my friend – call him M – had forwarded to me, I rang him at his place of work. He had told me almost nothing about the document in question, presumably so that I could approach it without preconceptions. Now, when I asked about its provenance he said, somewhat implausibly, that he'd transcribed the typescript from a holograph document found in a vestigial cellar or basement – I had an impression of a priest's hole – reached via a trapdoor in the floor of a wardrobe in a flat in Summer Hill where he used to live. I passed over this improbability without comment.

I did, however, have a number of other questions, particularly with regard to the mysterious woman the eight-year-old Ern meets in Rookwood Necropolis. She is named Iris and I thought I knew who she was. A quick check in one of the likely suspect's best-known books confirmed that the memoir quoted – or rather slightly misquoted – from it. This seemed to me to prove that M must himself have been the author of the work: it was just too unlikely that one of New Zealand's best and most prolific writers and poets of the era between the wars should have encountered the young Ern Malley in Rookwood in 1926. Never mind that such a meeting (with *someone*) is at least possible, given her documented trip to Sydney during that year and the fact that she probably – although not certainly – buried a child stillborn during that visit.

When I asked M about her, he said she was just a name to him. I told him who she was and pointed out that the passage about *a stranger sitting down in the house of the mind* is taken from one of her pseudonymous books. He remained silent. I did not know then if it was a silence of denial or assent. We seemed suddenly trembling at the brink of some catastrophe. I recalled M's history of psychiatric problems, his diagnosis of multiple personality disorder, recently revised down (or up?) to that of paranoid schizophrenia, his sometimes heavy use of medication, his propensity, at other times, to dispense with it. I remembered his anxiety about tenure, which he was up for that year (in the event it was not granted him). And his paucity of recent publications. I should have had the sense to pass on to other things, but I was too caught up in the matter at hand.

For the thought had occurred to me that, if M's ignorance was unfeigned, then my assumption that the presence of Iris Wilkinson in the memoir was proof of its fictional nature, might in fact mean the opposite: proof that it is, if not exactly genuine, then of genuinely unknown authorship. But when I recklessly advanced this proposition M took offence, I think at the implied questioning of his integrity; my attempts to reassure him only made matters worse; and, in the ensuing argument, he demanded I return the copy of the manuscript forthwith. In fact, he came round that very afternoon in his car to get it. Of course I gave it to him.

It is a peculiar danger of Malley studies that we might mistake the unreal for the real; nevertheless, in this instance, when the possibility that the work is genuine is almost unthinkable (unless the memoir was written by James McAuley and/or Harold Stewart – or indeed by Max Harris: all options that strain any ordinary sense of the word 'genuine'), we are yet faced with its seeming authenticity. I mean that what Malley or his surrogate(s) wrote, like the poems, does seem to carry traces of real events, however unlikely that may sound. It is tantalising to think that this mystery might yet find a solution. Perhaps sometime in the future we will find out what really happened that spring afternoon in Rookwood when, in a ghostly meeting, the lines of influence in Antipodean poetry became weirdly crossed.

Meanwhile I continue to wonder about my falling out with M in this almost inadvertent manner. Apart from the possible end to a long, if sometimes fraught, friendship, there were other consequences: I missed the opportunity to ask M for a chance to view the holograph he said he transcribed from; and I failed to secure a copy of the memoir. All I have left is the memory of my reading and the few notes I took at the time. Worse still, perhaps, I do not know exactly how I offended. Was it the accusation that he had written the work himself? The implication that he lied about or invented its provenance? Or some other insult, actual or supposed? Perhaps I should not have remarked, in passing, that any new contribution to the Malley debate really needed to show more wit, novelty and significance than this one did.

That M is a native Australian and I one only by adoption, may have had something to do with it, as it certainly did with regard to the Wilkinson misunderstanding. That we are contemporaries, perhaps rivals, may have been a factor as well. Then there is the circumstance that he has taken the path of the scholar, while I remain a freelance writer, with all of the precarious liberties and deficits involved in that choice. But there is surely something more.

If M did author the memoir himself, which still seems to me the most likely scenario, then it is a gamble on a Malleyesque scale, one that will either make his reputation or ruin him. It is therefore possible that, for reasons of confidentiality, he thought better of his decision to show it to me and that was why he took it so precipitately back. He may have felt painfully exposed. Or perhaps he suspected that I might rush into print with a description before he had the chance to publish himself. From a certain point of view it may even be thought that, in writing this paper, I am doing just that. However, I don't think so: this account is not intended to obscure M's work but to prepare the way for it. Indeed, I wish him well and hope that the manuscript I was lucky enough to read – whether it prove to be fiction, non-fiction or something else entirely – does in time take its equivocal place along with all the other dubious texts in the Malley opus.

In conclusion, let me return briefly to 20 Terminus Street. Bereft of both memoir and friend, still under the spell of the tale, I decided to visit this house for myself – why, I don't certainly know, only that I was drawn irresistibly to do so. It is, curiously, both derelict-seeming and inhabited. Long grass, rioting vines, sagging wooden fence, rubbish-strewn yard, the letter box stuffed with uncollected junk mail – and yet, day and night (I have been back several times), a light burns behind the brown curtains hung haphazardly before the windows of the front room. Somebody lives there, I am convinced someone labours within, in the very place where the young Ern dreamed his first dreams, poised over a desk lamp perhaps, or under the dim gleam of a forty-watt bulb – doing what? Reading? Writing? Or remembering paradise.

3
ILLUSIONS

Series of Dreams

I

After the party I make my way towards Town Hall Station. A pale face leans out of the darkness, attended by shadows. *I can smell money on this one*, he says. I am indifferent to his threats. Crossing at the corner, I see the City vanish. The road arches towards the harbour under a midnight blue sky. When a running man throws his antique flaming torch down on the asphalt, it does not catch fire. Two more men run hard by, both alike from the original race, their faces ancient with grief. No one knows whose production this is, nor why the City has disappeared behind hoardings. In a bitter fluorescent tunnel underground, I find the last train has gone. This is clearly the future. Not knowing what else to do, I walk further into sleep. When I wake, the war has already begun.

II

A rocky path leads through sparse trees along a cliff top. A sheer drop to the sea hundreds of feet below. It is the Marquesas. We are on Tahuata. Across a channel white and blue with spray and haze is another island, Hiva Oa. Boys clinging to vines suspended from the sky leap off and swing out over the ocean. They let go one vine and grasp another. Children honey-pot into the water below like small dark tiki. The warm brown arm of a slender girl is against mine. Then it becomes night. Entering a public hall, hoping she will be able to use her charm and intelligence to further the cause of her people, I see her, half hidden by a pillar, her face swollen from drinking and her beauty beginning to fall away. I know from her eyes that she knows this too.

III

A hooker comes up to me in a tunnel under the City. Through the fluorescent glare and hum she says: *Fifty-five dollars for you.* I pass on and in another underground place, near a door, with pale light falling on the red cloth of my bed, a Japanese girl slips in beside me. Her brown breasts brush my chest. Her skin is warm. She is wet when I part the rough curly hair over the plump flesh, the pink tender fold. And shy, so shy, her eyes closed, her face next to mine, looking down. How we cry out when we come together.

IV

I walk down a dusty road. My friend comes from the mountains ahead, bearing gifts, Chinese boxes wrapped in red paper. In a studio before a wide stage, he becomes she, directing cameras, standing at a central console as important personages sweep in and out of the tungsten glare of the lamps. At the rear of the auditorium I wait, holding chocolates from one of the Chinese boxes. I find her later in an elegant apartment where naked women run laughing through rooms with purple curtains. A blonde is making love to her. She lies rapt, her eyes turned up, her long body extended, the other's head between her legs. Two languorous women recline beside them, paying no attention. I sit on the edge of the bed watching the blonde lick love juice from the corners of her mouth.

V

On a still night, in a town of my youth, I meet the thin, determined ghost of my former self, walking the opposite way down the same street. We stop and face each other. Under a datura tree growing over the churchyard wall. Wordless, nothing to say. I no longer know what it is he is so intent upon: the face of an unknown woman, the timbre of her voice, the odour of the particular room where they first encounter each other? If he is a ghost then what am I? A phantom plucking at his sleeve, some slight resistance to his passage. Head down, unknowing, he continues on with all his enigmas buried in the cave of his chest. A white trumpet falls to the ground. The heavy scent hangs in the air. I listen for the sound of my own forgetting fading along the footpath.

Marine

I

We lunched on a beach with the odour of dead bird in our
nostrils, an equivocal relish to the soft white Vienna loaf,
browning avocado, vintage tasty cheese and quartered hard
green apple. Drinking water flavoured with rose geranium
leaves. Shoals of tiny crimson spiral shells lay in drifts in sand
hollows. Pellucid water, a desultory surf, waves overlapping like
the passing minutes. In the tide wrack, the keel of a shearwater,
the carapace of a crab. Thirteen godwits flew across the sea:
nine adults, four young, landing to graze the beach among piles
of weed while we ate, slapping at the stinging flies and feeding
them to a golden-flanked lizard. At Wreck Bay, in the odour of
dead bird.

II

In the Botanic Gardens we circumambulated a purple lake, in
whose darker depths the long-necked turtle lives. A fringe of
sand the colour of white ash, specked with black detritus. Red
carnivorous plants grew in the cropped grass of lawns where a
plaque was set in a boulder. The farm had belonged to a maker

of pianos. He had visited only rarely. Stock languished, pasture withered, men ran away into the bush until only an illiterate boy named Riley was left, whose fate is not otherwise recorded. On gravelled paths, sprays of water from circling sprinklers spotted our clothes. We chose our moment and ran laughing through the spangled light. In the pavilion, the ghost of a house we would never live in built itself around us. Outside time, at ease, we watched the agitation of wind in an horizon of trees across the lake, as if on every other evening of our lives together in this place.

III

Another afternoon we parked the car at the end of a road and walked through tunnels of scrub to the ruined lighthouse. The echo of the dome falling still hung in the air. The stones immemorial in their disarray. It had fallen out toward the sea, the highest point landing just inside the cliff-edge fence. A snake coiled in the shade of the keystone. What light had shone in the dome, who tended the fire, who brought the fuel? At the apex of the pile we took turns looking through binoculars at the opposite headland where another lighthouse stood, flashing its beacon at intervals of five-five-five . . . fifteen . . . five-five-five . . . fifteen . . . when shadows turned blue on the moon-coloured sand. A sea eagle passed the roofless ruin, the graffiti-ed walls, the fire-blackened grate, as if over a temple from which the goddess had departed.

IV

Again the odour of dead bird. Surf curling between crumbled headlands, pale lilies sticky with nectar at the margins of the yellow sand, cuttlefish transparent under the hammer of the sun.

Sculpted mauve plants in a rock pool, iridescent blue lichens, cockabullies speckled into the camouflage bottom. From one end of the half moon we turned to see a man on the rocks at the other make of his body a Y. The horizon no line but a turbulence of distant swell on salt-scoured eyes. I hurled myself shoreward on a long exhalation of the ocean, roaring, blind, an arrow of flesh up the tremendous beach. While you sat mute in shade near the broken albatross, lily flowers in the black band of your sun hat.

V

At night the walls of the tent were shaken by wind. Rain a faint braille on the nylon. Asleep in the air bed, we built a labyrinth of dreams where each wandered alone, seeking the other. In lost corners sand drifted, the shells of days whitened. Cast on to unknown shores, we heard the tongues of lizards speak a language in which each word was a pebble, each pause the pulse of a heartbeat under scaly skin. The cries of birds skirled half way round the world to vibrate the delicate bones of our ears. Stars circled and blazed, an intaglio of light on the black. When we found each other, I placed my hands on your neck where the gills had been, feeling your blood sigh within. Your mouth made an O, you bent your head until your lips touched skin. Salt dissolving in saliva, a taste of smoke, eucalypt and dust. It was to remember these things that we had come. Waking, we drifted up into the waters of another day.

El Camino Real

I

This is my summons of a dream, my dream of a summons. To the other side of the mountains you must go. There, Joseph Conrad waits. The town is flat, dusty, brown. A dusty inland town in the wastes of Gondwanaland. The address is wrong. One hundred and ten El Camino Real . . . there's no such place. I walk down the street parallel. Dark pigment stains the adobe red, green, black. Murals on the walls of all the houses. Through a door I see in the ochre light these paintings the colours of earth. A woman turns, smiling. Her body is a deer pierced by arrows. Through the arcade and back to El Camino. A friend joins me, together we search. A woman approaches, the same one older or another, I do not know. She takes my friend's hand and draws her into the cool dark. Joseph Conrad lies back on the big bed, his head monumental, his expression grave. He tells my friend: *I have met the Irish every place I've been. Welcome, I am glad you came.* She sits on a wooden chest against the wall. The woman stands on the other side of the bed, before a draped window; perhaps she is two women. In the swell of whitish light it is hard to tell. Joseph Conrad is lighting a cigar. I look at my feet. Cracked shoes, yellow painted boards. Why have I come? I belong to another century, a later one. Now I am here there is nothing to say. He lies back on the pillows smoking his cigar.

The head, monumental, the expression, grave. Perhaps it was not Joseph Conrad but someone else? No, this man was neither blind nor a librarian. He was a retired sea captain.

II

There was something I was trying to recall. A newspaper article about a hulk in Tasmania, once under the command of Joseph Conrad. Money was being sought to restore it. *The Otago* . . . I began. He shook his head. *No questions*, he said. *The details of my life are gathered like the shards of a great mirror in which destiny will be revealed. It is not so. Nothing is revealed.* The cigar fumes were making my friend uncomfortable. She said to the woman: *Could I have a glass of water please?* The women took a hand each. *Come with us*, they said. I was alone with Joseph Conrad. He drew on his cigar. Blue smoke layered the air, drifting toward the white window. The translucent drapes belled. *Oceans of paper*, he said. *Voyaging on. I lived at a time when kings were dying. We saw the ends of the earth. Contracted to a sphere. It was necessary to reinvent infinity.* I had not thought him contemporary with Einstein, Apollinaire. *C'est vrai.* He wrote letters in French, books in English. In what language did he think? *The man with the piano*, I said. *On the dock at Circular Quay. An Englishman. You spoke together for an hour. You were a young officer on a darkened deck. You never saw his face. His name was Senior.* The great head inclined forward once, acknowledging – what? That he had heard? Remembered? *We return to every place we ever were*, he said. *Oceans of paper, voyaging on. It is necessary to invoke eternity.*

III

The globe is small. It stands on three plastic legs, on the dresser before the dusty window. Outside, paint peels from a yellow wall. The sky is radiant, blue as ink. This is where we wake up. Sometimes it is dark, sometimes there are small brown stars we cannot name. Bats screeching in the avocado tree. Cats squalling in the laneway. Here blood threads our flesh with longing. Here is where we leave from on our inland journeys. We go together, or alone. It has happened that we set out for different places, only to find each other there. Other times we go nowhere. Comatose. Sunk in our bodies as into dank earth. Choking on flints, mumbling over bones, thirsting. Then water rises and we overflow, running into each other like underground rivers, sourceless springs. How do I know this is you beside me? How do I know it is me? There is no chest here, only the dresser, the mirror, the racks of clothes. The bed where we lie dreaming or awake, mingled or apart. The globe. I ask that the two women come forward as witnesses. In the works of Joseph Conrad you will not find them written, nor any mention of my friend, myself. Only Mr Senior is real. Leaning on a crate in the half-dark at semi-circular quay he smokes a cigar and converses with a man he cannot see. Wide-ranging, far-reaching, their words drift out towards the stars. We turn and turn. Sometimes we are one, sometimes two, sometimes many. Each night is an ocean. Waking, we find a shore, ochre and blue. We set out, maps in the palms of our hands.

Words on Maps

for Peter Baka

The map is (not) the journey. The journey is (not) the map. I once walked all the way from Gad's Hill along the Hope Range to look out, off Middle Head, over Broken Bay. From Gad to Hope to Middle to Broken: I saw no names along the way, just rocks and trees and birds and the great river running out to the sea. No matter what you call a place – hill, valley, swamp, river mouth, beach, headland – it will still be there after the name is forgotten. A map of forgotten names is the country of another time. If you know the names you can call back the country. Sometimes you can hear the country saying its names so that you can learn how to call it back. These voices rise at unexpected times in lonely places. You have to listen tenderly and move your lips slowly. Even so, you will make mistakes. Every mistake is an absence that cannot be recalled. Each forgotten name is a hole in the sky. But the nameless land endures. A map is a palimpsest: writing on the land which is rubbed out and overwritten, names obscuring older names, which themselves hide even older ones, like tattoo fading under tattoo under tattoo. You cannot excavate names, but you cannot wholly obscure them either: fragments will always show through, like skin showing through under a tattoo. Land is skin; map is tattoo. You can sometimes walk off a known map into an older time, when the names were different to what they are now. How do you know when you have strayed?

By the way the names have changed – from those that are known to those that are unknown. The unknown names are strange, and they afflict you with strangeness: you become a stranger to a place you thought you knew, and you wander. It is possible to be lost like this even when walking from one known place to another. Your return to the familiar is accompanied by feelings of relief mixed with sadness for the unknown country you have strayed into and are now leaving behind, perhaps forever. You do not need to know the name of a place to go there; but, having been, you are sure to call it by some name or another, adding it to the map of your wanderings. When I was younger I used sometimes to imagine my life as a tangle of journeys mapping all the places I had ever been, erasing themselves each time they were repeated. You can do the same thing with a day: picture it as a drawing on a map of where you have been. Some days I do not leave the house; yet still leave a snarl of paths. The map of names. The names of maps. The names are (not) the map.

Three

Nepenthe is forgetfulness, she brings the herbs of oblivion. Ariadne is guidance, she shows how to thread the labyrinth. Mary is mourning. There are three Marys: the Mary of forgetfulness, the Mary of guidance, the Mary of yearning. In the winter gardens, a statue of Nepenthe, cold stone under a rainy white sky. Ariadne wears gold bracelets on her graceful arms. She dances on the tiles at Knossos, and she laughs. There are three Marys, Mary mother of god, Mary Magdalene and who is the third? Ariadne threads the labyrinth. Nepenthe is forgetfulness. Memory.

Hawthorne Canal

Today there was that first faint chill in the air cold-climate people wait for. A cool wind whipping horse tails in the otherwise clear sky. A mix of nostalgia for winters past, anticipation for the one to come. Benign, anyway, in the temperate zone. In the afternoon I went for a walk, seeking the sea in this inland suburb. North, I thought. The Dog Park. There's a canal running through Summer Hill, it marks the border between the Leichhardt and Ashfield municipalities. Once it would have been a stream but that's more than a hundred years ago by the look of the sandstock blocks with which parts of the canal are lined. One of those neglected areas of a metropolis that belong to no one but the graffitists. That are not real estate. In parts even the tree trunks are tagged. Coming out by the canal I caught the river scent that is so much a part of my childhood. There's no cleaner smell than clear running water, even when it's only a trickle in a concrete drain. Three ibis were investigating the riverine wildlife. Schools of tiny transparent fish. Blue iridescent flash of a kingfisher's wing. Then startling green weed at what I took to be the intermingling of the fresh water and the salt. Two black teal beating up stream. A white-faced heron only feet away, pooling in the shallows. I ended up in a depot of some kind: old bricks, sandstone blocks, newly sawn timber, bark mulch, a disused bridge. I had to climb a hurricane wire fence to get into the Dog Park. Barefoot all the way to the bay without once stepping in the shit. There was the sea smell. Leaning over the side of the bridge leading back to the People Park I saw strange creatures moving through the khaki water of that arm of the Parramatta River which here was surely all salt. Medusas. They looked like uprooted brownish-grey mushrooms the size of a fat-headed man's head, with a stem trailing stumpy limbs and a kind of grilled or gridded cauliflower membrane that expanded and contracted rhythmically as they moved upstream. Images from the Bridget Riley show at the MCA came to mind . . . the Rileys gave me a headache as well as a dangerous sense of the instability of my perceptual world, but these medusas, though grotesque, were calm. There were plovers in the People Park. The tide was creeping up the canal. I saw toadfish in the shallows, more schools of the tiny transparents and then, splash! a big fish jumping. Mullet perhaps. There were schools of them, heading downstream to greet the incoming tide, undulating in slow waves from side to side in the canal waters, black from above but sometimes showing a startling silver flank. At the vivid green margin where salt and fresh mingled, the smaller medusas were a delicate lavender colour. Another flash of kingfisher wing, then another. I saw it perching in the branch of a tree, the dusty ochre colour they have on their breast. The nightsweet, which has nearly finished where I live, was here still covered with tubular yellow flowers. I imagine the heavy scent on the air now darkness has fallen and only the graffitists are out, inscribing that almost wilderness with their arcana.

Mighty Dread

I never go out to drive without a sense of dread, even impending catastrophe. Why is this? Nothing bad has happened to me yet and I trust will not. No, it is more psychological, some deep conflict between how I would like to imagine myself existing in the world and how, incontrovertibly, I do. And yet the feeling soon passes, I settle into the rhythm of the shift, the rhythm, let it be said, of the pursuit of money. Plus the ancillary social research I cannot help following. Every fare is a question or a conundrum. Who are they? Where are they going? Why? I am always trying to find out as much as I can about the Other(s) in these relatively brief commercial transactions. Because I work through the evening rush hour and also because I pick up most of my fares in the City, I get a lot of business people in the cab. Most of them do not interact with me in any meaningful way. Mostly they use the travelling time to catch up with calls on their mobiles or to work on their palm pilots. Or, if there is more than one of them and they are colleagues, they discuss work matters between themselves. The language of business is at once highly metaphorical and deadly dull. Phrases recur . . . *up to the next level* (architecture?); *driving the process* (transport?); *put our beefs on the table* (culinary?); and so on. What is perhaps interesting is that this language is almost entirely uninflected by whatever line of business is being pursued. In fact it is sometimes difficult to discover the line of business at all. Whether it is sports promotion, health care products, banking, travel . . . does not matter much insofar as the language itself is concerned. The universal subtext, largely assumed, almost never explicitly discussed, is the acquisition of wealth by means of struggle. 'Teams' use 'strategies' to 'get a win'. The sporting metaphor, derived ultimately from the practice of war, is ubiquitous, overarching. It too is never questioned. It is also, obviously, deeply implicit in the way we conduct politics in our so-called liberal democracies. Sometimes this world of contending factions in pursuit of wealth can seem very strange, sometimes I start to see it as if from very far away, like an alien observer of an equally alien culture. Every time I drive over the Anzac Bridge, that magnificent structure, and see the car-choked lanes of traffic heading towards and away from the lighted towers of the City, I experience a kind of vertigo, as if I really were from some other planet than this and could see with completely different eyes. The massed, serried ranks of red tail-lights heading one way, the similarly massed yellow-white array of head-lights going the other, can look very weird. This strangeness, this *stimmung*, is crystallised for me in an image: away to the left if I'm going to the City, on the vast flat wharfs of the Glebe Island container terminal, sit hundreds, perhaps thousands of brand-new vehicles, cars, utilities, vans, all painted white, all awaiting their turn to navigate the already terminally hardened arteries of this steel and concrete body, whose heart, the City, is made neither of stone, nor light, nor even language, but of some ineluctable substance, some ether or electricity, of which we humans are also a part. Then my feeling of dread returns, no longer for myself but for all of us; and, mixed in with it, a sense of wonder.

Westbound Train

The dawn wind clacks the palms. Crows on carved ledges of the sandstock spire of the church scream *Faaarrrkkk! Faaarrrkkk!* Vapour trails in the pale sky beyond. A white rabbit noses among the purple dahlias across the road then hops slowly back up the drive of the apartment block. It's too early for the commuters to be going to the station, though the trains are running. This time of day, they always sound as if they're coming here from my childhood before rattling away west towards old age and death. I only ever seem to hear the westbound trains, probably because they go through on this side of the tracks. It's always quiet for a bit after one passes. The spire looks white and bony this morning. Last night when I was sitting out here watching Orion settling towards the horizon, it was black, somehow admonitory, a summoning finger pointing skyward. I can't recall what denomination worships there. Anglican, perhaps. I've heard them singing. Churches are locked these days when there isn't a service in progress. Tough if you're seeking sanctuary. Not that I am. One of the pomegranates has burst. The bird of paradise is flowering. That pink hibiscus bloom will not last the day. *Quiet street for stories . . .* that was Johnny. He's gone west now. Lud and Blackspot too. Funny how I still hear their voices in my head. Even talk back to them sometimes. Another train goes through. Out east there are thunderheads, flotillas of them, but there'll be no miracle rain today. Johnny Bear would have had the street telling the story. He made everything sing: streets, lamp posts, taxis, even Luna Park. That guy in the cab the other night called three or four times on his mobile within ten minutes. Each time he said, so softly: *Where are you?* And then gave his location, in detail. Perhaps they were two lovers on convergent vectors, heading for an assignation; but I thought he was talking to God, checking their relative positions *vis-à-vis* each other. He was a Christian, no doubt, they have a way of thanking you so sincerely. What is the story? Or should I ask, is there a story? The trains go west with their complements of souls. The wind blows from the sun. The crows leave the steeple and flap this way, croaking to each other. Vapour trails dissipate, turning into long thin clouds lumpy like intestines. Now the skinny bronze wasps come to hover over the jade trees or settle on the ripening fruit of the palms. Now is forever. And a day.

Occultation

A jet flies in front of the sun, darkening my world. I call it Alexander, imagining, in the instant before light returns, that I am a Diogenes. Alexander goes on to occlude other worlds than mine. Later that evening I see the pinpoint that is Jupiter near the convexity of our moon and realise the moment of its occultation has passed without my observation. *It will disappear on the dark side*, said Dr Lomb. No matter, since it has surely reappeared. Was it then, as sister moon occluded gas giant and worlds seemed to but did not collide, that someone skimmed my bank account of all the little it contained? Was that when the violation occurred? *Man's luck is found in strange places*, said Pelsaert to two criminal Dutchmen he marooned on the West Australian shore, circa 1629. *When you think that you've lost everything / You find out you can always lose a little more . . .* sings Dylan. Premonitory words I've been entertaining for a while. If I could have got them out of my head would the disaster (= unfavourable aspect of a star) not have happened? Is it even a disaster? At the bank they are sympathetic but powerless to help. I must report the fraud to the police so as to get a case number for the counter claim. It will take twenty-one days. *Fill out this form*, the policewoman says. *Do you have a pen?* I ask. *No*, she says, then rummages through a drawer and comes up with a green one. I write my stat. dec. in bilious ink. Later, waspishly: *We're only following procedure. Everyone gets treated the same. I know*, I reply, knowing it isn't so. But the stars are indifferent. The planets too . . . or are they? My horoscope for yesterday says: *Power plays are going on around you and your working life is now in the hands of brokers. Learn the subtle art of manipulation* . . . Today's egregious suggestion is that I should *try to see the positive in the situation*. I'm not sure if I can. I need to be Diogenes for longer than the pause of an Alexander. When power confronts thought, is it always just a passing shadow? When thought encounters power . . . what then? Jupiter hangs now yellowy and pendant to the boneyard moon. Stars glitter in the cold air. Planets shine, I recall, stars pulse. The moon waxes. Then it wanes. I would like to think that there will be a reckoning.

Welladay

It was out west not so very long ago, a blue day, Sunday. We'd been to the jail, then we'd gone into town. There was a fair in the main street, stalls selling all manner of manufactured items as well as natural pieces like little plastic bags of semi-precious stones for fifty cents. We had lunch in a hotel called the Fitz then browsed the market; later we stopped in at a place down the other end of the strip for coffee. It was afterwards, walking past high colonial brick walls towards the muddy river, that I said: *You're a dragon, aren't you?* and she said: *No, I'm a snake . . .* looking at that moment so strangely ophidian my heart turned over inside me, full of wonder and yearning. Then we saw behind a dusty window of the museum a taxidermed cobra all dry and raggedy and long-gone coiled up there. Beside the brown river we returned to the car under wattles in bloom and I said: *It's unlucky to bring wattle into the house* and she said: *Well, I won't ever do that again.* And: *Thank you.* On the drive back we stopped to buy apples and mandarins and avocados and garlic and zucchinis at a roadside stall. When the trip was over and we were saying goodbye I couldn't hide that I was feeling delirious. At the end of the hallway was a park. The distant sound of children's voices, barred light under a golden sky. Since then, it's been a month of Sundays.

Local History

I

Every morning I woke into a future; but this future never lasted longer than a tick of the clock. It could not be prolonged, nor postponed, it could not be inhabited even for a moment. It was less a future than a fugitive, imperceptibly decaying into the present which itself decayed, perceptibly now, into the past. The past was easy, was all around, could be entered at will or involuntarily, as I pleased . . . in the grand deco entrance of the town hall I watched through glass as somnambulist couples turned about each other in a ring that also turned across the sprung floor. A rudimentary shuffle, some of the old ones orbited at arms length about a still centre that was nowhere – or everywhere – between them. They were moving to a muzak version of the 'Dance of the Hours'. A notice on the wall next to a telephone suggested dialling the local historian's extension, which I did, only to find myself apparently connected to my own voice mail: that is, as if I were the local historian. This was both true and not true, it didn't matter which. In the same way the square, squat tower over the entrance to 20 Terminus Street was and was not the citadel of the Prince of Tyre. Terminus Street ran between Crystal and Palace. There were no odd numbers on the left-hand side (walking east) but no houses on the right either, only train tracks. Would the local historian know if there ever had been? Her assistant wrote down the opening hours of the library at which, it may be, the answer was contained in some book. I wanted to ask where Taverner's Hill was but suspected I already knew. It was north of here, that line of dim shacks where ghostly children played with sticks and hoops and kerosene cans. White paint peeled from the balustrade, exposing grey concrete beneath. An ibis bisected the sky. I thought: pterodactyl. Wondering if it would rain. And if the pterodactyl thought: ibis? I hoped so. After all, there's no time like the future. I took another book down from the shelf, opened it and read: . . . *most of the universe consists of huge clouds of uncertainty that have not yet interacted with a conscious observer . . . a vast arena containing realms where the past is not yet fixed . . .* The couples had left the floor now, they filed into the tearoom next door to the auditorium and began to eat pieces of crumbly rhubarb cake. Rebarbative, now there was a word. It was what the future was. Or wasn't. How to remain there, in that moment of arrival in the fleeing moment? My mouth improbably fixed to two mouths and ecstasy rising, like smoke, through my veins?

II

Next time I went to the town hall there was just one couple turning on the wide floor. Nothing somnambulist about them: they were practised ballroom dancers, practising. He, thin, sandy, suited, peremptory; she, buxom, brown, skirted, dutiful, wearing lime green high-heeled shoes. No music played and yet, as I watched from the foyer through plate-glass windows, it was as if something unheard lay upon the air and guided them through their moves. The same telephone hung upon the wall as before but I made no move to pick it up. There was a poster of a painting by Pro Hart on the noticeboard, boys playing cricket with sticks and apple boxes in some stony paddock out back. Just over the way was the oval where Bradman made his first first-grade century. Broke his bat on 98. Run out at 110. I could not help eliding, every time I saw the famous name, that r, turning super hero to villain. Upstairs I met for the first time the local historian. She gave me a box of microfiche on which were recorded the names on every inscribed stone at the necropolis. The largest in the Southern Hemisphere I recalled reading somewhere. The names were indexed according to religion: Old Anglican, Anglican, Methodist, Catholic, Jewish, Indeterminate, No Religion . . . the one I was looking for was not there, nor did I expect that it would be. It might not even be the right graveyard: the only clues were *red earth and daisies, far out west.* And a pale child interred there, who would bequeath his name to his grieving mother. The archives were held in the old council chambers where the dark wood and red leather furniture remained bizarrely *in situ*, as if the ghosts of councillors gone still mumbled over the traces they had left. Minutes turning to centuries as they watched. It was History Week. The display celebrated the place of women workers in the industrial suburb of the mid-century years, with a brief nostalgic glimpse at the bucolics that had preceded it. Coming down the stairs later I remembered nothing except the picture of the General Motors plant opened with great fanfare in 1926 and closing abjectly only five years later. The resounding names along the front of the building: Oldsmobile Vauxhall Bedford Pontiac Cadillac Buick Chevrolet GMC Truck. The hall was empty, the dancers had gone; but the unheard music lingered. It carried me all the way back home, where there were lines out to places you could never go by car.

Oasis

It was one of those tears in the fabric, one of those rents, one of those places where you enter a stillness that is not so much outside time as more deeply embedded in it. I saw it first through the train window and only later found a way to get there past the derelict sheds, the daubed superannuated carriages, the dead engines, the great wheeled machines whose uses were forgotten and gone. A rectangular enclosure fenced with hurricane wire. A silver tank that had lost its bogies. Piles of blue metal on the beaten earth. Pampas grass. And everywhere, the ibis. It did not seem a likely place for them to be nesting, so far from water, nor could I imagine that they found food there either. It just seemed a place they wanted to be. I stood a little way off, close enough to see them clearly but not so close as to scare them away. In a patch of sun beside a pile of bricks. It was hot, I thought it was the heat making me dizzy; but when I moved into the shade and sat down on a piece of masonry, the buzzing in my ears increased to a near-unbearable whining hum and then suddenly accelerated out of range and I was through, I was there, in the oasis. Not pampas grass, papyrus. Lotus pools where brown earth had been. Flash of silver from the meniscus of the pond and a reflection of palms shimmering there. This was what the ibis saw, this was why they were there. The illusion lasted only a moment and then I was back on my stone, back in the dust of the abandoned rail yard, faint with longing. I heard the metallic sound of wheels on rails and saw the grey train passing. That was me at the window, one minute I was watching myself go by, the next, looking out through smeared glass at that enigma of ibis about weedy gravel mounds behind a hurricane fence.

Rain

Was that rain falling in my sleep? Or was that rain falling outside the window? Was it the same rain raining in my sleep and out the window? It was as if in this half-dreaming, half-waking state my mind – but not mind alone, body was also implicated – became a vast extension, flat, two dimensional, reaching perhaps as far as the edge of the rain cloud that hung over the City. How far was that? When the wind gusted and the curtains belled and sucked, those perturbations rippled the ridges of dream, they rucked the silks of thought, sent shivers across my skin and then it was all one, the distance to the end of the rain was no distance at all, it was I who lay over the City, over the ocean, over the cloud that clouded my mind; and this was where the humdrum hauntings showed their faces: books and papers specked with rain drops on the bar, the huddle of dark musicians sitting on beer crates, reaching their hands up behind them without looking to shake mine, the procession of martyrs from door to door, bound into their starched formalities, deriding all other faiths as they came uselessly a second time in the same door and out the other; and why was the wrinkled penis hanging out the front of someone's trousers considered an act of fealty by these pilgrims of despair? Why could I not go elsewhere, into the next room perhaps, where masses roared shoulder to shoulder at their pots and sawdust lay on the floor? There seemed no end to horror, as if the consequence of every act of bad faith was exile to this place I could neither be in nor leave. And thus the rain, falling in the window, falling in my sleep or not-sleep, whichever it was, laying the dust on the grimy floor, came to seem like a benison which, waking, I might at last receive. Grey wet streets, a fallen frond, melancholy cries of birds. A trickle of liquid spiralled in the cochlea of a shell like something running out of your ear. Streets, leaves, birds, a water droplet upon which, in the faint early light, a layer of pollen dust trembled.

There Is Joy In Being Where The Angels Are

I drive out to Rookwood, the cemetery a few suburbs west of here. It goes Ashfield, Croydon, Burwood, Strathfield, Lidcombe. Running more or less along the southern side of the Western Line the whole way until you hit Centenary Drive, a major north–south artery and go left and then right. Through a works depot, past the Lidcombe mail exchange – I was nearly assigned there once years ago when I worked as a postal officer – in the ornate sandstone and iron-lace gates and on to the fetchingly named Necropolis Drive. *Rockwood Necropolis is the largest cemetery in the Southern Hemisphere*, my Sydway says. *It is the final resting place of nearly one million people.* That's a lot of bones I think as I drive slowly through open grassy fields where tombstones stand, lean, or topple in all directions. It looks like some crazy chessboard, endless, as if a forgetful god was playing an infinitely complex game with himself before losing interest and going off elsewhere. The day is warm, blue, blustery, a buffeting wind blows from the south west, strong enough to rip small branches off the eucalypts and strew leaves along the paths. I'm not here for any special reason, I just want to get a feel for the place. I go right to the end of Necropolis Drive until it turns into Necropolis Circuit, with the Martyrs Memorial in the middle of it. Round the circuit and there, on the left, I see the old section I've sometimes looked at from Railway Street at night when I've been out in the cab. Down here the tarmac is pot-holed, the seal disintegrated, it's like being on some country road out back. I park the car under a tree, get out and start walking among the graves. They're mostly from the 1880s, English names . . . later I find out it's the Anglican sector, maybe even Old Anglican. There seem to be a lot of people *native of Manchester*. Even the Greek family, whose mausoleum is crowned with an impressive and intact white marble column, turns out to have had a Mancunian *materfamilias*. One of their daughters was called Aphrodite, she died young. There are odd names: Glasscock strikes me strangely, as does one Tan Dann, whose monument is so faded I can't make out anything else about him . . . or her. As I walk the landscape becomes wilder, the trees bigger, the gravestones more tumbled or, in many cases, missing altogether. I come to a place where a swarm of honey bees has made a hive in a crack in the bole of an old blackbutt tree. Bees returning bang into the back of my head as I stand there looking at it. Not far away is a set of commercial hives, about a dozen of them, which seems curious: who harvests honey from the fields of the dead? There is a metallic smell, clean, antiseptic, emanating from these hives, I don't know why. Here's a pond with the headless statue of a young woman in the centre; the water is cloudy with yellow weed and there is a new, newly abandoned brickwork canal leading to and from the pool, which is old. I wonder if this is the bed of a natural stream? Past the pool it's starting to look like real Australian bush and I recall that, when the local authority announced they wanted to clear the bones from some sections so that they could be re-used, conservationists answered that there are unique relict stands of the original flora of the Cumberland Basin in Rookwood, plant communities that no longer exist anywhere else. I turn and go back a different way, walking through fields of knee-high brown grass and wild flowering ixia and spraxia, thinking about snakes. A hare breaks from under a tree and goes drumming away down the hill. I see it sitting at the bottom of the hollow, its long ears raised up: my familiar, at least in the Chinese horoscope. I come to a grave that has been paved with beautiful old ceramic tiles, some of which have broken or come loose. I pick up a couple of fragments, then carefully replace them where they were, remembering the last line of Shakespeare's epitaph: *Cursed be he who moves my bones* even though these are not bones, just tile fragments. Near an enclosure fenced with heavy iron chains, anchors as posts, where sailors are buried, I find the daisies I've been looking for and pick half a dozen. Stark white with purple centres that crimson as they age. I take them back to the car and drive away, randomly. Near the Chapel for the Independents, someone has been practising topiary on the shrubbery, cutting the bushes to look like tombstones; truly bizarre. Then I'm in the Catholic section, which is shiny and bright and busy, like an open-air mall. Later I pass by the crematorium and with a pang recall that I have been here once before, Maundy Thursday, 2003, when Blackspot's body was burned.

B, D & M

At Births, Deaths and Marriages you have to take a ticket specifying which of these categories you are interested in. I go for Births: A42 is my number. It is called almost straight away, there's hardly anybody here this wet Wednesday morning. I show my letter of authorisation to the kindly older woman and explain my mission. She demurs. The letter is not enough, I need three forms of ID from the next of kin if the inquiry is to proceed. We spar companionably for a few minutes then I ask if I can see her supervisor. *I'm not trying to cause any trouble*, I say. *I know*, she replies. While we are talking a startlingly beautiful young woman dressed in purple and green, heavily made up, passes behind and smiles at me. I sit down to wait, wondering who has left their reading glasses on the grey unbacked courtesy couch nearby. An older woman, thin, dark, on crutches, labours up the stairs with an attentive young man beside her. She also smiles, dazzling, she looks excited, she might be one of the Stolen Generation about to solve some mystery of origin. A very tall young man appears behind the screen in the booth with A42 above it, he is the one who might be able to help me. I explain my mission again, in more detail this time, encouraged when he takes a sheet of paper covered with squiggles and begins to write the information down. The beautiful young woman passes and repasses several times while we are talking, each time with that wonderful smile.

The tall young man says he has to copy my ID and, further, I will need to pay a fee so my query can enter the system. *How much?* I ask. *Thirty-one dollars, Boss,* he says. I have a weakness for people who call me Boss. I fill out a form while he goes away to check something. The glasses belong to a distracted, middle-aged Asian woman who is also filling out a form at one of the stand-up desks. The atmosphere in the grey anonymous room is full of hope, a buoyant, almost effervescent sense of possibilities about to be fulfilled. The tall young man returns, he says my inquiry may proceed but, if it is successful, I may then, perhaps, he isn't sure, need to get those three forms of ID from the next of kin. He refers my case to another clerk, a balding man in his thirties with a moon face. I don't understand the instructions given this clerk, although I know all the words: some kind of bureaucratic arcana. The clerk processes my form. I give him a fifty-dollar note and a one-dollar coin. He puts the money in the till but does not offer any change. I wait. After a while I mumble something about *my change*. He smiles, he hasn't forgotten, it seems the procedure involves an unexpected delay between receipt of money and the giving of change. He completes his task and takes from the register a twenty and two fives. I am unsure if he has deliberately undercharged me or made a mistake, but I don't say anything. The beautiful young woman passes for the last time, for the last time I am gifted that gorgeous smile. I want to leap the barrier and embrace her but I don't, I fold the money away in my wallet, thank the clerk and turn to go. I am sure I will see her on the way out, she must be either in one of the other booths or behind the reception desk at the front, there's nowhere else she could go; but no, I'm wrong, she's not, it is as if she has passed into the air. Perhaps she was never there at all I think, going outside into the brightening street and walking away; the trace in my mind indelible.

Realia

It was a disturbance in the realia. A bird unzipped the sky. There was nothing behind it. The heavy grey clouds peeled back against a black without green or blue or purple highlights, no, no red either in that darkness. Unutterable. It might only last a second but how long is that? What first is it seconding? Is this the originary black, darkness moving upon the face of the waters? The bird's faint cry collapsed the air its wingbeat opened up, burning out like a spark. Fire, then? No fire. No air. No water. Earth . . . yes, earth. Urth was here. The envelope of urth, that was what the sky was. Those past tenses layered before the bird's wings like waves, sound waves, the barrier it had broken, gone through. An explosion then? No explosion. Who, what, would zip up the sky? Restore the atmos? The breathlessness of unutterability. Wanted. A signifier, some thing, one, to bear witness, speak, so that this atrocity might end. End? There was no such thing. Beginning then? Again? Start over . . . it was like a great soundless wingbeat, feathered, yes, shocking in its whisperless cacophony. No one saw, heard, felt the sky come back. The sigh come back. Realia . . .

The Avatar of Venus

I was lonely that year. Read 256 books though I can't pretend I looked at every word of every one of them. Remember almost nothing apart from a few titles. Went to 43 movies. Remember even less. Smoked 2987 cigarettes. Drank 184 litres of red wine, mostly while sitting out on the veranda looking at the stars blurring up in the night sky. Mornings, my kidneys ached. That might have been the painkillers. Coughed less than you might expect. Liver? Don't ask. My health stayed surprisingly good, perhaps because my mind remained active. Active? Frantic might be a better word. Slept occasionally, never enough. Someone was in love with me, I didn't love her. I was in love with someone else, she didn't love me. Such is life. Got to know all the passers-by, not by name, just by their looks, their routine sashays up and down the street. Invented histories for some of them, others didn't seem as if they had histories, just days. And nights. People are mysterious when you don't know them, less so when you do. Unless you're in love of course. Entertained many other phantoms, none of whom ever became quite real or never for long enough. One night Venus, the planet I mean, came down so close it felt as if I could reach out and touch – her? It? Whatever. Though it was clearly another illusion, I extended my hand anyway then closed it to a fist. The feeling was indescribable but I will try. Like clutching incandescent mist. Like wet fire.

Like a viscous bounteous mucous. When I couldn't stand the heat any more, I withdrew my hand and opened it. In the palm shivered one silvery drop, I'd say mercury but that's a different planet. Anyway this liquid was clear as water. I touched it with the forefinger of my other hand, it burned. No whorls left now on that fingertip. The little drop of Venus was undiminished. In a moment of recklessness, I licked it up and swallowed. It went through me like white lightning and nothing's been the same since. I've become her avatar. A tiny part of her, wherever she goes I go. Round and round the sun. Sometimes I see Earth like a single blue tear in space. Sometimes I see Pluto, disappearing. And I remember everything, every sip, every gasp, every image, every word. Every touch . . . it isn't enough. I sleep even less now and often find myself singing the old song: *It's never enough / it's never enough / until your heart stops beating / the deeper you get / the sweeter the pain / don't give up the game / until your heart stops beating . . .* that's how it goes.

Arrivée d'un Départ

Today it is yesterday in America. The wine we drank is all run away into the channels of the flesh. An ashtray of butts with gold writing on them, under the Christmas tree, for just a moment longer. Then they'll be gone too. Which indefatigable graffitist inscribed the black line down the centre of each lane at the pool with cock and balls? Three round strokes with a texta, then the slit for the glans, over and over. Why no vulva? A shimmer of amazement when the sun comes out, filling the blue water with gold spangles. I don't know where you are, just somewhere in America. I don't know when you are. The day after tomorrow feels too long ago for wonder; yesterday like a future lost forever. Now is only a breath after all. The wine . . . the smoke that drifted up from our cigarettes . . . smell of pine mingled with nightsweet, with frangipani . . . dumb shouts in the street . . . health that is like an affliction, affliction that is like memory, memory like a stone, stone like water, water like . . . nothing. Sometimes at night, when the small brown stars wheel above, I rise over all this and see the brightdark line of sun shadow fleeing towards us, gold spangled, across the blue Pacific, leaving America with all its yesterdays and tomorrows dark and bright behind it. Then day arrives, an absence enclosing a presence, waiting to be called.

Cirque

Along the road up to the Institution I saw cat-like creatures of a species unknown to me. They were dun-coloured, leggy and lithe, with large eyes and small padded feet, and they moved swiftly in packs across the bare grounds. Flights of birds that looked like their more colourful avian equivalent were caged in another enclosure, where the animal keeper apologised for the poverty of her zoo and the paucity of visitors. I said I much preferred it to the Metropolitan, where crowds invade the sacred precinct reserved for those moments when animal and human gaze mutely at each other across the abyss of a lost communality. Here, however, I allowed, most people who pass are in too much of a hurry to reach the hallowed halls of the Institution. When I mentioned the cats, her eyes softened so that for a moment they took on that feline darkness in which there is no depth but depth. My friend and I leaned companionably on the railings for a while, looking at the birds with their green heraldic crests, black wings and orange bibs. Our upper arms pressed warmly against each other and when we walked on, we held hands. This surprised me because she had previously refused to let me kiss her on the lips and later said that we could only ever be good friends. Her hands are rough and warm, larger than you might expect in someone so graceful and small. As we came up to her hotel, I let her go, intending to walk on by myself; but somehow

I was still there when she, having showered and changed, came out again. Near the hotel entrance was a collapsed wall exposing a niche, and my friend climbed up there and posed among the broken masonry and fallen timbers, looking exactly like someone modelling for a reminiscence of the Blitz. It was then I recalled that item two on the wish list she'd shown me earlier mentioned her desire to earn her living solely by acting – something her current commitments would never allow her to do. As we wandered through the crowds along the Strip, we talked about the way so many traditional occupations have been lost or are gone, how so many of us these days spend our time devising entertainments for others to enjoy, how the construction and enjoyment of amusements of all sorts has become the *raison d'être* of our society the way war or discovery was of earlier ones. So that, when we heard a blare of horns on the road ahead and saw a line of vehicles approaching, advertising themselves as the Dusty Highway Crew or something similar, with black-clad acrobats frozen in hieratic poses on the backs of flat-bed trucks and denizens with the parched and weary faces of road warriors staring disinterestedly from driver-side windows, we felt their apparition only confirmed what we were saying. And who could repress a surge of excitement as the whole long convoy swept through the Strip and round the bend towards the Fairground that materialised, just then, behind the dingy clubs and the gambling dens?

The Impossibilities

There is something about the City in the early evening that is productive of an intense melancholy – perhaps because, for one who spends his days at home, at the computer, or in the local area, to get on a train at 4.45 and ride into town is to reverse the pattern of most daily journeys . . . coming up the stairs from Town Hall Station into the fading afternoon, I find George Street full of smartly dressed office workers hurrying away from their places of employment towards their homes or to assignations with friends or lovers. The lights are just coming on and I am reminded, as always, of the cities of my youth, particularly of Wellington which, in my late teens or early twenties, seemed replete with all the possibilities in the world. I used to sally forth at this time of day with the feeling that I might meet any of my literary heroes, any of the queans of my imagination, during a stroll down Willis Street and into Lambton Quay. Or that, at a table in Barrett's Hotel, the secret of the universe would be revealed to me, most likely at the bottom of a glass of something or other. To roll out into night-time streets several hours later, on our way somewhere else – probably Macavity's, a restaurant named after the mystery cat – was to embark on another odyssey into the further reaches of possibility, even if what actually happened was only a drunken stumble up Plimmer Steps to The Terrace or, if it was still running, a cold ride on the outside of the cable car to Kelburn . . . it isn't that I don't still feel a leap of the heart at the chances that might come my way as I go down Druitt Street and into Kent, looking for number 400 where, on the eleventh floor, the book launch is taking place; rather it's that, even with my sense of expectation intact, I no longer believe in infinite possibilities the way I did then. And perhaps that sense of the infinite was itself a mere index of youthful vigour, youthful ignorance . . . ? Perhaps, too, it had its own melancholy, arising from my fear of exclusion from the all I wanted to be part of? Then, I did not know that most lives are made out of the humdrum, that even grand passions can lose, over time, both their grandeur and their passion, that most of what we do, we do over and over again. At the launch I feel, as I have always felt, younger than everybody else in the room although, when I look carefully around at those I am among, I have to acknowledge that this is my generation and we are all pretty much of an age. Later, I don't go with the authors and publishers to dinner in Chinatown, preferring to take a cab with a friend over the Anzac Bridge where we settle for a coffee at her place. Later still, having said goodnight to her, I'm rambling up Darling Street in the direction of Victoria Road, since I always like to walk a bit before catching a ride . . . and then, although it's not late and I'm not drunk and nothing's really happened, suddenly the potentials do return in all their infinite variety and I feel, just for a moment – but how long is that moment? – that all things are possible, even the impossibilities.

In Crocodilopolis

A plane passes into the empyrean, turning red-gold as it goes behind the steeple and climbs towards the light of the sun that has set here but blazes still over the western plains. A cloud like a crocodile, trailing the extravagant curlicues of a sea horse, drifts slowly northwards, eating the wind. *Astral Weeks* on the stereo, its nostalgic accents becoming ever more unbearable as they fade and fade but never reach vanishing point. I am beset by phantoms. Some have names and shapes, others, more inchoate and more dangerous, do not, or not yet. Are these future hauntings that I hurry towards? They are all succubi, and if I name and shape them, as I so easily could do, will they only possess me further, sooner? What to do with these seductive almost-presences? I do not know . . . recall how on that terrible night two years ago, the precognition of this place where now I live came: I knew, wherever it was, it looked west, as the places I lived at the beach, east-facing all, did not. Was that the tilting of some kind of fulcrum, did the see-saw shift irrevocably then? The smoke I suck in, the alcohol I gulp, are they hastening my death, my west? No need to search for an answer to that one. Jupiter now hangs yellow in the sky. The moon waxes. The proofs lie on the table in the next room, but what do they prove? Enterprise? Or folly . . . the Master has approved my delusion, it is beguiling enough for him to have been moved generously to words, all eighteen of them. *People disappear every day*, Maria Schneider said. *Every time they walk out of a room*, was Jack's incontrovertible reply. Shall I walk out the door? Yes, but not yet. Those future ghosts, those almost-presences, are they the importunate dead, beckoning? Houri? Or do they call to another kind of rendezvous, in some genizah where I will find the damaged, the discarded, the heretical? That which cannot be proofed or proved? Sebek, crocodile, horse of breath, sea, see, repair, the broken bodies of the dead . . .

4
VOICES

Ghost Who Writes

. . . it is not private thinking but, as Brecht once expressed it, the art of thinking in other people's heads that is decisive.

— WALTER BENJAMIN

I

In 1935, the Portuguese poet Fernando Pessoa believed he had two more years to live: time enough at last to order his literary papers. His horoscope, which he cast himself, made this certain. Unfortunately, as his literary friend and fellow occultist Raul Leal realised, Pessoa had made a mistake in the casting; but he hadn't the heart to tell him. Pessoa died on 30 November 1935, in Lisbon, leaving behind a trunk containing 27,543 documents, organised in a way only he understood. When, soon after, they were rifled, that order was lost forever. Those documents were written by one man, but that man wrote under seventy-two different names: like the seventy-two letters of the name of god. His own name, *Pessoa*, means person, or persona; it is old – there was a Pero Pessoa employed as a factor in Portuguese Malacca in 1512. Perhaps it was the anonymity of Pessoa which generated the drive towards other identities.

He called those multitudes under whose names he wrote *heteronyms*, adapting to literary usage a term hitherto employed to describe certain anomalous linguistic facts: the same word with different sounds and meanings, different words for the same thing. But what is the relationship of a heteronym to the author who writes him (or her: Pessoa's heteronyms include a hunchback girl called Maria José)? It gets stranger. For those works written under his own name, Pessoa used another word, *orthonym*, meaning *real name*; by this sleight of language making it seem that even when he was writing as himself, he was still someone else. How far is the remove of self from orthonym, with what subtlety might that distance be calibrated?

Elsewhere, Pessoa calls the art of Portugal a mirror in which the rest of Europe will see itself *without remembering the mirror*. One way of understanding his heteronymic project might be this: a heteronym reflects the self at the same time as the means of that reflection, the mirror, disappears. Further, the self which exists as reflection is perhaps otherwise non-existent. His own non-existence as a personality is a central insistence in Pessoa's work; paradoxically, from this insistence arises his ability to empathise with the existences of others. Pessoa the hermetic, the occult, the rarefied, has more passages of acute recognition of the dilemma of the common man or woman than any comparable writer (except that there are no comparable writers).

His great poem, 'Tobacco Shop' by Alvaro de Campos, begins with a confession of utter nullity – *I'm nothing / I'll always be nothing / I can't even wish to be something / Apart from that, I've got all the world's dreams inside me* – and ends with a revelation of the ordinary existence of others – . . . *'Hello, Stevens!' and the universe / Re-organizes itself for me, without hopes or ideals, and the Tobacco Shop Owner smiles.* Pessoa gave his life's work the title *Fictions of the Interlude*. It was to include the writings of all his heteronyms, excluding only semi-heteronym Bernardo Soares' *Book of Disquiet*. The interlude is the time between birth and death, as if consciousness itself were only a brief flare between two darknesses, and made up entirely of inventions of various kinds.

The questions raised by Pessoa's heteronymic project are multiple and mostly unanswerable: is it a master plan never put into execution, or a splendid ruin? An act of despair or a triumph? An example of total idiosyncrasy or a strategy with wider applications and implications? What can we learn about authorship from one who refused the simplicity of his own name?

In a literary essay written in English, Pessoa calls Shakespeare *the greatest failure in literature*: a startling proposition. He also suggests that Shakespeare must have been aware of this. Shakespeare's famous impersonality is interrogated in the essay, and found to have its source in both his temperament and his life experience. Pessoa divines that what he calls *unappreciation* poisoned Shakespeare's mind: he had to spend his life engaged in theatrical hackwork, when he was capable of so much more: *Great as his tragedies are, none of them is greater than the tragedy of his own life. The gods gave him all great gifts but one; the one they gave not was the power to use those great gifts greatly . . . his creative power was shattered into a thousand fragments by the stress and oppression of life. It is but shreds of itself. Disjecta membra, said Carlyle, are what we have of any poet, or of any man. Of no poet or man is this truer than of Shakespeare.*

It is not hard to intuit that, writing of Shakespeare, Pessoa was also writing of himself. He once compared his heteronymic panoply to a cast of characters without a play, a sequence of soliloquists who appear, not on the stage, but on the page and therefore in the interior theatre of the mind. The question is, are any writer's works different? What is the act of writing and how does it work?

St Augustine, in the fourth century of the common era, was the first person in history to read without moving his lips. In other words, the first to read without saying the words aloud, even if that 'aloud' is understood as silently aloud. Without moving his lips: the words he read went from the page, via the eyes into his mind, their status as oral facts concealed in the transition. Even so, whether accomplished in silence or out loud, all reading and all writing does involve the act of mentally speaking the words being written or read. But what is *mental speaking*? Is it somehow analogous to the interior monologue most of us engage in most of our waking moments, as our narratising selves talk us through our days? And if, however occluded it may be, mental speaking is intrinsic to the act of reading, does this mean that when we read we are inhabited by the projected voice of the author we are reading, hosting him or her the way an organism hosts a parasite or a virus?

When the American writer Richard Ford read aloud from his novel *Independence Day* at the Embassy Theatre in Wellington on the night of 9 March 2004, there was a moment between the end of his prefatory remarks and the beginning of the reading proper when his body seemed to shift slightly to one side, and upwards, if such a thing can be; a shiver went through him; and his voice, when it came, was pitched higher than it had been and seemed to have a trace, though only a trace, of a whine in it. Richard Ford had moved aside to allow Frank Bascombe to enter.

Or should we say to let Frank Bascombe out? Here is Pessoa again, this time speaking of one of Dickens' characters: *Mr Pickwick belongs to the sacred figures of the world's history. Do not, please, claim that he has never existed: the same thing happens to most of the world's sacred figures, and they have been living presences to a vast number of consoled wretches . . . it is a recasting of the old pagan noise, the old Bacchic joy of the world being ours, though transiently, at the coexistence and fullness of men . . .*

A vast number of consoled wretches: the readers of this world are not usually described thus, but why not? Whether the consolation be philosophic, poetic, fictional, non-fictional is beside the point: the living presence of an (insubstantial) other within us makes our own unreality a little easier to bear, for a while that lasts as long as consciousness does. The means of this sharing is a telepathic act whereby words first spoken in one person's head are, via the acts of writing then of reading, spoken again in another's; and this statement is not modified in any crucial manner by the distinction between fiction and non-fiction, or poetry and prose. It is as pertinent to a software manual as to a page of Wittgenstein, to a Mills and Boon fantasy as to *The Travels of Marco Polo*.

II

Constantin Cavafy was an older contemporary of Pessoa's, born in Alexandria in 1863 and dying in the same city in 1933. Like Pessoa he spoke English, having lived in London between the ages of nine and sixteen; and the two writers shared a passion for the works of Shakespeare, especially, Oscar Wilde, and other English writers – Robert Browning for Cavafy, Dickens for Pessoa. Like Pessoa, too, Cavafy affected English manners and dress all his life and is said to have spoken Greek with a slight English accent. While Pessoa spent his working life as a translator of commercial correspondence into English or French for Portuguese businesses trading abroad, Cavafy was for thirty years a special clerk in the Irrigation Service (Third Circle) of the Ministry of Public Works; this income he supplemented with speculative earnings, often quite substantial, on the Egyptian Stock Exchange. With Kafka, the insurance man, these two make up a triumvirate of nearly anonymous clerks who transformed European literature.

Cavafy is remembered as a conversationalist who would on street corners in Alexandria recount salacious gossip or scandalous anecdotes, sometimes at great length, about characters who had been dead for hundreds of years. A contemporary of Pessoa's confessed that, whenever they parted after meeting in the streets of Lisbon, he never dared to look back as his friend walked away – in case he was not there. With both writers, then, we are dealing with speculative existences as alert, almost anonymous, sensors, through which the past of the empires their cities had commanded, as well as the present life abroad on their streets, was filtered. In Pessoa's *Mensagem* (Message), the only book in Portuguese he published in his lifetime (there were two early books in English), both factual and legendary events in Portuguese history are incorporated into his own consciousness; Cavafy's trajectory is opposite, he sends himself into the past to become a living observer of it.

'Hidden Things', a poem written in 1908 and unpublished in his lifetime, begins: *From all I did and all I said / let no one try to find out who I was.* The poem refers to Cavafy's homosexuality which, while hidden from the world was, as an act of private disclosure, one of the major engines of his poetry; but it was not the only one: or perhaps we should say his sexuality was a facet of the forces which drove his poetry, others of which might be anonymity, historical consciousness, memory and fate. 'Hidden Things' ends in the conviction that *Later, in a more perfect society / someone else made just like me / is certain to appear and act freely.* That time, sooner perhaps than Cavafy thought, may already be here, though we might quibble over the phrase *more perfect*; yet a reading of Cavafy's oeuvre leaves absolutely no doubt that *later* also means *earlier*. In other words, *someone else made just like me* not only will come but has already been.

In Cavafy's world, past and present, though usually not the future, are contemporaneous. His poetry collapses the twenty-two centuries between Alexander's founding of the Hellenistic empire in the third century BC and Cavafy's own world of late ninteenth-century and early twentieth-century Alexandria. A few of his poems, like 'Hidden Things', are in his own voice, but most are not: through him speak people – typically but not always men – of other times. Some of these are historical characters, many are fictions: anonymous voices from the Seleucid Dynasty, say, or from that of the Ptolemys or Syrians who seem, by an act of ventriloquism, to appear out of an inky blackness into the clarity of Greek light to speak their piece before disappearing again. It is common for these anonymous or fictional characters to discuss, like Cavafy himself, the activities of real people from obscure parts of the historical record which, paradoxically, seems to increase the reality of both fictional character and real person. Cavafy's own voice is thereby given to others as hidden as he himself wanted to be.

The eerie dimension of his reach may be illustrated with reference to 'One of Their Gods', set in Selefkia which, founded around 312 BC by Selefkos I Nicator as his imperial capital, stood on the Tigris. The poem narrates the progress of a beautiful young man through the city *toward the quarter that lives only at night*; while passers-by watch and speculate: . . . *they would wonder which of Them it could be / and for what suspicious pleasure / he'd come down into the streets of Selefkia* . . . The young man is a god come down to debauch himself among mortals. He is as veiled as the author in 'Hidden Things' – and as immortal. But how can this be? It is commonplace among writers of antiquity to speak of gods coming down to earth and moving among men and women; but what they actually mean by that is as mysterious as what Cavafy means here.

If we were to think of it another way, and imagine that a mortal may become for a brief period the repository of the divine, possessed by some unearthly spirit of beauty or courage or delight, then that would trouble a modern sensibility far less than what is actually said – that a god has descended and moves among us. It is something which most of us cannot in any literal sense believe. Cavafy characteristically elides the difficulty by narrating the act(s) of the drama through the eyes of casual, anonymous passers-by. The effect of this is to contextualise belief in the everyday reality of the gods, granting it to the contemporary observer while allowing the possibility that it is nothing more than a quaint superstition from times past. But the poems do not privilege a rationalist, sceptical view. Rather, they go as far as they can towards unmediated belief, without ever taking that last step into complete acceptance.

Thus, as readers, we seem to hover in suspension before a world entirely interpenetrated by the divine or one in which history is made before our eyes; just as, in the erotic poems, we are suspended on the brink of a comprehensively eroticised reality, which is nevertheless out of reach – or reachable only in memory, whose agency is imagination, that is, the poem itself. Not that Cavafy has no time for scepticism itself, which takes its place alongside belief as a vital component of the sensibility that can see the world as divine, or erotically charged, or – the third critical dimension of his work – replete with the immanence of the fates of men. It is one of the miracles of Cavafy's poetry that he can, by elaborating upon obscure addenda to history, activate so many questions yet answer none of them.

As Marguerite Yourcenar points out in her definitive introduction to the 1957 French edition of Cavafy's works, if all of his poems are entirely historical, at the same time they are all also entirely personal: he is equally an inherited voice of the Hellenistic world, a conduit of memories of the past, and the site of the recurrence of remembered and re-remembered erotic encounters. Yourcenar's account of how Cavafy constructs what she calls *a timeless self* out of contrarieties has a *claritas* which is perhaps the French equivalent of the Greek light that illuminates Cavafy's Memory Theatre. She stresses particularly the way in which he evokes this theatre through an economy of means: unadorned language, vernacular speech, a paucity of description, a resiling from lyric effusion. But his central achievement is that forging of a timeless self: for when we read Cavafy's work, from which he seems absent and yet at the same time in which he is pervasive, indeed immanent, his absence leaves room for us, however briefly, if not to walk that antique stage ourselves, at least to stand not far off, watching the enigmas and ambiguities of love and fate unfold. We become, in this moment of psychic legerdemain, timeless selfs ourselves.

III

The German-Jewish writer Walter Benjamin died in the small Spanish seaside border town of Portbou on 26 September 1940, apparently by his own hand. He had already spent three months in a concentration camp in France, from which he was released through the intercession of friends; he returned to Paris, but fled as the Nazi armies approached. He had just arrived in Spain, having been guided on foot through a pass in the Pyrenees, carrying with him, despite his *angina pectoris*, a heavy briefcase containing a manuscript which, he said, was more precious than his life. Lisa Fittko, his guide, many years later wrote an extraordinary account of their journey.

The day before they were to leave, on fairly vague instructions given by the local mayor, they walked some way into the mountains to find the path. At the point where Fittko, who had never taken this particular route before, was satisfied she knew at least where it began, turned back, *Old Benjamin*, as she called him (he was 48), announced that he would stay the night there. Nothing she could say would dissuade him from this course, so she left him there. One of the arguments Benjamin used to justify his decision was that he had already carried his briefcase thus far and it would be silly to carry it back and then out again; and he could not of course leave it there. Next day, it turned out he had spent the night stretched on the grass elaborating, by a process of reasoning that left his guide incredulous, exactly how many minutes – ten – he would be able to walk for before needing to rest. Nor, on the way over, could she dissuade him from drinking water from a stinking pool, even though he risked catching typhoid: he was thirsty, he said, and it didn't matter if he got sick, so long as the manuscript arrived safely in Spain. *He couldn't act intuitively*, Fittko said. *He couldn't do anything at all until he had first developed an appropriate theory.*

At a hotel in Portbou, Benjamin was told by Spanish authorities that they now required an exit visa from France and, next day, he would be sent back to obtain one; unable to face this prospect, it is alleged that he overdosed on morphine, a number of tablets of which he was carrying. Alleged: the circumstances around his death are complex and ambiguous and no one has yet managed to give a clear account of exactly what happened. The briefcase was found next to his clothed body in the hotel room; it contained his personal effects, some of which had clearly been removed from his pockets: his watch, his tobacco and pipe, six passport photos, an X-ray, his glasses, letters, magazines, documents and money, but no manuscript. It had disappeared, and has not been found since. Nor has anyone yet offered a convincing theory as to what this work was: suggestions include a late revision (or duplicate) of *Das Passagen-Werk*, his magnum opus on nineteenth-century Paris; an expanded version of the *Theses on the Philosophy of History*; even some kind of politically compromising work which included a list of communist collaborators and/or traitors.

In fact, a manuscript of *Das Passagen-Werk*, along with Benjamin's sonnets and other notes, was safe in the Bibliothèque Nationale in Paris, secreted there by Benjamin's friend Georges Bataille. It is a discourse on the shopping arcades of Paris, *the capital of the nineteenth century*, and a meditation on the crowd in recent history. *Das Passagen-Werk*, as the title suggests, is itself a vast labyrinth, over a thousand pages long, about five sixths of which consists of quotations Benjamin derived from other sources. The remaining one sixth, written in his own voice, consists mostly of short pieces of dense, fiercely allusive prose.

Benjamin once remarked that, if his German prose was superior to that of his contemporaries, it was because he had long since sworn off the use of the first person singular, the authorial 'I', as the voice of his thought. He would write in the third person, or let others speak for him. He also conceived the ambition, never fulfilled, of composing a major work consisting entirely of quotations. In this it would imitate a city, where the most disparate facts – a wig-maker; a massage parlour; a video shop – abut against each other to make a kind of occult order which can be deciphered only so far as to elucidate its enigmatic splendour.

The literary figure at the heart of Benjamin's labyrinth, the writer who spoke most eloquently for him, is Charles Baudelaire. *Les Fleurs du mal*, said Benjamin, was the last lyric work that had *a European repercussion; no later work penetrated beyond a more or less limited linguistic area*. After Baudelaire, we are all swallowed up in the crowd. In the same piece (*Some Motifs in Baudelaire*, XII), Benjamin quotes from a passage of satirical prose which, he says, has been unfairly ignored by Baudelaire's editors. A poet, discovered in *a place of ill repute*, is asked how he came to be there. While hurrying to cross a boulevard, the poet replies, *midst this moving chaos in which death comes galloping at you from all sides at once*, he slipped, fell and dislodged his halo, which rolled away into the gutter. The poet did not have the courage to pick it up again and anyway decided *it hurts less to lose one's insignia than to have one's bones broken*. Besides: *Now I can go about incognito, do bad things, and indulge in vulgar behaviour like ordinary mortals*. Nor will he report his loss to the police, or inquire after the halo at the lost property office. It amuses him to think that a bad poet might pick it up and wear it, thinking it has some value or significance.

For Benjamin, this tale told *the price for which the sensation of the modern age may be had: the disintegration of the aura in the experience of shock*. The anonymity of the self in the crowd is our true condition, one that we share with everyone, even those who pretend to be exceptional. This is what has rendered the lyric project untenable. In Baudelaire's *On Wine and Hashish* (1851), subtitled *Compared as a means of multiplying individuality*, and in 'The Poem of Hashish' in *Les Paradis artificiel* (1860), he speaks at length of his agony at the proliferation of selves he feels during hashish intoxication, an experience which may be contrasted with Pessoa's lifelong anguish of self-less-ness; what is exemplary in both writers is their insistence on making this depersonalisation and/or proliferation of self central to their work.

Some eighteen months before Benjamin's death, the Spanish poet Antonio Machado crossed the same frontier in the other direction. He was fleeing Franco's Nationalist troops at the end of the Spanish Civil War, travelling in an old car with his aged mother sitting in his lap. Within a month both had died, worn out, in the French town of Colliure, Machado predeceasing his mother by a few days. Machado had also been carrying a briefcase full of manuscripts; but by some misadventure, it was left behind in Spain, and when it turned up again it was, like Benjamin's, empty. However, in this instance, we know more or less what was in it: a number of poems by an imaginary poet called Pedro de Zuniga, a putative member of the Spanish Generation of 1927; and an anthology of imaginary future poets.

It is unclear if Machado was aware of Pessoa's heteronymic obsession, although he may well have been; perhaps it does not matter. Like Pessoa, he invented other writers apart from those lost from his briefcase, though not as many as his Portuguese contemporary. Among them are two main figures: Abel Martín, a poet-philosopher; and a student of Martín's called Juan de Mairena, who, in the early 1930s, wrote a series of newspaper articles defending the Spanish Republic. 'Siesta – In Memory of Abel Martín' by Juan de Mairena concludes: *With our cup of darkness filled to the brim / with our heart that always knows some hunger / let us give honour to the Lord who created Zero / and carved our thought out of the block of faith.*

The poem is de Mairena's elegy for his master and comes with a commentary on the philosophical implications of this and other of Martín's poems: *In the theology of Abel Martín, God is defined as absolute Being, and therefore nothing which exists could be his work.* This definition harks back to the pre-Socratics, especially Empedocles, whose sphere where all elements mingle together under the power of love is analogous to Martín's Zero. In other words, we come from nothing and in that genesis is both our ability to conceptualise – thought begins out of the idea of zero – and, importantly, our ability to forget: . . . *and since the miracle of not-being is finished / start then poet, a song at the edge of it all / to death, to silence, and to what does not return.*

There is something inexpressibly melancholy about the loss of Pedro de Zuniga and Machado's other future poets, gone back in *to the great circle of nothing* from which they came, even though that is the condition of all work, and all people. They are like war dead, whose potential for love and valour has gone under in the cataclysm; theirs are voices we have never heard and, Cavafy notwithstanding, may never hear. It is as painful to contemplate Benjamin's lost manuscript, if indeed it was not a version of something that has survived in another form; almost all his late work is anyway fragmentary. But if he was a man who could not act intuitively, that does not mean he could not write prophetically.

In his last surviving work, the *Theses on the Philosophy of History*, he wrote (about a Paul Klee work in his possession): *This is how one pictures the angel of history. Its face is turned towards the past. Where we perceive a chain of events, he sees one single catastrophe which keeps piling wreckage on wreckage and hurls it in front of his feet. The angel would like to stay, awaken the dead, make whole what has been smashed. But a storm is blowing from Paradise; it has got caught in his wings with such violence the angel can no longer close them. This storm irresistibly propels him into the future to which his back is turned, while the pile of debris before him grows skyward. This storm is what we call progress.*

IV

German writer W. G. Sebald's first publication in English was *The Emigrants* (1996) which had previously appeared in Germany, in 1993, as *Die Ausgewanderten*; like all of the books which were published during his lifetime, its translation into English was overseen by the author, in such a manner that it is difficult to believe that the original was written in another language. Like Cavafy's and Pessoa's, then, Sebald's work has an organic connection to English literature. Sebald sometimes used the word 'novel' – *Roman*, in German – to describe the four books he wrote and published in the last decade of his life: in English, and in the order of their German composition, *Vertigo*; *The Emigrants*; *The Rings of Saturn*; *Austerlitz*; at other times he spoke of *prose works of indeterminate form*.

The Emigrants begins with the unnamed narrator and his companion, Clara, driving out to a place called Hingham in East Anglia *in search of somewhere to live*. In that same first sentence we learn that the narrator is about to take up a position in Norwich, where the real W. G. Sebald taught for over thirty years. What follows in the next twenty-odd pages is a seemingly straightforward description of the place they go to see, a brief account of the almost entirely uneventful period they spend living there, followed by a summary of further contacts they had with a certain Dr Henry Selwyn, who spent most of his time in the garden of the old priory at Hingham. There is nothing in the section to suggest we are reading anything other than a piece of autobiographical prose, not even the sudden, though not entirely unexpected, suicide of Dr Selwyn, who shoots himself with a hunting rifle; the narrator comments: *When we received the news, I had no great difficulty overcoming the initial shock.*

But certain things, he goes on, *have a way of returning unexpectedly.* Some time after Dr Selwyn's death, the narrator, on a train in Switzerland, reads in a newspaper an account of the finding in the Swiss Alps of the preserved body of a Bernese alpine guide who disappeared in the summer of 1914; this man, Johannes Naegeli, was known to Dr Selwyn. Indeed, in the year before the beginning of the Great War, the two became so close that Selwyn said *never in his life, neither before nor later, did he feel as good as he did then, in the company of this man.* When he disappeared just after mobilisation began Selwyn felt *it was as if I was buried under snow and ice.* We are left in no doubt that the disappearance of Naegeli had always haunted Selwyn, and contributed to his long-premeditated suicide; nor can we question the veracity of the reported reappearance, seventy-two years later, of the alpine guide's body: in the book, poorly reproduced, but date-stamped and written in entirely convincing French, is a newspaper report of the event, photocopied from a Lausanne paper.

Or can we? We turn the page to section two of *The Emigrants* and find another suicide of another man in his twilight years, this time Sebald's former primary school teacher. You start to wonder. Is it possible that the newspaper account of the discovery of the body of the guide in the ice inspired the story about Selwyn's loss of love, and not the other way round? Was there perhaps a man of that name or another, known to Sebald, who took his life with a hunting rifle, yet never climbed in the Swiss Alps? Did he put together two or more unrelated events to form the vignette of Dr Henry Selwyn?

It is impossible to know. And therein lies the genius of Sebald's writing: he persuades you to read his work as autobiographical non-fiction then, with immense subtlety, manages to suggest that, on the contrary, it may be *made up*. And in that doubt about the status of what is before you, you read on with a preternatural attentiveness to detail. *W. G. Sebald* is, in Pessoa's sense, an orthonym. As one writer put it: *Sebald's narrator is one W. G. Sebald, who lives in Norfolk, comes from the German village of W, and has a companion, Clara. Max Sebald was born in Wertach im Allgäu in 1944 and lived in an old rectory outside Norwich with his Austrian wife, Ute, and their daughter, a school teacher.*

Sebald was obsessively private and gave interviews only rarely: *I don't want to talk about my trials and tribulations. Once you reveal even part of what your real problems might be in life, they come back in a deformed way.* His sudden death, coming at a time when he had reluctantly relinquished a larger part of this privacy in order to publicise his last book, *Austerlitz*, thus seems both perverse and cruelly ironic.

Given the degree of artifice in his work, it is not surprising that Sebald knew what he was doing: *There was a vogue of documentary writing in Germany in the 1970s which opened my eyes. It's an important literary invention, but it's considered an artless form. I was trying to write something saturated with material but carefully wrought, where the art manifests itself in a discreet, not too pompous fashion . . . Every novelist combines fact and fiction. In my case, there's more reality. But I don't think it's radically different; you work with the same tools . . . It's the opposite of suspending disbelief and being swept along by the action, which is perhaps not the highest form of mental activity; it's to constantly ask, 'What happened to these people, what might they have felt like?' You can generate a similar state of mind in the reader by making them uncertain.*

Elsewhere, he was sometimes scathing about the processes of the conventional novel, describing how, in the act of reading, you hear the machinery creak as the novelist constructs dialogue to advance the story, or moves characters around their artificial world to illustrate a theme. His own work is seamless, shifting time, place and voice the way these qualities shift in dreams. There is something fluvial about Sebald's prose: to enter one of his works is to enter a river of language, which carries you along to confluences with other rivers, which also become part of the flow, until all of the tributaries meet and mingle in the great sea of silence that comes after the last page is turned. His chosen voice is the first-person singular, but that voice is typically speaking of another individual who might then take up the narrative in his or her own voice, speaking of another, who might in their turn begin to speak: as if memory is not a solitary accomplishment, but requires contributions from us all.

These are formal questions, but they have a thematic edge. The epigraph to that first short section of *The Emigrants* reads: *And the last remnants memory destroys.* All of Sebald's writing is about memory but in what way? Sometimes it seems that he is saying, look, after what has been swept away, these fragments remain; among all those who died, these people existed, these events happened. On the other hand, as the epigraph suggests, memory may itself be destructive. It has been suggested that memory does not record the events it seems to be about, but rather earlier memories of those events: your childhood recall of the grassy track to the bull paddock, full of fear and urgent anticipation, is not a record of the actual journey you took down that path, but a palimpsest, the memory of a memory. Memory is constructed out of fragments of past events, past people. However crucial it is for identity, it is still a *made up* record, not a true and verifiable one. We know this if we have ever tried to reconstruct an event – a car accident, the day Rachel died, that terrible argument – from multiple points of view. When Sebald says (Is he quoting? Who is he quoting? Paul Celan?): *And the last remnants memory destroys*, is he saying that memory is also a fiction?

Sebald's four novels are book-ended by two works of non-fiction, both published posthumously – *After Nature*, his first literary composition, a long poem in three sections, and *The Natural History of Destruction*, a sustained meditation upon the place of memory in literature. *After Nature* is an evocative, indeed precognitive prelude to his works of fiction, while *The Natural History of Destruction*, which at a crucial point invokes Benjamin's Angel of History, can be read retroactively as commentary upon his own practice as a writer. The title piece, a reworking of a series of lectures Sebald gave in Zurich in 1997, is an excoriating account of the Allied bombing campaign against German cities in the last three years of World War Two, focused upon the almost complete suppression of discussion of these events, not so much among the German people as among German writers. In the course of the essay Sebald introduces a concept, derived from Alexander Kluge, central to his own intentions as a writer: *retrospective learning*, defined as *the only way of deflecting human wishful thinking towards the anticipation of a future that would not already be pre-empted by the anxieties arising from the suppression of experience*. It is the literary equivalent of recovered memory syndrome.

The three essays that follow, on three writers (Alfred Andersch, Jean Améry and Peter Weiss) who were his contemporaries,

250

likewise deal with the place of memory in their (very different) work. While the first is a polemic against Andersch's bad faith, the essays on the two latter writers analyse their attempts to write the unwriteable. They include passages which explore memory as affliction, as in those torture victims, like Améry himself, whose remembering as a function of identity is irredeemably scrambled but whose recall of the actual torture they underwent is always with them. For such as these, memory is torment, and forgetting an unattainable grace. This perhaps clarifies what the fictional chronicles Sebald wrote are doing: they collapse the opposition of memory and forgetting, for that which is *made up* is neither remembered nor forgotten but exists in a different sense, a new thing added to the world. Furthermore: *For those whose business is language, it is only in language that the unhappiness of exile can be overcome.*

If Sebald's main subject is memory, then the theatre of that memory is essentially Europe, and particularly, though not exclusively, Europe since the French Revolution; but this Europe of his, what is it? Does it exist? Or, should we say, more terribly, did it exist and is now destroyed? Some recent histories – *Dark Continent: Europe's Twentieth Century* by Mark Mazower and *The Origins of Nazi Violence* by Enzo Traverso – suggest that the Nazi program was not an aberration but a coherent, if psychotic, synthesis of various forms of violence refined in mainstream European civilisation during the nineteenth and early twentieth centuries: the mechanisation of capital punishment, the Panopticon, the production line, the growing popularity of biological metaphors in politics, racism, anti-Semitism, the imperial extermination of Third and Fourth World peoples.

Sebald surely writes about *this* Europe, the Europe in which barbarism is a central, not a peripheral development. His is a generalised and non-partisan horror at what humanity has done, what we have become. One way to read him, then, is as someone who tries to recover, with writing, what has been destroyed in the world. At the same time, in the melancholy fall of his sentences, and their preoccupation with loss, he suggests that such recovery is ultimately not possible. And yet he persisted, perhaps because writing was the only way he knew to link back to a lost past and thereby make another future possible. The vehicle for the recovery of these losses is a free-floating intelligence called 'W. G. Sebald', about whom we know almost nothing in an autobiographical sense. What we do know are his obsessions – architecture, graveyards, maps, photography, prisons, street names, zoos – and his emotions, which are precisely logged in all their overwhelming imprecision. And, as we read, it is indeed as if the Europe that has disappeared under the rubble of war is reconstituted as a simulacrum – not what was, so much as what might have been and therefore could yet be: a future in the past.

V

Baudelaire's de-haloed poet, Cavafy's hidden self, Pessoa's heteronyms, Benjamin's third person, Machado's zero, Sebald's orthonym: who is the ghost who writes? As the author of five books and a few shorter works which are, in whole or in part, autobiographical narratives told in the first-person singular, shouldn't I have something to say about this? But 'I' is not me. It is as much a construction, and a strategy, as the other voices interrogated in this essay. Further, the process of the construction of this voice, I believe, does not differ in kind from other constructions, though the quality of the work it makes might. Perhaps a brief history is in order.

The Autobiography of My Father, which is a book of mourning, began out of frustration with poetry as a means of expression. I wanted to write about my father, yet when I went down the lane that beginning day to the writing room I rented underneath a friend's kitchen in Darlinghurst, a feeling of intolerable weariness at the persona of my poetry came over me. I was sick of the sound of my own voice. That was a liberating moment, and once I decided to try prose, in the first person, and address myself directly to my father, the writing flowed, without much anxious scanning back over what I'd written, nor any of those terrible moments of doubt that stop you mid-sentence in horror at the wasteland or exit-less maze you have got yourself into. The book, so unlike the troubled, ultimately clouded life of its alleged author, my father, had a charmed life. Part of this ease came from that simple decision to address myself directly to him; part was because the longest section in the book is in fact a transcription of an actual conversation; part because there are other real documents embedded in the text, speaking for themselves. Perhaps for some readers there was a voyeuristic thrill to be had from the disclosure of this intimate material; though I know for others my father is a palpable presence between the covers.

My next book, *The Resurrection of Philip Clairmont*, could not have been more different. Instead of a few weeks, it took almost a decade to complete. Every possible difficulty, all of those the first book had flown blithely past, afflicted it. That long period in the 1990s during which I researched and wrote it, remains in my mind an interminable haunting: sleepless nights, existential terrors, imaginary phantoms, actual apparitions. Some of these problems reflected difficulties with subject matter, some were the consequence of my own uncertainty in the face of the task I had set myself: I was confronting real spectres both in the world and in myself. I'm reminded of the medium who felt she had to exorcise the Clairmont paintings she saw in the Govett-Brewster Art Gallery. I also remember the departure of the spirit of Philip Clairmont from me, a day during which I spend some time convulsing on a bed in the midst of what resembled a panic attack but which was, unlike a panic attack, followed by a feeling of great serenity. In this case the ghost who wrote was not entirely my own, but one I entertained for a time, along with the various real or phantom other presences it trailed.

There is a radical change of tone in that book, from the first-person autobiographical voice which narrates the first section to a neutral voice that tells the rest of the story. I was trying, in part two, to channel the artist; in part three, the art; with varying degrees of success. It's impossible to know now, but I sometimes wonder if, had I continued in the first person, I might have written a book which would have travelled into the larger world as a classic tale of an artist manqué.

That yearning to write a book straight through in one voice was the inception of *Chronicle of the Unsung*, which began as a phrase drifting unbidden into my head one day. This phrase, which I knew instantly was a title, carried with it no other information. I didn't know what it meant, nor did I know what the book was to be about. A lament for dead friends who'd never achieved their potential? A book about the obscure of the world? My own unsung exploits? In the end, I decided to take the title in a literal sense and apply it to parts of my life story. In other words, to take some of the mass of failed, unfinished, unpublishable or just unpublished writings I owned and see if I could string them together on an autobiographical thread. These included a few poems, a couple of diaries, the memory of the first seventy-odd pages of a novel lost when I changed computers, two completed but unproduced screenplays and miscellaneous other pieces, mostly ideas for essays which I'd noted down but never written up.

I was nervous about attempting autobiography: what possible justification could there be for that? Hence, every time I introduced myself, I jumped off as soon as possible into some other subject presumed to be of more interest or importance. This foregrounding of digression was an integral part of the conception of the book but it wasn't an easy strategy to make work. Eventually I found I had to take myself seriously: the departures from autobiography wouldn't work unless I actually wrote autobiography. In this way, a book initially envisaged as quite impersonal became in some respects exceedingly personal. This was however an interesting process. One of the things I learned was that scepticism towards my own experience, while entirely justified, could nevertheless be turned to account. The way to unite disparate material in the same frame was through the use of a distinct voice. This voice would at once tell and doubt the story it told.

It might also be described as a merger of the personal narration of part one of *The Resurrection of Philip Clairmont* with the neutral channelling voice of the rest of the book; or as the naïve voice of *The Autobiography of My Father*, grown up. Or even as a conversation between two voices, one personal, one laid open to other voices. Part of the artifice of the personal voice is in its omissions: it is extremely partial autobiography. Each of the four sections of the book recounts a fragment of time, none longer than nine months, chosen essentially for its resistance to easy understanding. That is, they were difficult periods which were for that reason possible subjects for writing.

Another part of the construction of the voice is what is added: I suddenly found myself in a position where I no longer felt obliged, as I had previously, to present the documentary truth of my recollections. I felt free to include in the autobiographical narration inventions, exaggerations, possible truths, while practising a much stricter fidelity in the digressions. This was as liberating as not writing poems about my father. It doesn't matter what these inventions are; hopefully, it is the narrator's voice you come to trust and if you do you will believe what it says; and in that belief the documentary truth or otherwise of the recollections becomes irrelevant.

Those who doubt this might meditate upon the fact that the author of *Independence Day*, with its bitter-sweet evocation of a father–son relationship, has never had a child of his own. Essentially the same point was made by Gabriel García Márquez when he said in the recently published first volume of his autobiography what he learned from Kafka: *It was not necessary to demonstrate facts: it was enough for the author to have written something for it to be true, with no proofs other than the power of his talent and the authority of his voice.*

Despite the plethora of recent commentary about unreliable narrators, most readers still want to trust the inner revelations of character or thought an author presents them with. This need to believe what we read is deeply ingrained, so much so that even when we read the words of a known liar, we still like to think we can distinguish truth from falsehood. In the same way, in our reading of non-fiction, we tend to believe, within certain constraints, those factual details about the world an author tells us. In all cases, however, what we actually believe is the voice in which we are told these things, whether they be memories, inventions or so-called facts. If the voice is compelling enough, the alleged status of the tale we're being told becomes extraneous and this is just as true of factual writing as it is of imaginative writing. Probably there are no intrinsic differences between kinds of writing along the continuum from fact to fiction, only formal differences.

My most recent book, *Luca Antara*, written from the same template as *Chronicle of the Unsung*, is a more radical exploration of it. Like *Unsung*, it includes inventions among its facts; but these inventions are more extensive, more obvious and also more mysterious, in that their status has to be intuited from the context, which is not itself free from supposition, as if the very notion of fiction and/or non-fiction is questionable – which I believe it is. This leads to what might be called genre confusion: how do you describe a book that is partly autobiographical yet channels historical voices that have no other existence apart from that given them by expression in writing? The convention seems to be that inclusion of any invention whatsoever means the book must be a novel, but I am unwilling to subscribe to this because, perhaps paradoxically, it may render fact fiction.

In his majestic edition of Jorge Luis Borges' non-fiction, *The Total Library*, Eliot Weinberger notes that there is no term in Spanish for 'non-fiction'. It's also the case that many of the works Borges later published as *ficciones* appeared earlier as essays – as if a distinction the language did not make was therefore illusory in formal terms as well. The root of the English word 'fiction' is Latin *fictilis*, from *fingere*, to make, with particular reference to the potter's craft – and, by implication, to the clay with which god or the gods fashioned us. The term non-fiction is thus an anomaly: not made? And yet surely an artefact too? This absurdity might be called the fiction of non-fiction. The way I've worked around this thus far is by framing inventions within a construction that is, or purports to be, not invented, not made up, non-fiction. In this manner, I can continue writing in the way I started out – first person, notionally autobiographical, with digressions into matters that have nothing obvious to do with a personal narrative – while also producing strings or streams of language that please me simply because of their intrinsic qualities or else because of what they say or seem to say.

The trope whereby an author suggests a fiction is something that really happened is of course very old, much older than Defoe, who is usually identified as the one who made it over in the form most available to us now, the novel (It. *a tale, a piece of news*). The book I've recently completed, called *White City*, has a similar set up, but with this difference: it is a fiction presented as a non-fiction that cannot be true. In other words, a false memoir, authored by an alleged person who is known never to have existed. I thought this would be an interesting form to try just now, when genuine (and failed) attempts at deception routinely hit the headlines. My intent is not to deceive, or perhaps I should say my intent is not entirely to deceive; rather, I want to take readers far enough along the road to deception for them to have to ask where it is they are or are not going.

So am I writing something falsely true or truly false? How much do I need to practise fidelity? How detailed, how convincing should I be? Sometimes I feel trapped in a hall of mirrors and that's when I start to doubt. On the other hand, I served my apprenticeship as a poet, a field unbounded by the fences of fact or not fact. That I was never a very good poet is beside the point: nobody asks if a poem is fact or fiction, though they might

257

wonder if it is true, which is another question: perhaps the only one we should ask of literature.

Machado's Zero, like Mallarmé's blank page, is the beginning of all literary work. It is not so much a cancellation of what has gone before as an acknowledgement of it: the past like a great tsunami banks up behind us, sweeps over us, obliterating all we try to do as it rushes through the present to make the future. To write at all is to reserve a space from this process of flux, to make a provisional clearing of the wreckage of history in which to build a structure which may alter the flow of time in some previously unthought way.

The self is a user illusion, thought the Dane, Tor Norre-tranders. And after all, the voice we carry in our heads is not unitary but threefold: the one who speaks our thought (our 'self'), the one addressed (the 'other'), and a third, the silent audience of both. This tripartite division is reiterated in reading, when the one who speaks (the author) is entertained by the one addressed (the reader), while the silent third listens; if and when this third loses interest, we put the book aside.

For some writers, the best way of accomplishing this dramatic transfer is through the use of a denatured voice, a stripped-down voice, an authorial voice that is not author as personality but author as intent, with language its sole medium: *For those whose business is language, it is only in language that the unhappiness of exile can be overcome.* For others, it is the opposite: only a voice not distanced from personal preoccupations, in fact mired in them, and alive to the psychological complexities they entail, can properly cross over from writer to reader. Writers like these may want to draw attention to their 'I', not because it is immaculate but because it is not: intimacy always presupposes deficits which have to be made up somehow.

I think of the Lucidity Institute, devoted to the theory and practice of Lucid Dreaming, or Dreaming True. We all know fragments of reality enter into our dreams and are there transformed; but what if, as they surely do, fragments of dreams enter into reality and transform it into something resembling a dream? Lichtenberg wrote that *we live and feel as much dreaming as waking and are the one as much as the other. It is one of the superiorities of man that he dreams and knows it.* The exercise of the will over dreaming is one thing; the exercise of the dream's will is another. This is what authorship attempts. Writing is not so much a process of predicting a future as it is of working out how to make one happen. And to do that you must first find a voice in which to tell it. If it is an authentic voice – one that can be believed – then what it says may well come true.

Afterword

Only two of the pieces collected here ('Going South', 'Prospect Bay') were written for this book. The occasional appearances elsewhere of some of the others were obscure, even fugitive. Most have not been printed before. Any order they may have is inadvertent, a product of my obsessions or predilections: self and other; psychedelics and the nature of perception; landscape, with its intimations of paradise lost or found; the City; the far reaches of spacetime and the means used to probe it; love and longing; above all, the workings of memory and what it can tell us of time, mind and world. I will try to say how this came about.

I started writing with reviews of art shows that tried to find verbal equivalents for visual phenomena. I wanted to include some of these here but they could not be made to fit. Yet that attempt to find ways of saying in words what wordless things say has turned into a lifelong inquiry. This desire to cross-fertilise visual and verbal art forms began in the artistic and intellectual ferment that existed in Wellington in the mid-1970s.

Of all the many fruitful encounters of that time, the most crucial was with Alan Brunton who, as an editor of *Spleen* (subtitled *A Useful Organ*), helped fuse my attempts at art criticism with the notion that they might also be journeyman work towards real writing – for the press, for the theatre, for film, for books . . . or anything really. That sense of unlimited possibilities Alan brought with him and encouraged in others was my making as a writer.

'Waimarino County', which gives its name to this collection, was begun after I left Red Mole in 1980. It was meant to inaugurate a writing life. Here, where I started out as a child, I would begin again as a writer. The first draft, under the title 'A Quiet Corner of Paradise', was much longer than the piece is now. It was also unfinished and stayed that way for quite a long time. A failure, perhaps. When I gave it to one of my sisters to read, she returned it without reaching the end, saying it was just too sad.

One of the reasons it remained incomplete was that in the midst of drafting it I was offered my first film job. That is also why there is nothing else here from the 1980s, because in that decade most of my effort went into trying to learn how to craft film scripts. Screenplays, too, seek to find verbal equivalents for visual phenomena, not to elucidate them but in order to make movies. I haven't much to say about screenwriting because theory interests me less than practice.

I returned to prose writing at the beginning of the 1990s with 'The Hallelujah Chorus', commissioned by Alan Brunton for *Hamilton Hometown*, the issue of *Landfall* he guest edited. Alan also, later, suggested that John Geraets invite me to contribute to *brief* magazine. I doubt I would have essayed aesthetics without that initial offer.

Some of the other Meditations were written for, though not always published in, *brief*, including, under the editorship of Jack Ross, two essays that posthumously discuss Alan's life and work. They reappear on his author's page at the New Zealand Electronic Poetry Centre (nzepc) site through the agency of director Michele Leggott, who also asked me to give the paper, at Bluff in April 2006, that became 'Strangers in the House of the Mind'.

'The Abandoned House as a Refuge for the Imagination' was written to be given as a talk at the Antipodean Gothic Conference held at the Albany campus of Massey University in

December 2002, but for various reasons wasn't or, rather, only a garbled version of it was; it was later adjudged joint winner, with Tze Ming Mok's 'Race You There', of the 2004 *Landfall* essay competition. It also appears, illustrated, and in a slightly different form, in *Gothic New Zealand: The Darker Side of Kiwi Culture*.

Publishing in cyberspace is a relatively recent prospect and I did not take it up until, in 2004, Mark Young persuaded me to start a weblog. Apart from the three or four early attempts at prose poems, all the Illusions began as virtual texts, written directly into cyberspace. You don't need an editor if you have a blog, or rather you are your own editor; but I've continued to work with Mark and he has published some of the Meditations in his e-zine, *Otoliths*.

The final essay, *Ghost Who Writes*, was commissioned by Lloyd Jones to make one of the elegant little books that his Four Winds Press published. Lloyd was a generous editor, and I am grateful for the opportunity he gave me to write a purely literary essay. 'The Oblate of Unknowing' began as a draft of the fifth section of *Ghost Who Writes* but is probably happier where, and as, it now is.

All of these writings have been revised, some extensively, but even those seem obdurately to retain their original configuration; which is on the one hand a disappointment and on the other a kind of validation: what is essentially unalterable remains essentially itself. It isn't for me to say what might emerge from this collection; but those repetitions and cross-references that do appear were neither contrived nor suppressed. I don't know if a conclusion is even possible; but I can log, with thanks to their editors, previous incarnations: 'The Hallelujah Chorus' in *Landfall* 180 (1991); 'Diptych' in *Otoliths* 4 (http://the-otolith.blogspot.com/) (2007) and at *White City* (http://whitcity.blogspot.com/); 'an.aesthetic' in *brief* 20 (2001); 'Folk Tale' in *brief* 24 (2002); '. . . among the ruins with the poor' and 'Lighting out for the Territory' in *brief* 25 and 28 respectively, as well as at nzepc (http://www.nzepc.auckland.

ac.nz/) (2002–03) (all section-heading quotes in this piece are from 'Alan Brunton Gets Jaamed', originally published in *JAAM* 16 (October 2001); this interview is also available at http://www.nzepc.auckland.ac.nz/authors/brunton/); 'The Abandoned House as a Refuge for the Imagination' in *Landfall* 208 (2004) and also in *Gothic New Zealand* (OUP, 2006); 'The Inconsolable Song', 'Rosetta' and 'Entoptics' in *Otoliths* 1, 2 and 3 respectively (2006); 'Strangers in the House of the Mind' in issue 2 of *Ka Mate Ka Ora* at *nzepc* (2006); 'Hawthorne Canal' and 'Mighty Dread' in *Famous Reporter* 31 and 32 respectively (http://walleahpress.com.au/index.htm) (2005–06); 'Westbound Train' in *Fugacity 05* at *nzepc*; 'Oasis' in *Bluff 06* on the same site; other Illusions at *Luca Antara* (http://lucaantara.blogspot.com/) (2004–06) and *dérives* (http://fluvial.blogspot.com/) (2005–06); and *Ghost Who Writes* by Four Winds Press as a part of the Montana Estates Essay Series (2004).